The DRUID and the ELEPHANT

ANDY MORRALL

The Druid and the Elephant

By Andy Morrall

ISBN-13: 978-988-8843-33-6

© 2024 Andy Morrall

FICTION

EB199

All rights reserved. No part of this book may be reproduced in material form, by any means, whether graphic, electronic, mechanical or other, including photocopying or information storage, in whole or in part. May not be used to prepare other publications without written permission from the publisher except in the case of brief quotations embodied in critical articles or reviews. For information contact info@earnshawbooks.com

Published in Hong Kong by Earnshaw Books Ltd.

To my Wife and Son

Dramatis Personae

Agrippina: Roman Empress, wife of Claudius, mother of Nero. Intelligent, beautiful, deadly.

Amergin: Druid and first teacher of Cassibelanus. Cunning, expert with plants and animals.

Boudicca: Queen of the Iceni tribe. Indomitable rebel.

Britannicus: Son of Roman Emperor Claudius. Younger stepbrother to Nero, poor kid.

Caicer: Boudicca's Druid. Royal adviser and loyal friend.

Caratacus: Prince of the Catuvellauni tribe. Silver-tongued resistance leader.

Cassibelanus / Caz / Decimus: Druid and warrior. Narrator of the tale.

Catus Decianus: Procurator of Britannia. Tax collector, rent collector, and paymaster.

Cerialis: Commander of the Ninth Legion, in eastern Britannia.

Claudia Octavia: Daughter of Roman Emperor Claudius, unfortunate wife of Emperor Nero.

Claudius: Emperor of Rome. Limping, stuttering, and sickly. Bad at choosing wives.

Dervalon: Boudicca's war leader. Able to turn good advice into victory.

Dubhtach: Druid to King Verica of the Atrebates, and teacher of Cassibelanus.

Eppilus: Comrade of Cassibelanus and cavalry leader. Expert horseman and loyal friend.

Gamus: Centurion of the Imperial Palace Guard, who were known as the Germanii.

Gamo: The Emperor's personal bodyguard. A man not to be messed with.

Ganna: Druid and Priestess of the War Goddess Baduhenna. Dreamer and seer.

Halotus: Chief Steward of the Imperial Palace in Rome. Food taster for the Emperor.

Hospes: Senior member of the Imperial Palace Guard. Kills on command.

Irgaine: Daughter of Prince Caratacus. Loved by many, lover of none.

Lukon: Comrade and loyal friend of Cassibelanus, and ballista expert.

Melanipa: Princess and commander of Sarmatian cavalry. Takes ears as trophies.

Messalina: Empress of Rome, wife of Claudius. Mother of Claudia Octavia and Britannicus.

Micipsa: Elephant belonging to the Emperor of Rome. Giant intelligent tusker.

Narcissus: Ex-slave and Secretary to the Roman emperor Claudius. Powerful and intelligent.

Nero: Emperor of Rome. Son of Agrippina. Adopted by Claudius. Husband of Claudia Octavia. Poet, musician, singer, actor, chariot-racer, athlete, murderer, adulterer.

Pallas: Treasurer to Emperor Claudius. Extremely rich. Rumoured to be Agrippina's lover.

Rufrius Crispinus: Prefect of the Praetorian guard. Rich, powerful, and dangerous.

Segnorix: Assistant to the High Druid, and later High Druid.

Seneca the Younger: Philosopher, statesman, and dramatist. Tutor and adviser to Nero.

Sextus Afranius Burrus: Praetorian Guard Prefect after Rufrius Crispinus. Adviser to Nero.

Suetonius: Gaius Suetonius Paulinus, Governor of Britannia. Killer of druids.

Surus: Rider of the elephant Micipsa, from the Roman province of Syria.

Tenvantius: Boudicca's tattooed and grey-bearded war chief. Suspicious and argumentative.

Teuhant: War leader and charioteer of the Catuvellauni tribe.

Togodumnus: Prince of the Catuvellauni tribe. Brother of Caratacus.

Trenus: Comrade and loyal friend of Cassibelanus, engineer.

Vespasian: Commander of the Second Legion in the invasion of Britannia, later Emperor.

List of Places

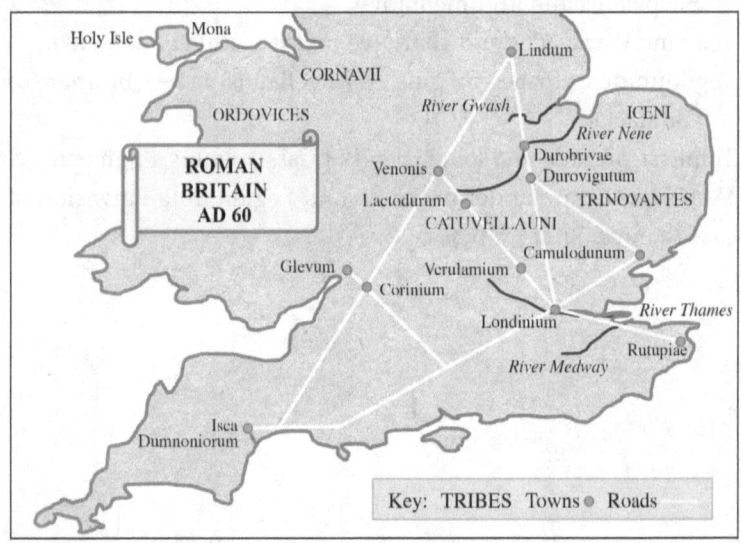

Baiae: notorious Roman resort town on the Bay of Naples.
Camulodunum: now Colchester, in Essex, was the capital of the Trinovantes and later the Catuvellauni tribes, then became a Roman base.
Corinium: Cirencester in Gloucestershire.
Durobrivae: Water Newton in Cambridgeshire.
Glevum: city of Gloucester.
Hibernia: Ireland.
Isca Dumnoniorum: Exeter, Devon.
Lactodurum: Towcester, Northamptonshire.
Lindum: city of Lincoln.

Llyn Cerrig Bach: lake in Anglesey, site of sacrificial offerings.
Londinium: London
Mona: Anglesey, Wales.
Oppidum Batavorum: now Nijmegen, a city in the Netherlands, near the Rhine.
Ostia: a port southwest of Rome.
Rutupiae: Richborough, Kent.
Sarmatia: now central Ukraine and the Caucasus.
The Holy Isle: an island in western Anglesey, Wales.
Tigranocerta: capital city in ancient Armenia.
Venonis: High Cross, Leicestershire.
Verulamium: St. Albans, Hertfordshire.

1

THE REBEL QUEEN

The sounds of distant battle pierced the forest: the blare of horns, the rumble of chariot wheels, and the clash of sword beaten upon shield. We left our horses in the deep woods and crawled to the edge of the trees. Across the adjoining fens ran a long narrow causeway, topped by a stone-flagged road, on which a century of Roman infantry had closed ranks to form a shield wall. My fists clenched at the sight of my enemies, those who had slaughtered my father and my fellow druids. The Romans faced north, towards a native warband formed up on a meadow at the head of the causeway. A thousand bare-chested tribesmen screamed death threats at the invaders. Mounted on a chariot at their centre, a tall, red-haired woman thrust a spear into the air. The gleaming gold torc at her throat marked her as the famous Boudicca, rebel Queen of the Iceni tribe. Around her stood her bodyguards, a white-robed druid, and musicians with war-horns and drums.

"The Iceni outnumber the Romans ten to one," said our druid guide, Segnorix. "After years of bloodshed and defeat, hope fills my heart. With any luck we can throw them off this island." He twisted his head to face me. "What are their chances, Caz?"

"See the bull mascot on those shields?" I said, "that's the Ninth Legion. They've been fighting here since the invasion,

THE DRUID AND THE ELEPHANT

when I was a boy. The Romans have beaten the Iceni before. They can do it again."

"Against so many? How?"

"Steel, spirit, strategy."

"Will that be enough?"

"Watch. You'll see."

The Queen stabbed her spear at the enemy, the horns blared, drums thundered, and a line of chariots charged forwards over the grass leading to the causeway. The charioteers urged their steeds into a gallop, screaming their war cries.

"They won't scare the legionaries," commented my engineer, Trenus. "See those drainage ditches on either side of the road? The chariots can't jump them, and can't get onto the causeway. They'll never get into combat."

As the chariots closed in, a dozen war dogs burst from the Roman ranks, and dashed towards the attackers, barking furiously. The horses shied at the sight of them.

"Those aren't warhorses," scoffed my cavalryman, Eppilus. "They're farm animals!"

The charioteers lashed their steeds on. Reaching the edge of the marsh, the warriors gave a great shout and hurled their spears. Driven by hatred of the invaders and the speed of the chariots, the shafts arced upwards, then fell towards the Roman ranks, bunched up on the road.

A signal rang out, and as one the legionaries raised their shields above their heads, interlocking like tiles on a roof, and the tribesmen's spears clattered harmlessly away. With the war dogs almost upon them, the chariot drivers slewed around and retreated at full gallop, to the jeers of the Romans.

Boudicca screamed in frustration. She leaped down from her chariot, and ran towards the enemy, howling her war-cry. Her bodyguards followed, and in a moment the whole warband was charging the Roman position. I felt the blood lust rise within me. I wanted to leap to my feet and charge, but I knew they were doomed and I would be throwing my life way, and those of my men. Better to watch and learn.

In front of the Roman infantry stood their slingers, and as the tribesmen charged, the first missiles whiplashed towards them. Boudicca's warriors sprinted, shields raised, into a hailstorm of Roman slingshot. Many fell, but their comrades leaped over the bodies and kept coming. The slingers fell back through their front line, and formed up behind, from where they began lobbing stones over their heads. The infantry readied their weapons.

At fifty paces the first volley of Roman spears slammed into the tribesmen. The long, narrow heads penetrated the shields of the leaders, hitting the bearer or lodging in the wood, weighing it down and rendering it useless in a fight. Casting them aside, the tribesmen charged on. At thirty paces the second volley of spears hit, and this time the tribesmen had no defence. Scores went down.

"Should have let the second rank take the lead," said Lukon, my weapons expert.

Leaping over their fallen comrades, the tribesmen closed on the Roman formation. The Roman slingers lobbed stones over their comrades' heads and into the leaders, stunning many at such close quarters. The tribesmen raised their shields against the hail of rocks falling from above. The front rank of Romans ducked, and the rear ranks hurled a volley of heavy war darts straight into the charging faces. Men fell, screaming. Undaunted, the following natives pushed past and closed on the Roman shield wall.

The Romans had one more trick. Every legionary carries a rounded stake for building fortified camps, and they had laid these down across the road in front of their shield wall. As the tribesmen crossed the last few paces, they had to run across these stakes, which rolled around under their feet, tripping many.

As the charge faltered, the front rank of legionaries stamped forwards. Roman shield bosses smashed into Iceni faces. Steel swords ripped into unarmoured torsos. Screams of dying men drowned out the war horns as Roman armour and discipline overcame naked bravado.

My body tensed and my fingers clawed the earth in frustration. I longed to be in combat. Years of training twitched my arms and shoulders, as battle-honed instinct took control. But I was in command, and my task was not to fight, but to watch and learn. Why were the Iceni not trying to out-flank the Romans? Was their only tactic a headlong charge? Where were their missile troops? Why no cavalry? Why attack the Romans on the causeway, where their flanks were protected by the marsh? Did Iceni warrior honour still look down on anything but face-to-face and hand-to-hand combat? Had they learned nothing about fighting the Romans in the long years since the invasion?

A pile of Iceni corpses grew across the causeway. Injured men staggered away, tumbling down the blood-soaked slope and into the marsh. Before long, Boudicca's bodyguards dragged her back out of danger, and the war-horns sounded the withdrawal. I heard a groan from beside me. Segnorix's face was as white as his druid's robes. "We've seen enough," I told him. "Let's get back to the horses."

Once there, his voice shook. "See what we're facing, Caz? Boudicca's rebellion will fail within days. The Romans will enslave us all. She needs you. Teach her how to win. I'll talk to her druid and set up a meeting. The High Druid has sent you as his war leader; she'll respect that. But it's up to you to impress her. Show her what you can do."

I nodded. I knew just the thing: how to build killing machines that would strike fear into any warrior's heart. With them, I would slay my enemies and avenge my father's death. I set my men to work.

The next night I met the rebel queen. Her command tent was warmer than the chill night air, but her welcome was icy. At the sight of me, Queen Boudicca's eyes narrowed. "So, this is the High Druid's spy, come to teach us how to defeat the Romans! Speak, let us judge your wisdom!"

"To beat the Romans we must divide them, out-number them, and overwhelm them," I told her. "Now the legions are far apart, the Ninth here, the Governor's forces in the west, and the Second in the south. We must cut them off from each other and defeat them one by one. I have been killing Romans since they first set foot on our shores seventeen years ago. I know their strengths and I know their weaknesses, but most of all, I know their commanders. I know how they think, I know how they fight, and I know how to beat them."

The tall, red-haired Queen stared into my eyes, searching for any sign of weakness. My eyes are different colours: one pale green and the other icy blue. In my home village they called it the evil eye, and my father had to send me away to be a druid when the villagers cursed me as a child of ill-omen. My eyes strike fear in the hearts of many. The Queen was not disconcerted. She had a commanding presence. But I am a druid and a battle-hardened warrior. We held each other's gaze.

"Why should we trust him?" rasped a tattooed grey-beard beside her. "His loyalties are as divided as his cursed eyes. He looks like a traitor to me!"

The Romans had whipped the Queen when they had seized her lands after the death of her husband, and I saw the anger that drove her, so I gave her a reason after her own heart. "I want revenge," I declared. "Revenge for the druids they killed on the Holy Isle, revenge for the sacred oak groves they burned, and revenge for my own father, killed in battle. The High Druid charged me to get the Romans out of the Holy Isle, out of our lands, out of our homes and out of our lives."

I stretched my arms aloft, then pushed back my hood to reveal the High Druid's gift to me, a gleaming bronze circlet, a crown of power, forged by the ancients, graven with images of the war gods. "Here is his symbol: his promise to our people to destroy the invaders. I vow that I will not remove it until the last Roman leaves our land. The High Druid has faith in me. Do you not have faith in him?"

The Queen snorted. "The High Druid just had his holy island taken from him by the Romans. The gods were not on his side. He's fortunate that we are rebelling now, so the Romans have come here to fight. I need warriors, not druids!"

Only a queen, made reckless by grief and anger, would dare question the High Druid. A violent demonstration of the consequences was demanded, and I had a plan to prove my mettle.

"As a warrior, I can tell you that this tent is a death trap. The firelight casts your shadows through the walls, visible from afar. You stand out: you are tall, your hair is long, your shadow is easy to spot." From my robes I took a horn hewn from the skull of a mighty bull, and blew a signal that reverberated across fen and forest.

The tattooed grey-beard sneered. "The camp is well-guarded. Nothing can touch us here!"

Three loud thuds smacked against the leather walls. Voices cried out and running footsteps sounded around the tent. Guards brought in a trio of blunted ballista bolts, and presented them to the Queen.

"My warriors can kill from afar," I told her. "These ballistas are now at your service."

The Queen's eyes gleamed. "Had you presented this to me before, I would have broken the Roman shield wall. We would have beaten them. Andraste, goddess of victory, has sent you to answer my prayers. Where did you learn such things?"

So I told her my stories, of the magnificent blood-stained horror that is Rome, and together, she and I went to war against the greatest empire the world has ever known.

2

The Battle of the Medway

"This is not honour," exclaimed the tattooed grey-beard. He snapped the shaft of a ballista bolt over his knee. "Killing from a distance is the coward's way, the Roman way. A real warrior defeats his enemy face to face, blade to bloody blade, and feels his enemy's dying breath. That is our way. That is honour!"

Queen Boudicca held up a restraining hand. "Let the druid speak, Tenvantius," she said. "You are my war chief, listen to his words and judge them for me." She gestured at me. "Tell us of your battles," she demanded.

"My first great battle was at the River Medway, just after the Roman invasion," I began. I had been young, beardless, and wanted to prove myself a man.

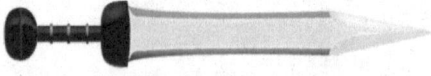

My first memory of that day is of my father, magnificent in his war gear, smiling down at me from his chariot.

'Don't worry, son,' he boomed, 'we'll soon have these Romans running for their lives. Look at our war host! We out-number them three to one! Victory will be ours!'

My brother, standing in the chariot beside him, grinned and gestured towards the enemy army on the opposite bank. 'Do you know why the Romans have such big shields?' I shook my head. 'It's so we can't see their knees knocking together!' Laughter sounded from the chariots all around. I so envied him, at my father's side, a brave young warrior, popular, and eager for battle.

'Now off you go,' said my father, pointing towards the river. 'Your druid is waiting for you.' Indeed, there was my master, Amergin, impatiently gesturing for me to get into a coracle.

I reluctantly jogged over, weighed down by my war-horn, which as a junior druid and trainee bard I was expected to blow before the battle. My master thrust the oar handle at me, and pointed towards another coracle, waiting in mid-stream.

I rowed us through the morning mist. On the other bank were the enemy cavalry. They were dressed head to toe in scale armour, which to my untrained eye seemed like fish skin. Behind us, our warriors were laughing and asking the mermen why they couldn't swim the river. Then a new group galloped to the river's edge. Their skin-tight armour gleamed in the sun, and by their shape we saw they were women. They let out a chilling war-cry and shook their spears. Our warriors promptly invited them to cross the water and enjoy the pleasure of their company and the hospitality of our halls, but not quite in those words. The women replied with mockery and derision. Some of our more impetuous warriors waded towards them, but were called back by their chiefs, who knew a trap when they saw it.

As we neared the other coracle, my reluctance was replaced by curiosity. In it was an old druid, grey-bearded and white-robed like my master, but beside him, instead of a male pupil, was a girl, the like of whom I had never seen. Her skin was white, but her eyes and lips were painted black. Around her waist was a wide leather belt holding a ceremonial sickle. She seemed about my age, but held herself with a confidence beyond her years. She had straw-coloured hair, bound by a headpiece made of antler. Few people had such hair. I wondered where she was from.

As our coracles met, the druids eyed each other up. 'You've put on weight, Dubhtach,' observed my master. 'Romans feeding you well?'

'Is your nose getting bigger, old man, or is the rest of your head shrinking?'

Ritual insults delivered, and secret passwords thus exchanged, they both nodded.

Dubhtach glanced at me. My master lifted his chin in my direction. 'This is Caz.'

'I'm Ganna,' said the girl, in a strange accent. Amergin nodded. I smiled, but she wasn't looking at me.

'No chance of stopping this battle, then?' enquired my master.

'None,' replied Dubhtach. 'The Romans want Verica to be King of the Atrebates. But I don't think it will stop there. The amount of effort they're putting into this, and given what they've done in Gaul, I reckon they're planning on staying.'

'So why are you helping them?'

'Verica is my King, and where he goes, I follow. He'll kill the usurper who took his throne, but I hope I can restrain him and limit the bloodshed.'

'Good luck with that. Any message for the High Council?'

'Tell them that the Romans blame us druids for raising rebellion in Gaul. They allow all kinds of religions in their empire, but they don't tolerate trouble-makers. You need to watch yourself. They'll kill you if they catch you.'

'Blood-thirsty brutes. But you need to be careful, too,' replied my master. 'There's a good chance your side will lose this battle. Our men will treat you with respect, but the Romans might blame you.' His stern eyes fell on the girl. 'And a battlefield full of warriors with their blood up is a dangerous place for a woman.'

Ganna had been looking at him, and pointedly ignoring me. Maybe she found my eyes disconcerting. Sometimes her gaze flickered past us, not only at our army, but upstream. At my master's words she did it again. Understandable, if she feared our warriors, but why was she glancing upstream?

I twisted round and followed her gaze. A gentle breeze parted the mists, and in the distance, past a bend in the river and so hidden from our forces, a figure emerged from the water, leading a horse. Further up the bank, in the trees, there was movement. I knew it wasn't our men, so it must be the enemy, trying to outflank us.

I shoved the coracles apart, grabbed my war-horn, and sounded the alert. Surging to my feet, I pointed upstream. Our warriors on the bank whipped their heads around, and seeing the danger, ran to the chariots. But the horses were all facing the river, and reared and snorted as the drivers desperately tried to wheel them around to confront the enemy.

My father and brother, at the front, urged their horses forward into the shallows, and drove in a wide curve. The first to get their chariot to a gallop, they headed towards the thunder of the hooves as the enemy cavalry began their charge. Sheets of spray rose from their wheels as they hurtled into battle. The foe, unfamiliar with the ground and unsure of the depth of the water, had stayed on dry land, and my father wheeled out of the water onto the bank, smashed into their flank, and burst through the nearest riders. My brother guided the horses behind the enemy line, and closed in on their leader in the middle.

Our other charioteers, realising that there was no time to turn their horses to face the enemy, formed a wall. The fighters leaped down and threw their spears. The cavalry commander, facing an impenetrable barrier, and with the element of surprise lost, decided to hit and run. He allowed his men one charge, then blew the retreat. They disengaged, leaving a scattering of dead horses and men behind, and galloped back upstream, followed by the jeers of our charioteers. But they were heading straight towards my father.

A British war chariot, with two horses unencumbered by riders on their backs, can outpace cavalry over soft ground, and my brother could have easily driven to safety. But that was not my father's way. They charged the enemy commander. Hundreds of charioteers roared their encouragement, the war horns blared and the battle drums thundered. My father ran up the yoke between the horses, and as they came together, plunged his spear into the commander's heart.

A great cheer rang out from our men. The enemy commander was thrown from his horse and rolled in the dirt. A moment later, the spears of the commander's bodyguard struck my father. He tumbled from the yoke, and my brother grabbed him and pulled him into the chariot.

'Father!' I yelled, and frantically rowed for the shore. But coracles are round and not built for speed. A frustrating nightmare of fruitless splashing lasted a few unthinking seconds before my master's voice cried, 'Jump in, Caz, it's shallow here.'

The water was freezing, but I didn't care. When my feet touched the bottom, I splashed my way ashore. Sprinting towards the battlefield, I searched for father's chariot.

I saw my uncle's chariot and ran up to him. 'Where's Father?' I panted.

'Climb in,' he said, and we raced to the medical tent, where I saw my brother carrying my father inside.

As a druid and a healer, this was my rightful place in battle, and I rushed in. My father was lying on a blanket, blood bubbling from a pierced lung. My brother was holding one of his hands, and I grabbed the other. He opened his eyes.

'Well done, my sons,' he whispered. Blood trickled from his mouth, and he coughed. 'Avenge...' But before he could get more words out, his breath left him. His eyes glazed over and his head dropped. I burst into tears, and my brother held me tight until the sobbing stopped.

The rest of that day was a nightmare of wounded men, screaming, and corpses. The Second Legion crossed the river, and there were massive casualties as our bare-chested warriors clashed with the armoured legionaries. I will never forget my first time holding down a thrashing man while my master amputated a leg, or the stink of seared flesh being cauterised. The battle lasted all day, but we fought them to a standstill, and neither side was victorious.

That night my brother and I placed my father's body on top of the funeral pyre, the rightful place for the hero who had led the first charge. The bodies of his enemies we threw in the river. Their heads we kept as trophies. They were Celtic auxiliary cavalry of the Second Legion, and next day we took our revenge.

3

Elephants

"I remember that day," said the Boudicca's grey-bearded war chief. "I was there. If you'd been keeping a proper lookout instead of gazing at women, you'd have seen the cavalry sooner, the chariots would have been ready, and your father wouldn't have attacked alone." Tenvantius' glare and sour expression revealed his hatred for me. It was a compliment in a way— maybe he worried that Boudicca would put me in command of her armies to take his place.

I refused to let him put me on the defensive. "Easy to judge in hindsight, but I don't remember you being there," I mocked. "The Iceni were friendly with the Romans back then. Were you with the enemy?"

The Queen broke in. "He was with my husband, Prasutagus, obeying royal orders. His allegiance is not in doubt. Yours is. You talk of revenge, so tell us, what did you do?"

So I told them of our vengeance.

On the second day of the battle, I was in the medical tent, helping my master care for the wounded, when I felt the ground tremble. I heard a chariot skid to a halt outside, then my brother ran in.

'Monsters!' he yelled. 'Run!'

Master Amergin didn't even raise his head from the slashed arm he was stitching. 'Go see, boy,' the old druid commanded.

I ran outside. The tent was on a long spit of land, with the river on one side and a marsh on the other. A hundred paces away was a line of monsters, advancing towards us. They were twice the height of a man, with gigantic tusks, and a box of Roman archers on top. On the face of each was a huge snake, and as I watched in horror, one of our warriors tried to stab one, and got too close. The snake grabbed him, picked him up, shook him violently, and then held him down while the monster stamped on him. Holding the body down with its foot, it ripped him in half.

Another group of our warriors, showing insane bravery, charged the biggest monster in the middle of the line. It speared one warrior with a tusk and trampled two more. The archers picked off most of the rest. A few who got through and tried to hamstring the monster from behind were cut down by cavalry following close on their heels. I recognised them as the same horsemen that had killed my father.

Running back into the tent, I, too, yelled, 'Monsters!'

'Are they breathing fire?' asked Amergin.

'What? No!'

'Then they're afraid of it.' And he continued stitching.

I frantically checked around the tent. The only fire was the brazier that we used for heating the cauterising irons, its coals glowing a dull red. It was in one corner, to keep it away from the medical supplies like the alcohol for cleaning wounds.

'I've got an idea,' I told my brother. 'Gather the slingers and chariots outside.' I loaded the flasks of alcohol into a sack, and, wrapping my robe around my other hand to protect it from the heat, picked up the brazier and carried them both out of the tent.

Outside, my brother had assembled the charioteers, with slings in their hands. 'Half take flasks, half take fire,' I told them. With my robe-swaddled hand I loaded up their slings with hot coals, while my brother passed out the flasks. The sound of fighting was getting nearer. I looked up the battleground at the monsters. The largest was heading straight for our tent.

'Mount up!' yelled my brother.

'Aim for the biggest!' I shouted.

The slingers jumped into their chariots and charged through our retreating army, spinning the slings around their heads. Their coals glowed red hot, then white. The chariots sped along the front of the line of monsters, and as they passed the biggest one, the slingers cast the fire and alcohol at it. Smashing on its armoured forehead, the flasks sprayed its head and neck with a cloud of alcohol, and the flaming coals set it alight.

As fire engulfed its head, the monster let out the most terrifying scream I had ever heard. It swerved violently and ran towards the river, heedless of anything in its way. Blinded by the flames, it smashed its way along the line of monsters. The sight and sound of their fleeing leader panicked the rest of the herd, which broke and ran. The cavalry behind them, taken by surprise, were too close, and many were run down and trampled as they tried to escape. Thus we had our revenge.

The fleeing monster had left a gap in the Roman line, and my brother rallied his chariots. 'Follow me!' he shouted, and charged through. Behind the cavalry were blocks of slow-moving Roman heavy infantry, and in the middle was the Roman commander. Seeing the chance of even greater glory for our family, my brother attacked.

The Romans were the Ninth Spanish Legion, who had fought under Caesar. They were highly skilled and disciplined veterans. Seeing my brother coming, they tightened their ranks into squares, leaving gaps for the fleeing cavalry and monsters to pass through. The outside ranks grounded their shields, and the next rank put their shields on top, forming a wall eight feet high. My brother's warriors leaped from their chariots and attacked, but could not break in.

The rest of our army assaulted the other groups of infantry, but they were also in tight squares. As the monsters and what was left of the fleeing cavalry ran between the infantry and disappeared into the distance, the squares started to move towards the commander. They were manoeuvring to trap my brother.

Running back into the tent, I grabbed my war horn, sprinted back out, and blew a warning. But in the din of battle, no-one heard.

My master emerged from the tent, wiping blood off his hands. 'Look, boy.' He pointed across the river. On the far bank were rank upon rank of Roman soldiers, wrapped in cloaks, with bundles at their feet.

'What do you see?' he asked.

'Romans, just standing there.'

'What's strange about them?'

'They're not moving?'

'Look at their heads.'

Their heads seemed small compared to the infantry in battle. 'No helmets!'

'Which means...'

As I watched, the Romans picked up the bundles at their feet and moved towards the river.

'It means, boy, that their helmets and armour are in those bundles. They're going to float them and swim the river. We have to get the wounded out of here now. We'll take the route through the marsh. Come and help.'

We dashed into the tent, got the casualties organised, with the walking wounded carrying the others, and made our way to the marshes. My master went in front, probing with his staff to find the hidden walkways under the surface of the water.

I was last. It was my job to set the tent on fire, so that the enemy couldn't use it, and in the hope that the sight of the burning tent would alert our army. I glanced down the spit of land at them. The Roman infantry had formed into one solid block, and were pushing our men back.

'Duck!' My master gave a warning yell. I bent, then jumped sideways as an arrow shot past my head. Spinning round, I saw the monster which we had set ablaze emerging from the river. The snake on its head pointed at me, and an archer on top nocked another arrow. I ran, and the monster bellowed and gave chase.

'Dodge,' yelled my master. I did. I couldn't run in a straight line, because that would present an easy target for the archer. But if I didn't run straight, the monster would catch me.

I sprinted and weaved. Arrows flew past me, but it's hard to shoot accurately from the back of a swaying monster. I heard the pounding footsteps getting closer and closer, and the beast made a sound like a hundred angry war horns. Fear sped my heels, but the marsh was too far away, and I wasn't going to make it.

'Go left,' yelled Amergin. I swerved, and the snake just missed me. The beast was so heavy that it couldn't swerve as well as me.

'Circle,' ordered my master, and I ran behind the monster. The archer on top was thrown against the side of the box as the monster tried to spin around, and his arrows flew wild.

I ran round the tail of the monster. It felt crazy to be so close to it. I should have tried to hamstring it, but I was too scared. Everything seemed to be moving unnaturally slowly, and I noticed the smallest detail of its pallid grey skin and pig-like tail.

From the marsh came a strange noise, like a swarm of irate bees. The monster paused, flapped its huge ears, trumpeted, and then made off towards the river, seeming to ignore me entirely. I seized the chance, and sprinted into the marsh.

The wounded had made their way to a low-lying island, and I caught up with them there. We hid among the long grasses and watched the battle. The Romans nearest us crossed the river, unpacked their armour and helmets from the bundles, put them on, and formed up in a line.

Our warriors, noticing the burning tent and the Romans beside it, saw that they were about to be trapped in a pincer movement. The foot soldiers retreated into the marsh, where the heavy infantry couldn't follow, and the chariots used the same shallows that my father had driven through the morning before to drive past the end of the Roman line and escape up the spit. The battle was over.

'What was that noise?' I asked Amergin.

'Magic!' he grinned.

'You always say magic is only between men's ears. Tell me!'

'When the news came of the Roman army gathering across the sea,' he said, 'I talked to our sages. They had heard of the Romans and their enemies using those animals. They're called elephants, and when the Carthaginian general Hannibal used them against the Romans, they learned how to defeat them. Elephants are afraid of two things: fire and bees. So I prepared this noisemaker to swing round and round on the end of a sling. It sounds like a swarm of angry bees. You're lucky it worked.'

4

THE BATTLE OF THE THAMES

At this part of the story, Queen Boudicca frowned. "Why would a beast so large be afraid of such small things?"

"Their mouth, ears, and eyes are sensitive, and they panic if a bee goes up their nose."

"Will we face them in battle soon?"

"No, my Queen. Never."

"How can you be so sure?"

"The Romans don't use them anymore, because they know that we have learned how to beat them, and because they haven't replaced Claudius' war elephants since I killed the last of them."

"My Queen, his tales are ridiculous!" protested her war chief, Tenvantius. "All he has are words and a few baubles that he probably looted from some grave. Why should we trust him?"

"Tell us something that only one who was there would know," she demanded.

"Were you at the Battle of the Thames, Tenvantius?"

"I was. Prove that you were. Tell me who was in command, and of the battle." He pointed a tattooed finger at me. "If you lie, I will know."

"I swear it by Toutatis, God of War, this is what happened. May he strike me down if I lie. After the Battle of the Medway in late spring, our warriors dispersed. The fields needed tending and the harvest reaping. The Romans pushed up to the Thames, but stopped, and we didn't know why. Druid Amergin was invited to a council of war, and he took me along. The Princes of the Catuvellauni tribe, Caratacus and Togodumnus, were in charge."

The Queen looked enquiringly at Tenvantius. He gave no confirmation, but had I been wrong, he would have pounced.

"What did they say?" asked the Queen.

I remembered that long-ago day well. Caratacus spoke first. He was tall, confident, his weapons and clothes practical, but of the finest quality, and a born leader. 'How can we beat them?' he demanded.

'The Thames is wider and deeper than the Medway,' replied Amergin. 'We can defend the fords, attack the Romans while they are still in the water, let them drown and the river will wash them away.'

'What about those Celts who swam with their horses?' asked Togodumnus. He was shorter but broader than his brother, with shoulders like a bull and bristling hair.

'Downstream, the river is too wide, and too far for horses to swim. Upstream, we can patrol the riverbanks, and call in reserves if we see swimmers.'

Queen Boudicca snorted. "Not much of a plan! Just sit back and wait?"

"That's what happens if you rely on druids' advice, instead of a warrior's expertise," sneered Tenvantius.

"So what went wrong?" asked Boudicca.

"The Romans had been waiting for their emperor to arrive. He brought more elephants and his personal bodyguard, the

Praetorians. They joined up with the Roman general, Plautius. That gave them four legions, the Second, Ninth, Fourteenth and Twentieth, so about twenty thousand Romans, and also the same number of auxiliaries. Their army was enormous."

"How did they get so many men across the river?"

I closed my eyes, and the memories came flooding back, memories of blood and death and horror.

Druid Amergin and I went upriver, to where he thought the invading Romans would ford the Thames. Caratacus ordered a fortified gateway built, and we hammered spiked stakes into the water around the ford so that anyone crossing was forced through the gate. We sometimes saw Roman cavalry patrols on the other bank, but they didn't try to cross.

Early one morning, as the mist shrouded the river, we heard the alarm. My brother was with us as part of the reserve, and we jumped into his chariot and sped downstream along the bank. As we drove, we heard the blare of trumpets, the thundering of drums, and the clash of arms.

We rounded a bend in the river and saw the Roman's trick. A line of boats was anchored from the far bank to ours, and between the boats were planks, making a floating road. Across this bridge were pouring rank upon rank of infantry, sunlight glinting off their armour.

Our warriors who had sounded the alarm were fighting bravely, but more and more Romans leaped off the end of the bridge into the shallows. They formed a shield wall and drove our men back.

My brother cracked the reins, and we surged forwards. In the distance, we heard another alarm, but this was a different signal.

'Elephants,' yelled Amergin to my brother. 'Take me there!'

My brother pulled the horses around, and again we dashed downstream along the bank. The alarms grew closer, but I saw nothing in the river.

We skidded to a halt beside one of our scouts. He removed the horn from his lips and pointed out into the river. 'Look!'

In midstream the water swirled, as if gushing over submerged rocks. In front of each swirl, a grey branch poked out of the water. A twig floated past one. The branches were not floating downstream with the current, but were making slowly towards us.

Amergin took out his horn and blew a summons.

'What are we going to do?' I asked.

'You'll see. I have a little surprise for them.'

'If those are elephants, where are the riders?'

'See around the swirls there are bits of reed? They're hollow for breathing through. The warriors are under water, held down by the weight of their armour and pulled along by holding the elephant harness. Clever, but not clever enough.'

The elephants were getting near the shore when a wagon arrived from behind us.

'At last,' said Amergin to the waggoners. 'All right, remember what we practised. Get moving.'

The men jumped down and opened the wagon. Inside were piles of bits of strangely bent metal. Each one had two bars joined in the middle, sharpened at the ends. They resembled a three-legged stool with a spike on top, as long as my hand. Whichever way round they were, there was always one spike sticking up.

'What're these?' I asked.

'Caltrops.'

'What are they for?'

'Elephants are heavy. We'll use that against them. Throw

these in the river where the elephants will come out.'

We followed the wagon along the river bank, throwing the caltrops into the water. While we worked, my brother's chariots arrived with another of Amergin's wagons. It drove into the water upstream of the elephants, and the waggoners rolled some barrels to the tailgate, and tipped something into the water.

'Oil?' I asked.

Amergin nodded. 'Things are about to get interesting. Let's get back up the bank, out of harm's way.'

The swirls in the water at the front had stopped, and the others drew close. Suddenly, one surged forward. An elephant lifted its head from the water and waded forward, trumpeting loudly. The others followed, and they charged towards the shore. Their warriors heaved themselves up onto their backs and pulled weapons out of baskets on the elephants' flanks.

The lead elephant was charging forward in knee-deep water when it must have stood on a caltrop, the spike penetrating its tender sole. It collapsed sideways, bellowing in pain. Amergin blew his horn, and the waggoners threw a flaming torch into the oily water.

Not knowing what had brought down the lead elephant, the drivers of the other elephants urged their mounts forwards to get out of the river before the burning oil floated downstream to them. Moving forwards, more of them stood on caltrops. Some fell over, trumpeting in agony, and that panicked the others, who fled back into the river.

The warriors from the fallen elephants waded out of the river and were met by my brother's charioteers. A brief and bloody fight followed, then the charioteers waded out to the elephants, scuffing their feet to avoid treading on the caltrops. The elephants were unarmoured, to allow them to swim, and slow in the water. Against such easy targets, the charioteers' spears were merciless.

The lead elephant, bleeding but alive, tried to charge on three legs, but must have stood on another caltrop, because it rolled in the shallows again.

'Leave them,' yelled Amergin. The burning oil drifted towards them, and the elephants tried to limp away. They were too slow, and as the flames caught up to them, their drivers made them kneel underwater with only their trunks out to breathe. Some tried to hold their breath, but the oil was slow-moving, and when they raised their trunks to breathe, the flames burned them, and they let out all-too-human cries of agony. The surviving beasts fled away into the river.

Amergin gave orders to the scout. 'I have to go. Follow the survivors, and if they try to come ashore, sound the alarm and throw the caltrops and oil. You've seen what to do.'

He clapped a gnarled hand my brother's shoulder. 'Let's get back to the bridge. Take us to a place where I can get a good view.'

We jumped aboard the chariot and headed for the sound of battle.

The fight was going badly. The Romans had pushed out from the bridge, and hundreds of them were clearing an ever-widening space as more and more crossed the river.

'We've got to break that bridge,' said Amergin.

I had never seen such a bridge before, and had no idea how to break one. I prayed to Toutatis. I breathed slowly, relaxed, and emptied my mind. A picture came into my head of the twigs floating downstream past the elephants.

'Got it,' I exclaimed. 'Let's find some fallen trees, or chop some down, and float them into the bridge.'

'Worth a try,' said my brother, and he led his chariots upstream to the next bend.

THE DRUID AND THE ELEPHANT

War axes are not great on trees, but there were enough charioteers to topple the first before too long. It was a willow. The long branches caught in the current and dragged the tree out into the river. Cries of alarm came from the bridge when they saw it.

Amergin called to my brother. 'Keep them coming. We'll be back soon.'

He strode off towards the bridge, and I followed.

As the tree floated into the bridge, Romans hacked at the branches to try to get it to go under the planks. The current was too swift, and as the river pulled the tree downstream, one of the anchor ropes holding a boat snapped. The bridge started to bend.

Orders were called out, and the Romans cut away the ropes holding the planks in place. A gap opened in the bridge, and the reinforcements stopped. The tree floated through, taking a bunch of planks with it.

'Well, that ought to hold them up for a while,' said Amergin. 'Let's go and find Caratacus. His reserves should be here by now. It's time to attack.'

We found Caratacus and Togodumnus arguing.

'We need to keep some troops in reserve,' said Caratacus. 'It's a fundamental rule of warfare. Always have a rear-guard.'

'No need this time,' yelled Togodumnus in frustration. 'The Romans can't get across anywhere except here, and we need every man we've got to push them back. Tell him, Amergin.'

'I'll stand rear-guard,' said Amergin. 'My scouts will keep watch.'

'Right,' said Togodumnus. 'I'll hit them from upstream, you hit them from down, and we'll crush them between us.'

They ran to their chariots and thundered away.

'Let's find a good viewpoint,' said Amergin. We climbed a

tall oak and gazed around. On the riverbank, the Romans had formed a square and were holding their ground until more reinforcements joined them. Across the bridge, men were carrying new planks towards the gap, and a new boat was being rowed into position.

A horn sounded the charge, and Caratacus' and Togodumnus' chariots sped towards the Roman flanks. At fifty paces, the Romans threw their spears. The charioteers pulled their horses to a halt, so the spears fell where the chariots would have been, and the warriors leapt off and charged. At thirty paces, the Roman soldiers threw their second spears. They slammed into our warriors' shields, weighing them down and making them useless. Throwing them aside, our warriors charged forward. At ten paces the rear Roman ranks threw war darts, felling a few of our men, and the front ranks braced for impact.

They came together with a thunderous clash, but the Romans stood fast. Our warriors' blades skidded off shields and armour, while the Roman short swords stabbed viciously at bare chests and bellies. Bodies soon littered the ground, the wounded limping and crawling away from the front line.

'We should set up the medical tent,' said Amergin. 'The wagon bringing it should be here by now.'

As we climbed down the oak, we heard an alarm from inland.

'Enemy cavalry!' exclaimed Amergin. 'Where did they come from?'

On the riverbank, fierce fighting continued. Another horn sounded, this time from where my brother and his chariots were, but Caratacus and Togodumnus didn't react. The noise of the battle drowned out the alarm. I pulled out my horn and sounded a warning. Caratacus heard it and broke off the attack, but Togodumnus was still fighting.

'Well done, but you've given our position away,' said

Amergin. 'Let's get out of here.'

We jumped down from the lowest limbs and ran to Caratacus. 'What's going on?' he yelled, pulling Amergin into his chariot.

I clambered into the chariot of one of his bodyguards. 'Cavalry raid from upstream!' I told the driver. Caratacus' signaller blew the "Follow me" and we disengaged from the Romans and drove off. I guessed Caratacus' plan was to go round the Romans and join his brother, but then the enemy cavalry emerged from the trees and charged Togodumnus' forces from behind.

I couldn't see who the enemy cavalry were, but they weren't Roman. They were dressed like Celts. We charged into them and gave Togodumnus just enough time to break off the fight and disengage. Then we wheeled away and left the field of battle.

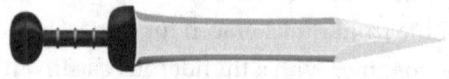

Queen Boudicca eyed Tenvantius. "Well?"

"All common knowledge. Maybe he talked to men who were there and pieced it together. Even if he was there, he might have become a Roman spy later. I still don't trust him."

"Only one way to be sure," said Boudicca. She stabbed a finger at me. "Bring me some Roman heads."

I nodded. "As you command, my Queen."

I left them in their brightly lit command tent, and returned to the cold, dark fens to meet my men. As I walked, I reflected on two things I hadn't told them: first, that after that cavalry raid I had never seen my brother again, and second, that I had found out later that the cavalry were Roman auxiliaries shipped around the coast, and then guided to the Thames by Iceni scouts. My revenge would not only be revenge on the Romans for my father, but also on the Iceni for my brother.

5

Ambush

The Queen wanted Roman heads, and her war chief Tenvantius would be on the lookout for any trickery, so they had to be real. I've never liked killing people: it's dangerous, messy, and there are always friends, relatives or comrades who want revenge. In the Roman army, some soldiers are in it for the glory, the thrill of killing, and the loot, so they're fair game. But a lot are like me when I was a recruit, young, only there because it's better than farming and the constant risk of poor harvests and starvation. They don't deserve death just for being in the wrong place at the wrong time.

To get the heads, I planned an ambush in the fens. The Romans had built a military road across the marshes, and we commandeered some boats and rowed out there. Our ballistas we towed with us on punts, flat-bottomed boats designed for hunting ducks. The road was on a causeway which zigzagged from island to island, surrounded by pools and reed beds. I'd learned to build Roman roads during my time in the army, and this one was in bad shape. The stones and the causeway were too heavy, and it was slowly sinking into the mud. Three large culverts let the rain-swollen marsh water flow out beneath the road, towards the distant sea.

We stood in some alder trees on an island, and I briefed

my men. "Right, lads, listen in. Our mission is to take Roman heads, to convince Boudicca that we are on her side. We're going to ambush a small party as they cross this causeway. See those culverts under the road? Our ambushers will hide there."

"We'll conceal the ballistas in the reeds, near the islands, so they can shoot along the causeway, but not too close, where they might be seen and attacked. I will be by the biggest, and give the signal to shoot. The medium ballista will be at the other end of this stretch of causeway, to hit them from behind. The small ballista is the reserve, to shoot anyone that tries to escape. When the ambushers in the culverts hear the first ballista shot, the ones in the middle culvert will charge the flank of the enemy. The men in the other culverts will climb onto the causeway, spread caltrops to prevent breakouts, and then charge in to hit the enemy from the front and back. You'll find sacks of caltrops in the punts. To help the ambushers escape after the trap is sprung, we'll build walkways underwater, made of bundles of wood. Collect fallen branches from among these trees, and use tufts of bog plant to mark the way. We must hit fast, hard, and get away quickly. I want at least three heads, with helmets. If things go wrong, we split up, and meet on that island," I said, pointing into the distance. The password challenge is 'Sunlight', and the correct reply is 'Moonshine'. If you say 'Moonlight', we'll know you've been caught, and will let you come forward, and try to rescue you. This job is vital. We need Boudicca to trust us, so we can lead her forces. Without us to lead them, the Romans will beat them, just like they did before. Then the whole revolt will fail, and the Romans will butcher the men, and enslave the women and children of our tribes and our allies, like we've seen in the past. These are our people. We can't let that happen. This is a simple ambush: we've done these before. You know what to do. Let's take some heads!"

All seemed ready, but in war, things rarely go as planned.

We allowed several large patrols to pass unmolested. Crouching in the stinking marsh, we rubbed mud on our skins to keep the biting insects at bay. Late in the afternoon, a target presented itself: a mounted messenger with an escort of five cavalry troopers. From their gear they were from the Ninth Legion, one of those who had invaded when I was a boy, and fought in the battle where my father had died, so I had no qualms about taking my revenge on them.

When they reached the middle of the causeway, Lukon, my ballista crew chief, pulled the release rope. The arms whipped forward, and the bolt flew through the air. It was a special bolt: a hollow wooden tube, filled with lead slingshot bullets, and open at the front. The tube cupped the air and slowed rapidly, but the slingshots were small and round, and flew straight and fast. As the tube dropped back, the bullets spread into a hail of lead, and peppered the horsemen. Two went down, and the others fled up the road, straight into the shot from the ballista behind them. Another fell, leaving two.

They fled back the way they came, but Trenus, one of my ambushers, threw a bag of caltrops onto the causeway. It split open and covered the stony surface with spikes. The cavalrymen tried to leap over them, but one didn't make it, and his crippled horse crashed to the ground. The rider was thrown and smashed helmet first into the stony road surface, stunning him. Deciding that the road was a killing ground, the cavalryman who jumped the caltrops swerved his horse down the bank of the causeway into the marsh. He dismounted, took cover behind his animal's body, and led it into the fen, using his lance to probe for safe passage. Such a large, slow-moving target was easy for the third ballista crew, who send a heavy bolt straight into the horse's heart. It collapsed with a splash, leaving the cavalryman standing alone in the bog. He tried to run, but our ambushers were lighter and faster. They surrounded him, and he fell on his own sword rather than be captured.

The only survivor was the messenger. His leg was pinned beneath his fallen horse, and as the ambushers climbed towards him from their hiding places in the culverts, he pulled out his horn and sounded the alarm. A few heartbeats later it was kicked out of his hands, and his throat was slit.

My men were pulling the dead Romans into the marshes when a distant horn sounded in response to the alarm. In groups of three, the ambushers dragged the corpses towards the reed beds, two pulling and one covering their tracks and laying caltrops on the underwater walkways behind them. The ballista crews hastily reloaded.

The men had just got into cover when a cavalry troop galloped onto the causeway from the furthest island. Dead horses and blood made the ambush site obvious. The troop halted, wary of a trap, and sent scouts forwards.

The blood was still wet and the horses warm. The scouts found the slingshot bullets and the wooden tube, and took them back to the commander.

I thought furiously. What would he do? His cavalry were useless in the marsh, and he knew we had a ballista. The missing men were probably dead. Would he move on and bring back search teams from the nearest fort, or would he try to avenge the fallen?

Their scouts were examining the horse with a ballista bolt in its heart. From the angle it penetrated, they made a rough guess about where it came from, and pointed out into the marsh. They guessed wrong, but unfortunately gestured in my direction. The commander shouted orders, and half his men dismounted and spread out in a line down the causeway. Then they faced the marsh, and, using their lances to test the ground in front of them, advanced into the bog in my direction.

When I was young, I would have only seen two choices, flight or fight. Running through a marsh wasn't a good plan if the cavalry had slings or archers. Fighting was suicide, as we were heavily outnumbered. My military instructors had taught me to take a deep breath, pause, and consider. See it as a tactical problem, not a terrifying premonition.

We couldn't move without being seen from the high ground on the island and causeway. We would have to hide, but how? I rubbed the heavy war crown around my brow. Then I remembered the elephants in the Thames. The ballista was big and heavy, so use its weight. In the bottom of the punt was a hole sealed by a bung, used to stop the punt filling with rain when beached. I pulled out the bung, and water flooded into the punt. We cut some old, dry, hollow reeds to breathe through.

It seemed to take forever for the punt to fill, and the Romans were wading closer and closer. Fortunately, as the water level in the punt rose, it got heavier, so we all pulled down on one side of it, and water flowed over the edges. It sank like a stone.

As the punt went under, we held onto the ballista arms and were pulled down beneath the water. I heard the sloshing as the nearest Roman waded up to us, and swishes as he poked his lance into the reed beds. He was coming straight towards us. I drew my knife.

The hollow reed transmitted the sounds of the search from above the surface to my head, and just as the Roman was about to walk into us, I heard a shout, 'Found something!'

The Roman stopped. "What?"

"Underwater pathway."

"Hold on, I'm coming."

He waded away.

"Trooper, get back in line! Scout, investigate!" ordered a new voice.

The Roman obeyed, but he had moved around us, and waded past, an arm's length away.

The scout followed the walkway and found a caltrop on it. "See, hardly any rust and mud," he reported. "It's new."

"Looks like a trap. Take it to the commander."

The search continued, but the Romans found nothing else, and it started to get dark. They called back the searchers, and after we were sure they'd gone, we crept away.

My men had saved three heads. We returned to camp, and I planned my next move to gain Boudicca's confidence.

6

THE STORMING OF CAMULODUNUM

The next evening, I was escorted into Boudicca's tent. She had not yet arrived, but another man was there waiting. From his white robes, he was a druid. His black beard was not yet greyed with age, and his eyes were keen. He was feeding scraps to a pine marten, sitting on his shoulder. As I approached, it hid in his cowl. The druid and I introduced ourselves using the secret password.

"Lurking in the shadows, old man? Boudicca ask you to spy on me?"

He sniffed. "Is that bog I smell on you, young snake, or your own foul odour?"

Ritual three-stage insults complete, we exchanged names.

"Cassibelanus, taught by Amergin. Call me Caz."

"Caicer. I'm Boudicca's druid. Segnorix told me about you. Amergin was a friend of mine. Rumour was that his apprentice disappeared after the Battle of the Thames. People assumed you were dead. What really happened?"

So I told him about the storming of Camulodunum, so many years before.

THE DRUID AND THE ELEPHANT

After the Battle of the Thames, Prince Togodumnus died of his wounds, and his brother Caratacus retreated to the ancient capital at Camulodunum to regroup. The Romans went north to put Verica back on the Atrebates throne, then made for Camulodunum.

Caratacus' capital was a big place, where two branches of the River Colne flow east and come together. To close the gap, on the western side there are earthworks, with ditches and wooden walls. Caratacus and Amergin spent a whole day walking the perimeter, discussing how to strengthen the defences. The southern branch of the river was narrow, so they planned a wall along it. The northern branch was wider, but we knew the Romans were good at crossing rivers, so they planned a wall there too. Caratacus put his warriors to work, and everyone else prepared for a siege.

As the sun set, Amergin tested my tactical knowledge. 'What would you do?' he demanded.

'The southern river is shallow; the elephants and cavalry can wade across. The wall needs to be strong enough so that elephants can't break through. Caltrops in the river might help, but the Romans know that trick now, and will send men to clear them. We need walkways round the walls for our warriors to stand on and shoot at anyone trying to cross the river. We can use your floating burning oil trick as well, but it will only delay them.'

'And the western wall?' asked Amergin.

'The ditch is good for stopping the elephants and horses, and the gateways are well-defended. The Romans will use their infantry to attack there.'

'The northern river?'

'Better. It's wider and deeper. The Romans might try another bridge, like they did on the Thames. We need to move all the boats to our side.'

'If you were the Roman commander, how would you attack?'

'Our walls are too long. We don't have enough men to defend them. I'd attack in many places at the same time. When all our warriors are busy, I'd strike again in a new place. Wherever the defenders are thinnest, I send in more of my warriors. I'd pretend to attack in the north, really attack the west, and then later attack the south.'

'So what should Caratacus do?'

'Have watchers on the walls who can call for reinforcements. Have a mobile reserve of horsemen who can dash to any danger point. And have an inner stronghold to retreat to if the Romans get in. In the last resort, have an escape plan, just in case.'

'Why?'

'They outnumber us, their emperor is here and won't let them leave until they win, and our defences are weak. They can surround us and wait until we starve. We need some kind of trick.'

'What trick?'

'We can drop bee hives from the walls onto their elephants.'

'What else?'

'Hide cavalry in the woods, and when they attack, hit them from behind.'

'Will that be enough?'

'Probably not. So what can we do?' I knew he'd have something up his sleeve.

'Use magic,' he grinned.

'What magic?'

'Remember how I told you that magic is what you make people believe?'

'Yes.'

'So how can we make them believe that there is something more important than attacking us?'

'I don't know! Poison them? Make them sick? Find a bigger and more dangerous enemy to attack them?'

'No. We're going to kill their emperor. He's the reason they're here. If he's dead, they'll have to take his body back to Rome.'

'He'll be well-guarded.'

'Of course. But I have a plan.'

Over the next few days Prince Caratacus' charioteers skirmished with the Romans and delayed their advance, while in Camulodunum the people built walls, and slaughtered their spare animals for winter meat.

Amergin and I rode around the surrounding countryside. It was flat and thickly wooded with beech and hazel, ideal for hiding cavalry. 'This will do nicely,' he said.

When the Romans arrived, we first saw their scouts sneaking through the woods. But our scouts were locals who knew all the good ambush spots, and their commanders, worried about rising losses, called their scouts back in to their main force.

The cavalry were next, in units too big for our scouts to handle, so we let them ride around, until they got near the walls of the town, when we sent arrows their way.

Amergin and I climbed a tall chestnut with a good view to the south-west of the town, and watched the legions deploy. They dragged forward large stone-throwing machines, and I watched as they threw rocks at the gatehouses. They worked together, and when they shot, all the stones would hit the same place at the same time. It wasn't long before they smashed wooden doors in the gatehouses. Then they changed targets, and starting throwing balls of fire over the walls into the buildings behind. Soon the thatched roofs were ablaze and smoke darkened the skies.

The Roman commanders galloped around, getting the infantry into position, and then they attacked the western wall. The elephants led, carrying tree trunks on their tusks, and dropped them into the ditches to fill them in. Accompanying archers hid behind infantry shields and shot at any defender trying to throw spears or shoot arrows at the elephants. The elephants were armoured, and the few arrows that did hit them just bounced off.

When the ditches were full, a cheer went up, and the centurions led their men forward to attack the gatehouse. Behind them were slingers and archers, who shot at our warriors on the walls and behind the gates.

Meanwhile, the elephants were filling in the ditch in a new place. Then three of them stood side by side. They reared up on their hind legs, put their weight onto the wall, and pushed. The wall slowly buckled and fell. The Roman reserve infantry saw their chance, and charged forward.

'There he is!' Amergin pointed, and for the first time I saw Claudius, Emperor of Rome. He was atop an enormous elephant, sitting on a throne with two guards behind him, and the beast was walking forward to give him a better view. Around him was a guard of horsemen. I didn't know it at the time, but these were the Praetorian guard, the best regular infantry in the Roman empire, from the unit who had found Claudius cowering behind a curtain after Emperor Caligula's assassination, and had put him on the throne. He had rewarded them with five-years' worth of pay each, and now they were protecting their investment in the hope of further generosity if he continued to rule. It was time for Amergin to mess up their plans.

The Emperor's forces were now inside the walls of Camulodunum, but it was a trap. We had instructed Caratacus' men to build a second wall inside the first one, lower so that the Romans couldn't see it from outside. The legions were now stuck between the two walls because the gateway in the inner wall was far away in the east, and the elephants were still outside. The carnyx blares of the defenders mixed with the trumpeting of the elephants and the screams of the dying. All eyes were on the city, and it was time to spring the trap.

The Emperor was outside the walls, with the Praetorians and a few remaining forces. Amergin waved a signal to our scouts below, and they sent word to our cavalry hidden in the forest.

'Now watch this,' he said. 'The Emperor is in for a surprise!'

Our horsemen cantered to the edge of the woods, about two hundred paces behind the Emperor, and just as the Roman guards saw them and raised the alarm, they charged. They smashed through the guards and galloped towards the Emperor. The Praetorians sent half their cavalry to meet them. But a cavalry clash was not Amergin's plan. As our men got within bow range, they halted and shot their arrows at the Emperor's elephant. It was well-armoured on the head and flanks, but its rear was uncovered, and was a large target. Amergin had improved his noise-maker that sounded like an angry bee, and put it on some of the arrows, so the elephant was simultaneously stung by the arrows and alarmed by the bee sounds. It let out an angry trumpet and charged off in the opposite direction.

The Praetorians were divided. Some had charged our horse archers, who now galloped away into the woods. Others followed their emperor, who was clinging on to the jolting platform for dear life. Arrows were sticking out of the back of his wooden chair, and his face was white with fear. As the elephant went forward, it came within range of our archers on the town walls, giving them the target of a lifetime. The Emperor was only saved by the bravery of the Praetorians with him, who used their own bodies as living shields. When the elephant finally stopped, the pursuing Praetorian cavalry found their emperor cowering on the floor of the platform beneath the bodies of his guards, covered in their blood.

I paused in my tale, memories of the Praetorians stilling my tongue. I both hated them for their part in the invasion, but admired their bravery and fighting prowess. In Rome, I had fought alongside them, and knew them to be ruthless enemies. They were the armoured fist of the most powerful man in the world, and something told me I had not seen the last of them.

"I see," said Druid Caicer, interrupting my premonition and dragging my mind back to the present. "The story I heard is that the Romans stormed the city and Caratacus escaped. How did that happen?" I returned to my story.

The war elephants that had made the second breach in the walls smashed through the inner wall in the same way, by pushing it over together. The legions got in and sacked the city. Amergin and I were still up the chestnut, and watched new smoke rising as the Romans set fire to the houses.

'Time to go,' said Amergin.

We climbed down, and following our scouts into the woods, headed east.

We had moved all the boats from the River Colne down to a port on the estuary. Half the cavalry crossed the river and prepared to head north to the River Stour, then west to avoid Iceni lands. The other half stayed with us.

Caratacus fought long and hard, but the Romans had heavy infantry and war elephants, so he couldn't win. The inner stronghold lasted until dusk, and then Caratacus slipped away to Amergin's escape route on the river. He had made rafts out of pairs of thick tree trunks tied together side by side, with a small gap in the middle. Caratacus and his men swam between the trunks. They left the legions behind inside the town walls, and the Roman auxiliary archers and slingers on the river banks peppered the trunks with arrows and slingstones, but to no avail.

When we saw them coming, we did a cavalry charge to clear away the Romans, then picked up Caratacus and his men in our boats, and sailed away out to sea. Our half of the cavalry crossed the river to join the others, and trotted away towards the pre-arranged meeting place, far to the north-west, away from tribes friendly to the Romans.

7

THE HIGH DRUID'S PLAN

Druid Caicer stroked his pine marten thoughtfully. "So," he asked, "the Romans won at the Medway, the Thames, and at Camulodunum. What makes you think you can beat them now?"

"The High Druid came up with a good plan, and me being here is a part of that plan."

"That was a long time ago, Caz," said Caicer. "Things have changed. The Romans invaded the Holy Isle and took it away from the High Druid. If his plan is so good, how come he lost the island?"

"Fair point," I replied, "but there's a good reason." So I told him the story of the High Druid's secret plan to defeat the Romans.

After the loss of Camulodunum, the druids knew that military victory was impossible, and held a high council meeting to decide what to do. My master, Amergin, was a member of the council, and as his pupil, I went along.

We met in a sacred oak grove at full moon. Around the fire sat the High Druid, his council of advisers, guests, and men who were to speak of what they had seen. I was surprised to see the druid we'd met on the Medway, Dubhtach, among them, but Amergin said he had a right to be there as a senior druid, and was part of the High Druid's plans. He was talking to his pupil Ganna, and they didn't notice me.

The High Druid first invited the witnesses to describe their experiences, from those who had first seen the Roman ships on the south coast to those who had fought at Camulodunum. When all had spoken, he rose to his feet. 'There is yet hope,' he proclaimed. 'All seems dark now, but a new dawn will come. The Romans have been beaten before, and can be again.' He gestured to a man in dark robes sitting beside him. 'This is Wulthus, of the Cherusci people, who beat the Romans at Teutoburg. His grandfather fought there. Welcome, Wulthus. Tell us of your victory.'

Wulthus rose. He was a tall, broad-shouldered man, white-haired around the temples and chin. 'Thank you, High Druid. Listen now to how my ancestors beat the Romans, of the hero Hermann, known to the enemy as Armenius, and of how we defeated the legions and captured their eagles.'

'Hermann's father, Segimerus the Conqueror, chieftain of the Cherusci, sent him to Rome as a hostage, where he learned to be a warrior. He became the trusted adviser to the Roman leader, Varus the Cruel. In secret, Hermann united the tribes and prepared them for war. His chance came when the Romans withdrew eight legions to send them to suppress the Illyrian revolt, leaving only three under Varus' command. Hermann deceived Varus with false news of a rebellion, and when Varus decided to march his men against it, led them into an ambush. The legions were mixed with auxiliaries and camp followers, in a long, thin line. Our warriors came together, attacked the line where it was weakest, and broke them. The Romans tried to escape, but Hermann's men had built a wall and ditch, and beat back the Romans when they tried to storm it. Their cavalry fled, and were run down by ours. We killed tens of thousands, and captured many more. Varus killed himself, and Hermann took his head. The glory of that day will live forever in our hearts.'

The High Druid stood. 'Thank you, Wulthus. You have shown us how to beat them. Here is my plan. First, the Romans are here to make Verica king of the Atrebates. We will allow them to do that, and then see if they depart, as Caesar did in my great-grandfather's time. Verica is old, and when he dies, we will choose his successor.'

'If, as Dubhtach foretells, the Romans don't leave, we will continue to fight them. We will make their stay on this island so costly that they will withdraw, as they have done from Wulthus' lands. To encourage our people to keep up the fight, we need to show that the Romans are not invincible. Their Emperor will parade through Camulodunum soon, and Amergin has a plan to make him seem a fool. He will then leave, and we can whittle down the legions, who will be weaker without him.'

'However, as we saw on the Medway and at the Thames, beating them is not easy. It may take time. What we need is a long-term plan. We will learn from Hermann. We will send young men to Rome to learn how to beat them, and then when our people revolt, as the Illyrians did, these men can return to lead us. The Romans will be wary of a repeat of this trick, so we will hide their origins. Wulthus has agreed to take our young men with him across the sea, and teach them foreign tongues and ways. Dubhtach will go with them to vouch for them if the Romans get suspicious.'

'To get the military training Hermann had, these young men will go to the Batavii tribe, where the Romans recruit the Imperial German Bodyguard that guards their emperor. Those who pass the tests will go to Rome. There they will learn Roman ways, they will rise to lead Roman forces, and they will carry out two tasks. First, they will take revenge for this invasion. The targets are the Emperor, and all his followers who have violated our lands. The second mission is to draw away the Roman legions. Hermann won when the Romans withdrew most of their forces, so our young men must cause wars between the Romans and their enemies, or revolts among people like the Illyrians.'

'Think on this tonight, and tomorrow evening bring me young men with the cunning of the fox, the heart of the warrior, and the thirst for revenge.'

The next evening, Amergin and I went to see who had been chosen. I was about to tell Amergin that I wanted to join, when he said, 'Don't even think about it, boy. You're too young, far from full grown, and this mission is fraught with danger. The Romans will have learned their lesson from Hermann, and be on the watch for spies. If you go, chances are you'll be caught, tortured for information about the others, and killed. The years of training I have given you will be wasted. You stay with me, finish your druid education, and lead our people here. This is the place to avenge your family. You can't do that if you're dead in Rome.'

How I wished I was older! How I wished I was a warrior! My family honour demanded revenge.

The other druids had brought their young men, all fine young warriors. Wulthus examined them and chose those who he thought could pass as Germanii. To send them off, the High Druid blessed them, and Dubhtach performed a good luck ceremony.

Then Ganna came forward, to curse our enemies. She was dressed all in ghostly white, with a pale face and a black stripe across the eyes. The skulls of small animals and birds were woven into her hair, and a necklace of wolf and bear fangs hung down to a wide leather belt tooled with the symbols of her gods. She held two chains, each with a hollow metal ball full of burning coals, which she spun round, leaving trails of sparks. She danced around us, chanting prayers foretelling hideous misfortunes that would befall any who opposed our warriors.

In the midst of calling on her war goddess, Ganna's eyes rolled back in her head and she began frothing at the mouth. Her movements became jerky, and she staggered around screaming about death. We all stood, frozen in awe, as the goddess possessed her. Her voice changed to a deep growl. Suddenly, she leaped over and pointed at me. 'He, he, he', grated the voice of the goddess. 'He is the doom of Rome.' The fiery balls shot up into the sky, and Ganna collapsed to the ground.

Amergin glared at Dubhtach and me suspiciously, but we were as stunned as everyone else. 'Well,' said the High Druid, 'not much doubt about what that meant. You can't be the doom of Rome staying here. You're going with them, young man.'

Dubhtach tapped me on the shoulder. 'Help me carry her, lad.' I looked back at Amergin. He nodded, and I picked Ganna up. I didn't know it then, but I would never speak to him again. I would have liked to see him once more, to tell him that his sacrifice was not in vain, and to reminisce about the good times we spent together. His training has given me the edge to survive and win too many times to count, and without him, I would have gone to the gods years ago.

I only saw him one more time, because I did see what he did to the Emperor, and that was hilarious.

8

THE EMPEROR'S PARADE

Queen Boudicca arrived, accompanied by her war chief Tenvantius. I upended the sack I was carrying, and three helmeted heads clattered to the floor. "Cavalry of the Ninth Legion, on their way from Lindum to Camulodunum."

Boudicca picked up a head by the helmet knob. "He seems foreign enough."

Tenvantius sneered. "How would you know what legion he was from, if you've been abroad for so long?"

"I saw them in Camulodunum, when the Emperor Claudius had his victory parade, and the kings surrendered to him."

"Oh, did you? What a coincidence. You always say you were there, but so was I, and I never saw you. Strange, that."

"I was there," said Boudicca, "and I remember it well. Prove that you were there. Tell us what happened."

So I told them the tale of how Amergin made a fool out of an emperor.

The Emperor of Rome has the best security in the world: the Praetorian Guard are the best warriors in the regular army, no-one gets near him without being searched. His spies constantly watch out for threats, the Emperor's food is tasted before he eats it, and doctors with cures for all sorts of venoms and poisons are on hand day and night. But the High Druid had ordered Amergin to disrupt Claudius' victory parade, and Amergin was the most cunning druid I knew.

The Romans had spent the summer taking control of the lands south of the Thames, and with their victories in battle and by putting Verica back as leader of the Atrebates, they had taken control of many small kingdoms. After Claudius' arrival, they had stormed Camulodunum with war elephants, and Caratacus had fled west. For Claudius' parade, these kings would now ceremonially surrender to him.

'What's going to happen to all these kings?' I asked Druid Dubhtach.

'Their lands will become part of the empire, or client kingdoms. Either way, they'll be paying taxes or tribute. The Romans will take cattle, grain, and young men for their armies. They'll bleed the tribes dry, and if they revolt, they will crush them.'

For the ceremony, the Romans had taken the marketplace, and enlarged it to fit their legions and the delegations of the surrendering kings. In typical brutal Roman fashion, they had enlarged the market by destroying the surrounding buildings, trampling it flat, and covering it in gravel so mud would not stain the Emperor's fine toga.

I was standing with Dubhtach and his pupil Ganna, in King Verica's retinue, at one end of the market. The Romans had not yet arrived.

'Where are they?' I whispered to Dubhtach.

'Ssssh,' he said. 'Their spies are all about, and their scouts are hiding in nearby buildings, in case of trouble.'

But they hadn't calculated on Amergin's deviousness, and

THE DRUID AND THE ELEPHANT

Claudius was about to fall into a trap.

The parade started with the Praetorians marching in. They were in full ceremonial armour, gleaming like the sun off the sea, cloaks as red as blood. The leading standard bearer was wearing the skin of an enormous cat.

I winked at Ganna and purred. She meowed back. Later, I saw living lions in Rome and learned what it took to kill one. I don't laugh about them anymore.

They were followed by the legions. Rank upon rank of men, in their thousands, marching in unison to the beat of drums and the blare of horns. At the head was the Second Legion, led by their commander, Vespasian. My fists clenched at the sight of them, and I silently vowed revenge.

Then came the Emperor, mounted on the biggest elephant I have ever seen. The ones at the Medway and the Thames were North African elephants, but this giant was from far to the east, from the fabled lands that the great Alexander had conquered. On seeing it, Ganna gasped and clutched my arm, her nails digging into my flesh.

No wonder she was horrified. Besides its enormous size, its tusks were tipped with vicious blades, its trunk armoured in gleaming scales, ankles protected by spiked bands, and its body shrouded in a coat of a hue I had never seen before, but found out later was Tyrian purple, the colour of the emperor. On its neck sat a dark-skinned boy of my age, dressed in gold cloth and guiding the beast with a hook. Behind him was the Emperor's platform, with Claudius regally sat on a throne of gold. To the rear of the platform were the champions of the Praetorians, ready to pounce on any threat.

The Romans had learned from their mistakes at the Medway, the Thames, and Camulodunum. The beast's feet were shod in metal, and its eyes were protected from fire by something else I had never seen before: glass. It was armoured all around, and the Emperor's throne was shielded from behind. But Amergin had a devious druid trick up his sleeve.

The beast halted in the middle of the market, and slowly sank to its knees. A dozen young girls skipped forwards with baskets of flowers and strewed a path leading to a raised dais. Attendants lifted the Emperor down, carried him along this floral path, then lifted him to a golden throne in preparation for our obeisance. He let out an enormous sneeze.

Old King Verica stood slowly, and shuffled forwards towards the dais. With him was a boy carrying a laurel wreath of victory, interwoven with sorrel and dock leaves. The boy helped Verica up the steps of the dais, and the King, with a shaking hand, crowned Claudius with the wreath. Another enormous sneeze echoed around the market. Claudius tried to stand, but seemed weak at the knees, and had to be helped by attendants. One of them held a scroll for him to read a speech, but after a few words he started to stammer, sneezed again, and slumped back onto the throne. The attendant read the speech for him, in Latin, which none of our delegation understood. Claudius was sniffing, and every now and again he interrupted the speech with another loud sneeze. The audience were desperately trying not to laugh. His head and voice shook, and the attendants picked him up, carried him back to the elephant, and beat an ignominious retreat.

Vespasian took his place, and the rest of the ceremony was uneventful. But that night the kings met, talked of the emperor's weakness, and the seeds of rebellion were sown. The audience went home, told the story to their friends and family, and whenever someone sneezed, people would cry, "Hail, Caesar!"

It was only later, in Rome, when I got to know more about Claudius, that I realised the genius of Amergin's plan. The Emperor suffered from hay fever, and had been in poor health

THE DRUID AND THE ELEPHANT

for years. Almost dying at Camulodunum had shaken him. The flowers, sorrel and dock leaves were all plants that made his affliction worse. His doctors figured out what had happened, and his spy-masters knew that druids were plant experts. From then on Claudius hated druids, and if he had found out about me, he was evil-tempered enough to make my death a long-drawn out agony. King Verica died shortly afterwards, and rumour had it they killed him in revenge for the wreath. And in going to Rome, Dubhtach, Ganna and I were about to put our heads in the lion's mouth.

Queen Boudicca nodded. "I remember that day. I was one of the flower girls. We were told to wave the flowers high in the air. So that's why. And I remember the druid and the girl next to you. She appeared so strange. But I don't remember you."

"Neither do I," Tenvantius interjected. "And why should we believe your tale? Maybe the Emperor was simply ill that day. It's well known that the Romans don't like the cold."

"And I remember the elephant," said Boudicca. "It wasn't frightening at all. Just like an enormous horse."

"That was Micipsa, the Emperor's riding elephant," I replied. "Wonderful animal. I got to know him well. We spent years together. A gentle giant. He didn't get on with the war elephants, though."

"By all the Gods," objected Tenvantius, "you're not going to ask us to believe that you rode the Emperor's elephant, are you!"

"Give me a large beer and an apple, and I'll show you how it's done."

Boudicca nodded to a servant, and I told them how to make friends with an elephant.

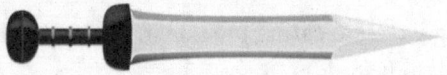

Claudius had made Vespasian and his general, Plautius, wait all summer for him because he needed to show the Roman people that, despite his physical weakness, he was fit to be emperor. And to do that he needed a conquer somewhere, then return to Rome and have a victory parade. For the parade, he needed prisoners of war, and representatives of conquered kings. Dubhtach was ordered to accompany the Atrebates delegation to Rome, and Ganna and I went along as his assistants.

The Romans were used to Dubhtach and Ganna being in their encampment, and being with them, I got to experience a new way of life. The legions had their marching camps of perfectly straight lines of tents, but outside the surrounding trenches was a whole horde of other people: the camp followers. There were blacksmiths and wine sellers, horse traders, leather workers, and merchants of every description. People from far-off lands, with strange clothes and accents, all speaking in their common language, Latin. Dubhtach spoke it, and I picked it up fast as I ran around camp, getting to know the place. Downwind were the tanners and fish sauce sellers, and upwind were the Greek doctors, who swore that their patients needed fresh air. But what fascinated me most was the elephants.

They had to be kept on the edge of camp, away from the cavalry, because horses fear elephants. The war elephants were a family herd, some male, some female, and the males did not like Micipsa. To them, he was a rival for their females, and as he was bigger than them, their only option was to gang up on him. So, to prevent trouble, they kept him on the other side of camp.

THE DRUID AND THE ELEPHANT

One morning we were eating breakfast, when Ganna said, 'I had a strange dream last night.'

Dubhtach raised an eyebrow.

'Don't laugh, but me and Caz were riding on the Emperor's elephant.'

'You have two choices,' said Dubhtach, dipping his bread into olive oil. 'Either you can do nothing, and see if fate makes it come true, or you can grab fate by the scruff of the neck and make it happen.'

'I can't see how this one's going to come true,' said Ganna. 'Caz is scared of elephants. We've heard about how one chased him and he thought he was going to die.'

I was too young and inexperienced with her challenges to know how she was manipulating me.

'I'm not scared,' I protested.

'Prove it.'

'I will.'

'How?'

'I'll think of something.'

'Gods, that will take forever. I'll just work my magic on the elephant rider. Bet I can ride on the elephant before you do!'

Challenge accepted, I spied on Micipsa and came up with a plan. Every day, the boy who rode him would take him out into the woods to eat long grass and tree bark. The horse doctors had taken the arrows out of his rear, and he was recovering with rest and good food. Most of all, Micipsa liked apples. Each morning his rider would go to the fruit seller in the camp and buy some, then use them as a reward, like scraps of meat when training a puppy. So I asked the local farmers, and they told me about a farm, abandoned because of the fighting, that had an apple tree.

Next morning I was waiting between Micipsa's shelter and the fruit seller, and I offered the boy some apples for half what he usually paid the fruit seller. He bought them, and the following morning I went to the elephant shelter with more. We got chatting in broken Latin.

His name was Surus, after the place he was from, far to the east of the empire. His father had owned Micipsa, and brought him and his family to Rome. When his father had died of an illness, Surus inherited his job. The other elephants were from Carthage in the south-west of the empire, so their riders spoke a different language, and handled their elephants in a different way. He was lonely, hated the cold weather, and was longing to go home.

Micipsa was named after a king of Numidia, who had given the Romans some war elephants to use in Hispania. It was a name given by the Romans, because Micipsa's real name was in Surus' language, and so unfit for an emperor's elephant.

Surus and I became friends. I showed him where the good grazing was, and he let me ride on Micipsa. I invited Ganna along, and she charmed Surus by telling his fortune, and that if he stuck with us, he would get back to his own country, and live a long and happy life.

I don't know if he believed her, but it wasn't wise to show any doubt of her prophesies. And on the journey to Rome, he and Micipsa were the only survivors of all the elephants and riders, which was my doing.

9

How to Kill a Herd of War Elephants

"I suppose now you're going to claim that you killed the war elephants all on your own," objected Tenvantius. He sneered. "Oh, Mighty Druid," mocked the war chief. "Tell us how you killed a herd of war elephants single-handed!"

"I didn't do it alone. I used a far greater power."

"What power?" demanded Boudicca. So I told them how a druid can harness the power of nature to do his bidding.

After the parade in Camulodunum celebrating his victory in the invasion, Claudius decided to return to Rome. He took the Praetorians and his elephants, and went south to the port of Rutupiae on the coast. I was with Druid Dubhtach and Ganna, following the High Druid's plan to go to Rome and wreak revenge and destruction. My chance came sooner than I thought.

It was winter now, and the sea passage to Gaul looked rough. The Emperor's naval officers advised staying in port until the weather improved. Surus, Ganna and I took Micipsa out of the port into the fields and forests to eat. One day we were returning to town, and had just started to walk along the beach towards the harbour when Micipsa suddenly stopped and went quiet. He lifted his trunk and inhaled. From my seat on his back, I could see over the roofs into town. People were running. There were yells and screams and crashing. Elephants were hurrying away from the huts and warehouses. One of the young females emerged onto the beach and started running along the sand. Then the cause of the trouble emerged.

We found out later what had happened. In the battles of the Medway, the Thames and Camulodunum, some of the war elephants had been killed, and the pecking order of the herd had been disrupted. The eldest male had died, his young successor wanted to breed, and went into what Surus called 'musth', or breeding frenzy. A clear liquid started to drip down the side of his head from behind his eyes. The rider had noticed too late, and when he tried to chain the elephant to a tree, it had attacked him. Realising what was going on, the other riders had fled, raising the alarm. The rogue bull went crazy, chasing the females around town and destroying anything that got in his way.

The young female elephant on the beach saw Micipsa, and instinctively knew that he was her best chance of protection. As she rushed towards us, the rogue bull elephant appeared. Seeing Micipsa as another male, and therefore a rival for breeding rights, it trumpeted a challenge, and charged.

'I'll get Dubhtach,' said Ganna, and slipped down off Micipsa's back onto the sand. She ran off into the dunes.

Amergin had taught me that when in trouble, people tend to get tunnel vision, and to beat them you need to check around for opportunities they don't see. The elephants, danger and the water reminded me of the Thames.

'Into the sea,' I yelled. 'They can't fight there.'

Surus wheeled Micipsa, and we ran towards the water. Wading in, Micipsa forged forwards, up to his eye level. The rogue bull followed, bellowing challenges, but the water came over its head, and it had to swim. Offshore were some flat-topped rocks, and the way the waves were breaking indicated a shallow beach on one side.

'Onto the rocks, that way!' I pointed.

Surus urged Micipsa on, and after a little more wading, we emerged up the beach.

The bull was swimming closer, and we just managed to rotate Micipsa to face it in time.

They were going to fight, and I didn't want to be on top when it happened. 'Jump!' I yelled, and dived into the cold sea.

Surus hit the water with a splash behind me, and we swam round the back of the rocks. From there we witnessed the most awesome fight. Micipsa charged the bull as it emerged from the water, and the sound of their heads coming together was like Toutatis and Mars battling to see who was the champion of the war gods.

Micipsa had the high ground, the size and the weight, and flipped the bull sideways into the sea. He trumpeted in triumph. The bull, maddened by musth and fighting fury, attacked again and again, but was ever driven back. Slowly, the effects of the freezing water took their toll, and each charge became more of a struggle. Exhausted at last, it slipped back into the water, and drifted away.

Meanwhile, Ganna had found Dubhtach. He had commandeered the local fishing boats, and they used their nets to catch the exhausted bull and drag it to the beach. Claudius had arrived with a guard of Praetorians to see what all the commotion was about, and he ordered the bull chained and dragged up the beach to the trees. The riders, who would normally have never gone anywhere near an elephant in musth, had no choice but to obey the Emperor. Before the bull recovered they managed to chain its legs together, then Surus swam Micipsa back to the beach, and dragged the bull into the trees, where he was chained up until the musth went away.

I swam to Dubhtach's boat, and he fished me out. The fishermen took me home and warmed me up with hot drinks and a cosy fire.

When I was feeling better, I stretched out my arms and told the fishermen, 'Now you can say "I once caught a fish this big."'

'Ha,' said Ganna. 'I've seen your future in my dreams, Caz. You'll fight lots of strange animals. Cats the size of wild boar, birds as tall as bears, and one animal so ugly I don't know any words to describe it. You even fight a whale!'

'A whale?' said a fisherman. 'We killed a whale once. It got stuck in the channel at low tide, and we went out in boats and speared it. Its fat was so thick we couldn't hurt it, so we had to climb on its back and spear down the hole in its head where it breathes. It drowned in its own blood. Fed the whole village for a month, and lamp fat for a year. But it smashed up two boats with its tail. If you have to fight one, beware!'

The Emperor was pleased with Surus and Micipsa. They were given accommodation in a big warehouse, with plenty of apples, and straw to keep warm. Claudius observed that Micipsa couldn't travel in the same ship as the other elephants, so would cross to Gaul on the imperial flagship, while the others would go back the same way they had come.

Surus was pleased. 'I don't want Micipsa in with them. They don't know how to control their beasts properly.'

'How can they control an elephant, if it gets like that male today?' I asked.

'My father taught me that riders should always carry a hammer and spike. If a war elephant runs amok and attacks its own army, the rider has to drive the spike into the back of its neck. The animal will collapse and die, but better to lose an elephant than a battle.'

'Could you really do that to Micipsa?'

'He's not a war elephant, so it won't happen. But my father told me to think of it like putting down an old or injured dog. Sometimes death is kinder. If the time comes, and it's for the best, I hope I will have the heart for it.'

The imperial flagship was down at the docks, but floating in the channel leading from the port to the sea, because it would have taken up too much room at the docks, was the biggest ship I had ever seen. I found out later that it was built to transport giant rocks from Egypt to Rome, but now Claudius was using it for his elephants. It was more of a barge than a ship, but it had a mast and a sail. None of the other ships was suitable for elephants, so I knew that it was the one, but the plan didn't come to me until that night.

I was sitting round the fire with Dubhtach and Ganna, chatting about the day's events.

'Did you foresee it all?' I asked her.

'I dreamed of running to Dubhtach, but I didn't know why. A lot of times I don't remember the dream until something happens that jogs my memory, like it did today when I saw the female elephant being chased by the bull. Then I know what I should do.'

'What do your dreams say will happen next?'

'The Emperor being furious, shouting on the deck of his ship, and Micipsa being terrified.'

'Terrified of the Emperor?'

'Just because two things happen at the same time doesn't mean that one causes the other, Caz,' said Dubhtach. 'Maybe something else is angering Claudius and scaring Micipsa.'

Ganna grinned. 'Who knows?' She dropped her voice to a whisper. 'Maybe it's you, Druid Doom of Rome. I foresee many battles in your life as you follow the High Druid's plan. How many Romans have you killed?'

'None. I'm a druid, not a warrior.'

'Three battles, no heads? And never on the winning side. The war goddess doesn't approve. Not very impressive.'

'Stop it,' said Dubhtach. 'Killing is wrong unless you have no choice. I could have left that bull elephant to die today, swept out by the tide until the cold killed it. But I didn't. It was no threat if it was handled right. It's only an animal doing what nature tells it. No need to be so bloodthirsty.'

'Yes, because it's on our side.' Ganna looked at me. 'How many of your people did those elephants kill? How many will they kill in future? You're on the same side now. Have you forgiven them? Maybe you'll need them one day.'

Her questions kept me awake that night. I wanted revenge, but they were just animals. Killing them wouldn't teach a lesson to other animals not to attack us. I couldn't make up my mind until I remembered the mission given to me by the High Druid: take revenge and weaken the empire. And the war goddess might be pleased, and give me more good fortune. I got the feeling I was going to need it. The major risk was Claudius' anger. I would have to be above suspicion. But how was I going to do it? It took days to devise a plan, but the weather was bad, the rogue bull was slowly recovering, and there was time. At last I figured out what to do. As my druid master, Amergin, had taught me, I would use their own special qualities against them.

I went to visit the local druidess, and introduced myself. By good fortune she knew Amergin, and in return for news of him, she let me borrow her coracle. She also showed me where some wild bees were nesting. Together we blew smoke on them to make them sleepy, and put them in a pottery jar, with a cloth over the mouth to stop them escaping, but let them breathe. We shared the honey, and as I left she said, 'Now you listen to some advice, young man. You mean well, but you're up to no good, I can tell. Your eyes are ill-matched and your future ill-omened. Danger and death await those around you.'

She wagged a finger at me. 'You be careful. Don't let innocent people get caught up in your schemes and suffer. I don't know what you're up to, but I smell trouble. I'm going to visit distant relatives for Samhain. But others lack the wisdom even to take shelter when they smell rain coming. Don't get their blood on your hands.'

I promised her I'd be careful, but she only snorted. As I left, she was packing.

That night it was raining and moonless. I paddled out to the big ship, threading my way between the supply vessels, the piling barges and the war-galleys. The sailors on guard were taking shelter from the downpour and passing the time drinking and gambling. They didn't see me climb aboard and leave them a little surprise.

Next morning the weather was better, but gusty, and the waves outside the harbour had white crests. However, the ship was so big that it wouldn't be a problem. The Romans brought the ship up to the docks and loaded up the elephants in the shallow hold. They shackled their ankles with one long chain along the middle of the hold from fore to aft to stop them from moving too much.

Surus and I helped load Micipsa into the flagship. He was smiling.

'Going home!' he said. 'Rome is good. Warm. Good food. Music. You'll like it, Caz.'

I nodded, but was not so sure. Ganna had said that I would fight animals, and I wasn't looking forward to that. And if my plan with the elephants worked, I was worried the Romans would figure out who did it. I'd be in big trouble.

The imperial Roman fleet put out to sea. The wind was blowing in the wrong direction, so a galley towed the big ship out of the port. Once they were in the open water and had space to tack, the captain ordered the sail hoisted.

Surus and I were watching. 'Big ship, flat bottom, moving a lot,' said Surus. 'Elephants not happy. This ship better.'

From my position on the flagship with Surus and Micipsa, I saw the crew hauling on the ropes, and as the sail rose, it unfurled. It was too far away to see, but the pot of bees that I had hidden in its folds must have fallen out, dropped into the hold, and broken open.

A swarm of angry insects must have flown out among the elephants. From our ship we heard the cries of the panicked beasts, and saw the tops of their backs moving about in the hold as they tried to flee, but they were chained. The largest of them moved to one side of the ship, the others followed, and their weight tipped the hull. The port rails went under, and waves flooded the hold.

Cries of alarm went up from the lookouts. 'Come about!' ordered our captain. The other ships in the fleet changed course to help, but it was too late.

The panicked trumpets scared Micipsa, and Surus and I stroked his trunk and whispered soothing sounds in his ears. In a few heartbeats, the big ship capsized and slid beneath the waves, dragging the elephants down with it. The crew and the elephant drivers dived into the sea.

The Emperor was livid, striding about the deck yelling, until he had one of his fits and was taken below. The swimmers were picked up by other boats, so fortunately I had not taken any human lives.

The captain, crew and elephant drivers were dragged in front of the Emperor. I was worried that heads would roll and the smell of blood would spook Micipsa. Fortunately, level heads prevailed. On listening to the reports of the bees suddenly appearing on the ship, the Emperor's adviser Narcissus cried, 'Druid magic!' Claudius hated druids so much after Camulodunum that he believed him.

He stood up from his throne and pointed at the captain. 'For losing your ship, a hundred lashes.' He pointed to the crew. 'Fifty lashes each for not securing the elephants properly.' He gestured to the elephant drivers, quaking on their knees and now useless without their beasts. 'Your animals sank my ship. Twenty lashes each!' Finally, he pointed at the shore. 'And send a ship back to port. Catch the druid who did this and crucify him!'

I was so frightened, I hid in Micipsa's stall until we reached land.

When we docked, the elephant riders were sent back to Africa by sea, because seeing them would remind the Emperor of the loss. For the same reason, Micipsa and Surus were told to make directly for Rome, while the Emperor went on an inspection tour north of the mountains.

Dubhtach and Ganna were on another ship, with the Atrebates delegation. After we docked, he took me aside. Ganna followed. From the angry glare in his eyes, I knew what was on his mind, so I decided to get in early.

'Did you do that?' I asked.

'No!' he hissed. 'Did you?'

'Me? I was on the flagship with Surus and Micipsa. And I'm just an apprentice. How could I do something like that?'

He wasn't fooled. 'You be careful, my lad. It only takes one look at your eyes to remind people that you're a druid's apprentice. If the Romans even suspect that you were involved, you're a dead man.'

Amergin taught me to never go on the defensive in an argument, but attacking would only annoy him. Time for a diversion.

'I'm more worried about you. The Romans know you're a druid.'

Ganna helped. 'Yes,' she said. 'Let's leave before they think of you.'

Dubhtach rounded on her.

'You put him up to this! You and your talk of war goddesses and taking heads. It'll be our heads if you can't guard your tongue.'

'Yes, Dubhtach', she said, dropping her eyes. But she didn't mean it. From then on she used her powers of persuasion on me when he was not around.

Dubhtach scowled. 'You've put me in danger because you didn't consider what would happen afterwards. You both need to grow up. Making a plan is like shooting a bow. You need to check past the target, in case you miss and hit an innocent bystander by accident. Now get out of my sight.'

Thinking back, I still don't know whether I did the right thing. Those elephants might have been useful in the wars I have fought, or they might have been used to attack me or my friends. I might have brought them to Britannia to fight with Boudicca, or maybe they would have fought against us. And who knows what the future will bring? Friends become enemies, and enemies become allies against stronger enemies. But one thing I have learned. Now I make my own decisions, not rely on what others tell me is my mission. I guess my experience in command has made me understand that leaders don't know everything. They give simple instructions because complicated ones get misunderstood, but in simplification there are not enough 'if's'. The best results are when the one who receives the orders thinks for himself, and does what he thinks is right.

Was it a decision that a druid would make? Probably not, especially according to Dubhtach. Was it a decision that a warrior would make? Depends on the warrior. The simple advice, "If in doubt, kill it", sounds good to the fearful, but good leaders don't make decisions based on fear, they make them with careful estimation of risk and reward.

The Emperor hated druids so much that the Atrebates delegation didn't want Dubhtach with them, and told him to leave before he got them into trouble. So he was free to guide us to the town of Oppidum Batavorum, where the tests for Claudius' palace guard took place. By the time we got there, he was in a better mood, and wished me luck. I needed it, if I was to pass the trials and enter the Imperial German Bodyguard, as the High Druid had ordered. The risk was intimidating, but the potential for revenge, immense.

10

THE WAY TO ROME

Tenvantius scoffed. "You expect us to believe that you were in the bodyguard of the Roman Emperor when you were just a beardless boy!" The war chief shook his head. "I don't believe it. They wouldn't let a stripling like you in."

Queen Boudicca shushed him. "The night is long." She nodded to me. "Entertain us with your tales."

So I told them of the tests, and how I tricked my way into Claudius' palace guard.

His conquest achieved and his reputation bolstered, the Emperor Claudius returned to Rome through Gaul. But the High Druid's visitor Wulthus led Druid Dubhtach, his pupil Ganna, the other young warriors and I east to the lands of the Germanii, arranging to catch up with Micipsa the elephant and Surus his rider later. If, of course, we passed the tests to become recruits in the Imperial German Bodyguard, as the High Druid had planned. Ganna taught us their language as we crossed northern Gaul. She forbade us to speak our own tongue, and cursed us so badly if we disobeyed her that by the time we got to the camp where the Romans selected Germanii recruits, we were fairly fluent, excellent at insults, and good enough to hide our origins. As long as I kept my eyes shaded, no-one would associate me with the apprentice druid in Britannia. My beard started growing, but it was still embarrassing fluff. 'The Germanii will make a man out of you,' teased Ganna. 'Looking like a beardless Roman might even help.'

Every year a Roman officer and some Germanii veterans came north, recruiting. But they wouldn't take just anyone. A palace guard has to have some special abilities, and not only in fighting.

On the appointed morning, about sixty of us gathered at the Roman camp for selection. They told us to stand in a line, with the tallest on the left, and we were each given a small clay tablet with a number on it. I was Number Fifty-eight. Number One was a giant of a man, bald-headed with a huge blond beard, and I prayed that fighting him would not be part of the tests. I inspected the other hopefuls, bigger and older than me. How could I beat them? But Dubhtach had told me that the gods were on my side, and Ganna said she had had a dream of me in a group of men, following a Roman officer south. If you doubt yourself, you are halfway to losing, so I lifted my chin and decided to give it my all.

The first test was simple: press-ups. Stamina versus body weight. 'Up, two, three, down, two, three', ordered the instructors. We raised and lowered our bodies in time to the commands. I was a farm boy before I was a druid, used to pushing carts up hills to market. I managed fifty. Some big, heavy men got fewer. But most were strong, trained warriors and got more. Not a good start for me, but at least I wasn't rejected, unlike those who did less than thirty. The instructors rearranged the line in order of press-ups managed, and explained the second test.

It was a simple race: across the field to the tree line, then run back. The field had been ploughed recently, and was muddy and furrowed. The men with the most press-ups went first, and the instructors set us off in order. Big men might have long legs, but they skidded more, and sank into the mud. I was in the middle of the pack getting back to the start.

'Again!' ordered the officer. Off we went. The field was churned up by the first run, and I had to look ahead and plan my route carefully to stay on firm ground. I was among the top twenty back.

'Again!' demanded the officer. The field now was rutted like a herd of boar had rooted it up, and was a nightmare to run on. I went round the edge. It was longer, but the footing was better. I got back in the first ten.

The instructors put us in line in finishing order, and paired us up with the man next to us. Luckily I got a medium-sized man who, like me, had run with his brain as well as his legs.

'Pick up your partner, carry him to the tree line, put him down. Then he picks you up, and brings you back here. Team One, go! Team Two, go!'

When our turn came, I jumped on the man's back, and we set off. 'Go around the edge', I called to him, and he did. By the time we got to the trees, he was gasping. I picked him up and set off back. I tried to run, but I staggered under his weight.

'Don't run. Walk fast. Keep your legs straight,' he wheezed. So I did. What followed seemed like an endless struggle to put one leg in front of the other. The man on my back kept me going. 'That's it lad, keep it up, you're doing well, not far to go. You can do it.'

Without him, I might never have made it. At the end, I collapsed to the grass. Twisting round and looking down the field, there was no-one behind us. We were last. I felt crushed, all that effort, wasted. What would I do now? My partner hauled me to my feet. The instructor pointed us to a group, and as we joined them, to my surprise, they slapped us on the shoulders. The other group were men who had put down their partners, and they were out.

With hindsight, I know those were tests of stamina and determination, designed to see if men would keep up on the march, and weed out stragglers.

The next test was one of trust in comrades. In battle, standing in a shield wall, you need to have total confidence in the man beside you. Those who cannot trust their comrades will break and run from battle.

The test was simple, but effective. The instructors demonstrated. One man stood on the back of a cart, and the others stood behind the cart in two lines, facing each other with their arms forward, holding the wrists of the man opposite. The man on the cart faced away and fell backwards, with arms folded and keeping his body straight. His comrades caught him.

'Pay attention,' demanded the instructor. 'Fall back with arms folded, legs and body stretched out. If you hit your comrades' arms lying flat, it will spread your weight over all their arms, and they can support you. But if you bend or sit, you will break through.'

They divided us into teams of nine, and on the command of the instructors, we took our turns. Fortunately, this was not new to me. As young druids, playing in the winter, we used to jump off trees into snow drifts, competing to see who jumped from highest. If you fell with all your body hitting the snow at the same time, it would cushion your fall, but if you fell bottom-first and penetrated to the frozen ground beneath the snow, you'd land on your tailbone, which was extremely painful. So I stood at the front, and got chosen to go first.

'On the count of three!' ordered the instructor. 'One, two, three.' I closed my eyes and fell back. Being light, the team caught me easily. But the heavier the fallers were, the harder it was for the team to keep a grip on the wrists of the man opposite. And it's hard for some men to trust those who they've only met that day, and who they are competing against. The final two men fell back wrongly and smashed through our arms into the ground. Fortunately, it was wet and soft, but they still rolled around in agony. They were rejected, as were failures from other teams, and we were down to half the men who had started.

The next test was a river crossing. The instructors took us to a river bank and pointed to a beech tree on the other side. 'Go round the tree and come back. Last man back is out. Go!' The river was about thirty paces wide, and the smooth surface told me it was deep. A hundred paces upstream were some rapids, with green slimy rocks sticking out of the water. Men started running towards them, but not me. Crossing rapids is always dangerous. The rocks are slippery, move under your feet, and you're liable to fall and smash your knees. I looked around for a better option. Across from us was a steep bank about six feet high, with sand-martin holes. Climbing that would be hard. Downstream the other bank was lower, pitted with hoof prints where animals came to drink. I ran downstream to some bushes across from it, and started to remove my clothes.

I didn't tell the Queen or Tenvantius, but as a young druid, Amergin had taken me to the druid's holy isle of Mona, on the west coast. It was a good place to train young druids, but every few years there would be a pirate raid, after slaves and priestly valuables, so the druids had secret hiding places. One was a sea cave, and the only entrance was underwater. To get in, you had to dive deep and swim through the cave mouth to get to the shingle beach beyond. The druids taught us to swim, and we had fun diving off the rocks. Inside the secret cave was a cache of dry clothes, because after a dip in the ocean, you didn't want to sit around in wet things and catch cold.

I left my clothes under a bush, swam the river, ran around the beech and swam back. By the time I had climbed to the top of the bank, some men had already finished. I grabbed my clothes and ran. The man laughed as I sprinted up, holding my clothes in front of me. I arrived at the finish cold, naked, and panting, but I wasn't last.

The last test before lunch was spear throwing. The officer addressed us.

'This,' he said, 'is not a spear. It's called a pilum. See how the head is long, narrow and sharp? It will penetrate a shield far enough to hit the man holding it. Even if it doesn't get him, it will lodge in the shield, weighing it down and making it useless. He can't charge like that, so he drops it. You throw your second pilum at him, and he has no defence. You need to throw the first one when he is still far enough away so that you have time to throw the second. No run up allowed, because in a battle there isn't room or time.'

My heart sank. How was I to compete against trained warriors? I stood at the back of the line, watching the others. Each man was called forwards, told to select a pilum from a pile, and throw. If their pilum fell shortest, they had to stand to one side, and stay there until someone else threw shorter than they had. The men were making distances of twenty-five to thirty paces. There was no way I was going to get close to that. As small boys, my brother and I had competed to throw the farthest, and my best was about twenty paces.

The Roman soldiers and their pilum reminded me of the Battle of the Thames. The Roman infantry there had thrown fifty paces. Later I had asked my druid master Amergin how they did it. He told me they used a leather strap which they wound around the shaft to spin the spear as they threw. I had tried it before we got to Camulodunum, and it had worked. I took off my rope belt and got it ready.

When my turn came, the big men were laughing, and betting on the distance my throw would go. The wagers were as low as ten, which was annoying, and I was determined to prove them wrong. I went to the pile of pila, and saw that there were two types: light and heavy, made of fir and ash. The light one I guessed was for long range, and the heavy one for impact, so I picked a light one. I tied one end of my belt around the end, wound it once along the shaft up to my hand, and put a loop around my forefinger.

'What is he doing?' some men mocked. 'Don't tie it to yourself: you're not bow fishing!'

I stood facing away from the throwing line. 'Over there!' teased the men. Although I wasn't allowed a run up, I knew a stone thrower's trick. I stepped away with one leg, bent my knee, took a deep breath, and went for it with all my strength and coordination. Snapping my knee straight by shoving with my thigh muscle, I rotated my shoulders as my brother had taught me. I shot my arm up and forward, and as I released the pilum, the rope made it spin. The loop came off my finger, the pilum rose into the air, vibrating from the force, and gracefully arced across the sky, landing point down in the grass. The instructor paced it out, with the men counting his steps. 'Twenty-three, twenty-four, twenty-five.' There were cheers from the men who had believed in me, and groans from the others. I was last equal, and trudged over to the loser's spot to join the other man there.

THE DRUID AND THE ELEPHANT

'It's not fair,' he complained, 'that's cheating. And he's just a boy, not a warrior.' He stepped towards the instructor, arms out, pleading and clasping his hands like a spoiled brat, begging not to be punished. The instructor frowned. I was worried that he was going to dump both of us, so I tried to appear totally different. I stood to attention, as I had seen the Roman soldiers do, and gave the other man a stare of withering contempt. He appealed to the crowd. 'You saw him cheat! You know it's not fair. Look at his eyes: he's cursed. He'll bring bad luck to you all. Take me instead!' No-one moved or spoke: they didn't want a whiny weakling for a comrade.

The instructor was furious at this attempt to go around his authority. 'Get out!' he yelled at the man, and stalked off. I was left standing there. The man I had carried in the earlier race beckoned me over, and I joined those still in the running.

We broke for a big lunch with plenty of bread, roast venison, and beer. The men in cold wet clothes from the swim warmed themselves up with hot food. We had a splendid meal, but it was strange that the Romans were being so generous, especially with the beer, as Romans usually drink wine. So I pretended to dig in, but actually ate little, and drank less.

After lunch, the next test was also devious in its simplicity. We stood in the middle of the field, in a circle facing outwards.

'There's a stag in the trees,' said the officer. 'Be silent. Clasp your fists behind your back, and when you see it, hold out the same number of fingers as there are tines on its antlers.'

We waited, and waited. And waited some more. The effect of stomachs full of beer made some of us yawn. It was hard to concentrate. Time passed slowly, and no stag appeared. I feared the others had seen it and I was the only one who hadn't. Were they already holding out fingers? Should I fake having seen the stag? How many tines were likely? Four? Six?

My worrying kept me alert, and I spotted something odd. The woodland birds had gone quiet. I concentrated and scanned the woods carefully, especially where the birds had stopped flying. A stag's head rose from behind a fallen log. One of its antlers was damaged, and it had only five tines. I held out five fingers, and the stag's head slowly went down. But it seemed wrong. A stag would lean forward to eat, but this dropped straight down. Must be a Roman holding a stag's severed head, circling us through the woods, showing the head to each side of the ring of men.

I waited with fingers out. Time passed. The instructor nearest me put his finger to his lips and beckoned. I stepped forwards quietly, and he directed me to the side.

I looked back at the circle. A dozen men were still there, fists still clenched, or holding out the wrong number of fingers.

'All those still in the circle, follow me,' ordered an instructor, and they were taken away. The unobservant, the inattentive, and the unreliable make bad guardsmen. That left less than twenty.

It was getting late in the afternoon, and there were two tests left. The first was a horse race. The Germanii are famous for their cavalry, and they don't want men who can't ride. But the remaining potential recruits were all older, taller, and heavier than me, so I got the smallest horse.

'Ride around the wood and back,' ordered the officer. 'Last one to return is out. Go!'

We galloped off. The route was about two miles, ending in a track through the woods that led to the finish in the field where the tests were. My horse was short-legged and slow, and we fell back and back until there was only a single rider with me, a big man on an old horse. His weight made it hard work for his mount on the soft ground.

As we reached the track through the woods, we were neck and neck. But the track was narrow, and as I tried to ride up beside him, he kept barging me, trying to knock me off the trail into the trees. Ahead, the track emerged from the woods, forded a small stream, and led into the finishing field.

The other rider barged me again, and I almost crashed into a holly bush. If I didn't do something, I'd be out. He was shoving me, so I had no reason to be sporting with him.

I took off my rope belt and wound the end around my fist. As we came to the stream, the other rider slowed his mount to get the stride right to jump it. Just as the horse gathered itself, I aimed for its rump with my belt. The end of the rope cracked like a whip, and its tip stung like a hornet. The horse was thrown off its stride, and instead of using its hind legs to jump, it instinctively tried to kick backwards. Its weight and speed carried it forward, and its forelegs slid into the stream, where they stuck in the muddy bottom. The rider flew over the horse's head and rolled in the grass.

My horse jumped the stream and swept past him. We cantered up to the finishing line, and I avoided elimination.

The ultimate test was fighting, and this was the one I had been dreading. They put us in two lines facing each other, paired up with a man of similar size, given gloves with padded knuckles, and told that if we won to move left, and if we lost to move right. What they didn't tell us was that if you stopped fighting, gave up, or seemed like you were taking it easy, you lost as well. But if you fought well and lost against a bigger opponent, you stayed. They can teach you fighting skills, but it's a lot harder to teach courage.

Before Amergin came to our village and chose me to be his apprentice, my father had been training me and my brother to be warriors. We fought as brothers do, with each other, and together against the other boys in the village. Even as a trainee druid, I had learned fighting, to fend off pirates and wild animals. I remembered my father's words, 'Fighting is simple. Find your enemy's weakness, and exploit it.'

'What if he doesn't have a weakness?' I had objected.

'If he doesn't have one, you make one.'

My first opponent charged me, hoping to knock me down. I faked indecision, and at the last moment stepped to his left and used my elbow to smash into his lower ribs. He bounced off and circled me warily, clutching his side. I tried a front kick, and he jumped back, so I did two more to get him moving backwards, then ran in and punched his nose. He went down.

The next opponent was bigger than me. I faked throwing a rock at him, and as he ducked, charged in and side-kicked him. He got angry and ran at me, so I curled up into a ball and dropped at his feet, and he tripped. I jumped on him from behind, kicked the back of his knee, and when he fell, grabbed him by the hair and started pounding his head into the ground. The instructor stopped the fight.

The other fights were still going on, so I prepared for the next one. I knew the opponent would be a winner, and good at fighting. Trickery was called for. I took off my rope belt, and knotted the middle of it to make a sling. One of the instructors saw what I was doing. 'No slinging stones!' he warned.

The last opponent was the biggest man yet. It's hard to use a sling while wearing padded gloves, but the range was short and he wasn't expecting it. I swung the sling and shot my Roman clay number tablet, hitting him in the middle of the forehead. He bent forward, wiping the clay dust from his eyes, and I ran up, grabbed the top of his head, jumped and smashed my knee into his chin. It hurt me. A lot. He fell on me, knocking the wind out

THE DRUID AND THE ELEPHANT

of my lungs. He recovered first, choked me out, and I lost. When I woke, the Romans gave me a new clay tablet. The number on this one was X, and they give me a Roman name, Decimus.

A dozen of us passed the tests, including four Britons: me, Lukon of the wolfish grin, Trenus the Strong, and Eppilus who loved horses. We formed a gang, which kept the bullies off my back. Next day I limped into line, and we were off to Rome. So far, the High Druid's plan was working.

11

THE ROAD SOUTH

"You expect us to believe that the Roman Emperor is guarded by men with no fighting experience?" protested Tenvantius. "Men who just take a few simple tests that a boy can pass, walk south, and that's it?"

"Give me another beer and I'll tell you about the fighting."

Boudicca nodded to a servant, and I continued with the tale of my boyhood.

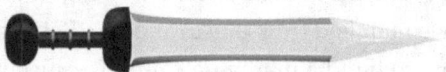

After passing the selection tests to get into the Guard, we went into the town of Oppidum Batavorum, to the barracks there, to get kitted out. I didn't know it at the time, but I was going to need weapons far sooner than I thought. We met up with men who had passed selection in other places, so there were about forty of us, enough to replace the retirees and casualties from the Guard in Rome. The odds of survival were low, but I was there for revenge. The war gods have brought me through, so I can take part in this rebellion.

Because we were raw recruits on the edge of the empire, the kit we got was cast-offs and repair jobs. Most of our men got chain mail and a long cavalry sword. As I was small, I got kit from dead or retired Romans: a dented set of armour made of wide overlapping strips of iron, and a short stabbing sword called a gladius, like the infantry carry.

I was happy because my armour and weapons were light, compared to what the others were carrying. But because of my Roman armour and beardless face, my new mates teased me. 'Ave, Decimus!' they saluted me, which means 'Hail, Decimus!' in Latin. In return, when the instructors weren't in earshot, I would pretend to be a Roman centurion, and deliver ridiculous orders. 'Polish those hobnails!' I would snarl. 'Get those teeth in line, you're an embarrassment to the legion!' Unfortunately, one of the instructors overheard me, gave me a sound beating, and forced me to polish the hobnails of my marching sandals every day.

We set off south, along the wide river that forms the boundary between Gaul and Germania. There's a string of forts along the border, and we marched from one to another. Between them, they taught us how to build a marching camp. Because it was winter, and the nights were long, the instructors divided us into five squads. Three would sleep, one would guard, and one would try to sneak in and steal the standard. If they succeeded, the guards would have to do their dirty jobs the next day.

Every few days, they gave us more things to carry from the baggage train. First was a shield, then a helmet, shin-guards, a digging tool, and so on. Besides building our strength, they taught us military skills: how to fight, how to obey trumpet commands, and how to guard.

I'd left my war horn behind, but I'd taken a simple flute with me, just to while away the winter hours, and because a good musician is always popular. As a trainee druid I had been taught basic bard skills of music and storytelling. The other men would drum on their shields, and we played marching songs. The instructors were always on the lookout for those with useful abilities, and the trumpeter who taught us signals found a horn for me in the stores in one of the forts. In the Roman army, if you've got a special skill, you are immune from having to do the boring jobs, so I was in luck.

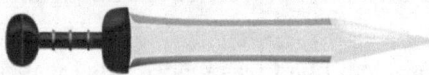

"Get to the point," interrupted Boudicca. "What about the fighting?" I fought back the desire to retort. No one should interrupt a druid. It shows a lack of respect. Interrupting a druid will get you cursed. Interrupting a warrior will earn you a beating. But interrupt a bard, and he will include you as a character in his tale, tell the audience about your physical shortcomings, then your mental deficiencies, and if you still don't shut up, your lamentable love life. But Boudicca was a queen, and I needed to keep on her good side. Tenvantius, however, was another matter. I went on with my story.

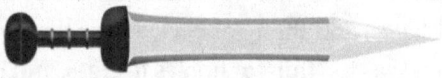

We'd been marching towards Rome for about a month when one day we heard galloping. We got off the road to let the horsemen pass, but they pulled up next to our officer and gave him new orders. The river had frozen, and our scouts had seen the tribes massing across the border. The orders were to get to the nearest fort and report to the commander. We left everything except weapons and armour with the baggage train, and speed-marched to the fort.

Outside the fort was a village for the camp followers, and they were building a wall of logs around it. From a distance I noticed a large grey shape, and as we got closer, I saw it was Micipsa, with Surus on his back. I looked around, and sure enough there was Druid Dubhtach directing work, but I couldn't see Ganna. Maybe she'd had the foresight to get out of danger. If so, I was happy that she was safe, but worried she might have dreamed of something bad.

The other problem I had was whose side I was on. The tribes were the same people as Wulthus, the one who had told the High Druid about Hermann. I didn't want to kill them, but the risk was that they would try to kill me. And maybe Ganna, Dubhtach, and Surus, too."

Boudicca's servant moved to refill my beer, but Tenvantius stopped him. "No more beer until he tells us about the fighting." He had seen how I disliked interruptions and was deliberately winding me up. While I carried on, I planned my retaliation.

"You're both commanders," I replied. "This is what the commander of the frontier did. His problem was that the tribes banded together in the forest, crossed the river on the ice together, raided our villages, and then got back across the river before we arrived. The ice was too thin for horses to cross, and they couldn't go far on foot. He sent us out to set up observation posts along the river, with a signaller in each with a horn. If we signalled a raid, the sound would travel along the line to a marching camp where our cavalry were waiting to ride out."

I took a bit of half-burned stick out of the fire and drew them a map with the charred end.

"This is the river, here's the camp, and here are the observation posts." As their eyes followed the stick, I dropped a little flavouring into my beer with the other hand. Neither of them noticed.

"The first raid was on a riverside village. The tribes rushed across the river, threw blazing torches onto the thatched roofs, captured the people and animals as they fled, and retreated across the river before the cavalry arrived."

Tenvantius took my beer. "You're not getting this back until you tell us the juicy bits. Stop beating about the bush."

I wanted to beat him so much, but I needed to be patient and aggravate him into drinking the beer. I continued my story as if he had not spoken.

"The tribesmen were not stupid," I went on. "They had heard our signals that called the cavalry, and for the next raid they changed their tactics, trying to sneak intruders across the river unseen. One night I was sitting in a bush with Lukon and Trenus, watching the river and taking turns to sleep, when I noticed something strange. A white lump was creeping over the ice. It was hard to see in the dark. Maybe my tired eyes were playing tricks on me. I didn't want to wake the others, so I watched and waited. The lump got nearer and nearer, making for where a clump of willows overhung the water's edge. As it got closer, I realised it was a man, dressed in pale sheepskin covered in frost, crawling over the ice. I roused my comrades, who slipped away, Lukon to get to the other side of him and Trenus to get inland. The raider made it to the trees, and once he was out of sight from the other bank, we charged him from all sides."

"Seeing us coming, he charged back, and as I was smallest, he charged me. As we came together, I did what we did in training: braced my shield and stabbed round the right side of it. He must have fought the legions and seen this move before, because at the last moment he leaped into the air to my left, and thrust down with his spear into my shoulder. Had I been wearing chain mail he would have stabbed through the rings into my muscle, making me drop my shield, but I was wearing banded armour under my cloak, so the spear tip skidded off the sheet metal, and he stumbled at the unexpected lack of resistance. I span and jabbed him in the side of the knee with the bottom of my shield, and his stumble became a fall. Then I threw myself on him, with the shield between us. At close quarters his spear was useless, and before he could draw his knife, Lukon and Trenus ran up and kicked him half to death. We bound and gagged him, and the next morning, when our replacements arrived, we took him back to camp and handed him over."

"That's it?" exclaimed Tenvantius. "You missed him, then you fell over? Only one enemy? You call that fighting?"

"For me, yes. You can't expect me to be involved in everything. Other men in my unit fought larger raids, but it was me who found a way to stop the raids altogether, without spilling a drop of blood."

"Oh, really, how?"

I continued the story.

After a few days, the Roman commander changed strategy because too many men in observation posts were being killed by raiders. The new system was to use cavalry patrols, with infantry like us defending towns and villages. We marched back to the fort for new orders, and as soon as I got off-duty, I went to talk to Dubhtach.

Micipsa was suffering from the cold, so the Romans had commandeered a barn for him, and that's where I found them.

'Oh, there you are,' said Ganna. 'We've been waiting for you.'

There were greetings all round, and I fed Micipsa an apple that I had saved from my rations.

They were looking at me like they were expecting something. 'What?' I asked.

'I had a dream,' said Ganna. 'You were on a ship, and you were leading Micipsa up and down the deck. But it can't be about the voyage over here, because Surus says Micipsa stayed in the hold. Then the ship that capsized sailed past upside-down with Dubhtach in command. It was weird.'

The pieces of a plan clicked together in my mind. The gods were using Ganna's dreams to talk to me.

'That's it! That's how to stop the raids! Here's what we need to do.' And I explained my idea.

The next day Dubhtach went to see the Roman commander, and then he, Surus and Micipsa set out south with an escort of Roman soldiers. They went upstream to where the water was flowing too fast to freeze, and put my idea into action. A few days later I saw the plan working. We were guarding a village on the riverbank, when our lookout let out a shout.

'Ship!' he cried, pointing out into the river.

Floating midstream was a large barge, moving downriver with the flow of water and breaking the thin ice with its prow. Lining the rails were Roman soldiers, watching the banks for enemy tribesmen. At the sides of the barge were chains leading to a sail, which was hanging in the water under the vessel and catching the current. As we watched, the barge drifted to a halt.

'It's stuck,' said the lookout.

On the barge were Surus and Micipsa. Surus led the elephant to the back of the barge, and its prow lifted out of the water. The current pulled the barge forward, the front of the keel rising into view and sliding over the ice. Surus led Micipsa to the front, and the ice beneath the prow cracked loudly under his weight, before breaking apart and raising jagged plates of ice on either side. The barge went forward again, leaving a wide channel of cold, dark, open water in its wake. Slowly it drifted off downstream, and we continued to guard the village, feeling much safer that the tribes would no longer be able to cross.

The weather wasn't cold enough to refreeze the river, and the Romans were well-pleased with Dubhtach, Micipsa and Surus, but it was Ganna who did the best out of it. Knowing the plan, she had set up a shrine to the gods of river and winter, and prophesied that the raids would stop. When she proved correct, the people of the camp follower village made offerings of thanks at her shrine, and held her in awe.

She bought a wagon with a team of black horses, and converted into a mobile temple to her war goddess, Baduhenna. To keep the Romans happy she also said it was for Mars. Warriors are a superstitious lot, because so much of warfare depends on luck, and she got a lot of donations. The soldiers offered captured enemy weapons, and she hung tribesmen's shields around the edges. At the corners she stuck up spears topped with enemy skulls. I went to make an offering of the knife of the raider who had tried to stab me, and Ganna explained her plan.

'The spirit world is the battleground of the gods. The more we venerate them in the real world, the more powerful they become in the spirit realm. When Claudius has his victory parade in Rome, this temple will take part, and the crowds will not only glorify him, they will exalt Baduhenna, too.'

A few days later there was good news. Our officer addressed us on morning parade.

'Pack your kit. Break camp. We're marching to Rome. Our spies report that the tribes have dispersed. No more river guard duty for us. For protection, all those going south will stay together in the same convoy, and our mission is to guard that convoy.'

So me, the Germanii recruits, Micipsa, Surus, Dubhtach and Ganna all went in the same convoy. Ganna told everyone that she had dreamed that I would ride Micipsa into battle, and when Surus caught a severe cold from sitting on top of him in the wind and the rain, I took over for a while. Riding an elephant into combat makes you feel unstoppable, and I dreamed of commanding a herd and coming back home to destroy the Roman invaders. I rode Micipsa in the war games that our instructors used to train us, and they liked us taking part, especially when they got to be the crew on the platform or sit on the Emperor's seat. That's why I entered Rome riding the Emperor's elephant.

Boudicca and Tenvantius shook their heads. "What a pathetic story! No fighting, no bloodshed, no glory. No beer for you," declared the grey-beard. He raised my mug to his lips and drained the beer, then spat it out. "Gods, that's disgusting!" The bitter herbs that I had dropped in earlier, when I guessed how the lack of killing in my story would influence my listeners, merged into the trampled grass on the floor.

"That'll teach you not to steal from a druid," I laughed.

12

Fire, friend and foe

"What happened to Ganna and Dubhtach when you got to Rome?" asked Boudicca. "Women and druids can't join the Germanii. And where is Ganna now? Her foresight would be useful in the battles to come."

"And why," demanded Tenvantius, "didn't the Germanii throw you out as soon as look at you?"

"Ganna and Dubhtach set themselves up in the religious quarter. Because of Claudius' parade, lots of people were curious about her temple, and wanted to see the barbarian trophies. She got lots of donations. Money, sacrifices, and ears."

"Ears? Why ears?" So I told them why.

We arrived at the Germanii barracks in Rome and formed up for inspection. The commander of the Germanii, Centurion Gamus, watched us march past, then inspected us one by one. He was a giant of man, who must have been twice my weight, dressed in a bearskin cloak and gleaming armour.

When he arrived in front of me, standing next to Micipsa's left tusk, he looked me up and down, and walked around the elephant.

He returned to in front of me and barked, 'Report!'

'Decimus, Sir, rider of this elephant, called Micipsa, who the Emperor rode to receive the surrender of the kings of Britannia. The Emperor's orders were to bring him to Rome and station him where he would be available at the Emperor's convenience.'

He pointed up at Surus, who was sitting on Micipsa's neck.

'Who's that?'

'One of the Emperor's staff, Sir, called Surus. He does the civilian jobs, like parades, and I do the military ones, because he's not a trained soldier.'

'What use is an elephant to the palace guard?'

'He can break down a locked door in a coup, break up a mob in a riot, break through a shield wall of rebel infantry in a civil war.' I paused, and took a gamble on the rivalry of military units and his pride in being an elite guardsman, and added, 'And the Praetorians don't have one, Sir!'

He regarded me critically. 'You're small for a guard.'

'Makes the elephant seem bigger in comparison, Sir.'

'You won't always be on it. Eat more meat. I want the guard to look dangerous.'

'Yes, Sir.'

'And get caligae with thicker soles, to make you taller.'

'Yes, Sir.'

'And a full-face cavalry mask, so no-one outside these barracks sees your baby face, and you don't scare the slave girls with those eyes.'

'Yes, Sir.'

He leaned forward and loomed over me. 'I'm taking you on against my better judgement, Decimus. Orders are orders. But don't you or your elephant do anything to embarrass the guard, or I swear by Hercules that I'll sell you to the amphitheatre for lion food, understand? Make sure you do us proud!'

'Sir, yes, Sir.'

So I was accepted into the guard, and so far, so good, for the High Druid's plan. But it wasn't long before we were in trouble.

Our march south and guarding the river had limited the military training that the instructors gave us, so for the next four months we worked hard to finish it off. I loved it. Learning new fighting skills, wrestling like boys in a meadow, playing music on the march, and plentiful food: what's not to like? The centurion would beat us when we messed up, but no more than my father used to punish me for my escapades as a boy. However, because of the training, and because the Germanii were not part of Claudius' invasion of Britannia, we had no part in his victory parade. I was glad: I didn't want anyone linking me to Britannia, or worse still, recognising me by my eyes. And I had no desire to celebrate Claudius' victories, or the deaths of my father and brother. But I was concerned about Dubhtach and Ganna.

When the parade was over, I went to visit Surus to find out how it had gone. He and Micipsa were stationed in the elephant lines near the palace, well away from the horses. When I got there, Ganna was visiting too, and someone else was with her. I felt a shock of recognition and apprehension, because she reminded me of the Battle of the Medway. She was one of the famous Sarmatian cavalrywomen, and was dressed for the parade, from head to toe in tight-fitting gleaming golden scale mail. Her face was pale from being under a cavalry mask, and her hair was a dark coppery colour.

'This is Decimus, a Tiro in the Germanii,' Ganna told her. 'Decimus, this is Melanipa. Her mother is leader of the Sarmatian cavalry.'

She brushed her hair aside and nodded at me.

'I'm just introducing her to Surus and Micipsa,' said Ganna.

I took out my knife, cut the apple I had brought for Micipsa in halves, and offered one to her.

'Micipsa likes apples,' I told her.

'Come,' said Surus, and we led her to our elephant, where she fed him the apple. He let her climb up his trunk and sit on his neck, and they walked around the stable yard. Her horse, tied to the gate, started to get skittish. Melanipa clambered down, went over and calmed him. He was a magnificent stallion, clad, like her, in scale armour. She beckoned us over, and I stroked his muzzle.

'You like horses?' she asked me.

'Yes.'

'Are you in the cavalry?'

'Not yet.'

She looked disappointed.

'You are a warrior.'

'Yes, in the Imperial German Bodyguard.'

'How many battles?'

'Three.'

'You must have killed many enemies to be allowed into the Germanii so young. How many heads have you taken?'

'None. I guard lives, not take them.'

'I have taken two enemy heads.' She grinned. 'I need one more before I can marry. Your head would look good in my collection.'

I grinned back. 'And how many heads has the man you want to marry taken?'

She drew herself up proudly. 'My mother has not yet found a man worthy of me.'

'And have you?'

'Maybe. Ganna dreamed of me charging into battle beside a man, but she couldn't see who he was. Perhaps my fate is not yet written.'

THE DRUID AND THE ELEPHANT

On the other side of the yard, Micipsa lifted his trunk and gave a nervous snort.

'Can you smell smoke?' asked Surus.

I sniffed. 'Yes.'

A strange expression crossed Ganna's face. 'Trouble,' she said. 'We need to climb higher to see what it is.'

Melanipa mounted her stallion, and the rest of us ran back to Micipsa. From his back I could see over the nearby buildings. There was an orange flickering glow in the distance. The wind was blowing towards us from that direction, and I heard shouting.

'That way,' I told Surus.

'Isn't that the stables?' asked Ganna.

At those words, Melanipa kicked her stallion into a gallop.

The palace has a maze of courtyards, which I knew from my guard training. Melanipa was taking the long way round, heading for the stable entrance, but I knew a shortcut.

'That way!' I guided Surus, and he urged Micipsa on.

Our route took us to the back of the stable block. It was well on fire, and the neighing of panicked horses came from within.

'Smash down the wall,' I cried, and Surus guided Micipsa up to the wall and shoved. The wall was just wooden slats between brick buttresses, and gave easily. The elephant shook his head to clear a wider gap with his tusks, and then backed out, followed by a stream of frightened horses.

Inside, some stall doors were still closed, and horses tethered inside. I jumped down from Micipsa's back, and ran into the stable. The straw in the hayloft was on fire, sparks and burning embers were raining down, and smoke filled the building. Hammering sounded from the far end. The heat was intense, so I dunked my cloak into a drinking trough, then wrapped it around me. I took a deep breath and ran up the central aisle, slashing the tethers with my sword, until I got to the main doors. Squinting through streaming eyes I saw they were barred, and the bars were tied down. Two human figures lay on the floor beside them. I slashed the ropes, lifted the bar, pushed open the doors and staggered out. Hands grabbed me and pulled me away. I was coughing violently, and my cloak was on fire. Someone threw a bucket of water over me, and I collapsed.

The Romans have a group of men called the Vigiles whose job is to put out fires, and they arrived with buckets. People in the area had rushed to the fire when the alarm was raised, and the fire was gradually brought under control.

Someone threw more water on me and slapped me into wakefulness. I was hauled to my feet by two burly Vigiles, and found myself face to face with their centurion, who slapped me again.

'Who are you? What were you doing in the stables?'

'Decimus, of the Germanii.' I coughed. 'My elephant broke through the back wall.'

'There's no elephant, don't lie.' He back-handed me. 'Why were you here?'

'We smelled smoke and heard shouting.'

'Can anyone vouch for you?'

'Ganna, Surus and Melanipa.'

'Never heard of them.'

'The Germanii can vouch for me, too.' But he ignored me, because of the sound of hooves. A group of riders swept into the yard. They were Sarmatian cavalry. Some ran to the rescued horses, others to the smouldering remains of the stable. One group rode up to us.

'Who commands here?' demanded their leader, a tall woman on a magnificent stallion.

'I command,' stated the centurion. 'Who are you?'

'Amage, daughter of King Zorsines of the Siraces.'

'What do you want, Amage of the Siraces?'

Amage spoke to the rider beside her, in words I did not understand.

The rider walked her horse over to me, put her lance tip under my chin and lifted my face to see my eyes. She was wearing a cavalry mask, and firelight gleamed from the golden scales of her armour. She glanced over her shoulder at Amage, and nodded.

'I claim this man,' declared Amage.

'By what right?' demanded the centurion. 'You're not a Roman citizen. He's a suspect in a crime on Imperial property.'

Amage's escort pointed their lances at him and moved threateningly. One of the Vigiles holding me drew a knife and held it to my throat.

The masked rider moved forwards. 'I bear witness to this man's innocence. He was with me when we smelled smoke.'

'And who are you?'

'Melanipa, daughter of Amage.'

'You say he's innocent? Prove it: what is his name, and how did he get here?'

'He is Decimus of the Germanii, and he got here on an elephant.'

'I'll believe it when I see this elephant.'

Melanipa gazed around. 'Where's Micipsa?'

'Behind the stables, last I saw.'

Amage issued terse orders to her riders. Melanipa galloped away with two other riders. Her mother addressed the centurion. 'You ask by what right? These horses are our remounts. We are guests of your emperor, here to celebrate his victory in the parade. Where are the grooms we left with the horses? Where are the rest of my horses?'

'We found two dead men. Their bodies were inside the stable doors, which were bolted until he opened them. These are all the horses we found.'

'I saw the horses,' I said.

One of my captors slapped me. 'Speak only when you're spoken to.'

Amage walked her horse forward. 'Where did you see the horses?'

'When the elephant knocked down the back wall of the stable, some ran out.'

'Where did they go?'

'Towards the elephant lines. Over that way.' I nodded in the general direction.

She issued more orders, then regarded the centurion.

'I'm leaving an escort here with you. Release this man when the elephant comes. I go to find my horses. I will speak to the Emperor tomorrow. Pray that I have no reason to mention you to him.' She led her riders away, leaving four with us.

The centurion commanded the Vigiles, 'Stay here with the suspect. I've got better things to do.' He walked off towards the fire.

In the guard they teach us that it's at this time prisoners imagine they can escape, and that the guards should discourage this. The usual method is a punch to the kidneys or stomach, and knocking the prisoner to his knees. So I coughed and sagged in their arms. They didn't want to support my weight, so they let me down to my knees and grabbed me by the hair. But at least they didn't hit me.

It wasn't long before Micipsa arrived, ridden by Surus, Ganna and Melanipa, and followed by Melanipa's riders leading her horse. Micipsa charged over to me and the Vigiles backed off quickly.

'Let's get out of here,' said Ganna. 'Surus, take us to the Germanii barracks. Decimus had better tell them what happened before anyone else does. Melanipa, what do you want to do?'

Melanipa talked to the riders who had stayed with me, and decided she'd better help her mother find the runaway horses. Micipsa took me back to barracks, where I reported what had happened. My centurion was called, and I was in hot water.

A few weeks later, the Vigiles caught a Sarmatian spy trying to leave Rome through a smuggling network, which unfortunately for him had been penetrated by a Vigiles agent. He confessed to setting the fire, and I was called in as a witness to see justice done. Amage and Melanipa were there, and Amage asked me what I wanted as a reward. What I really wanted was for Melanipa to like me, but I couldn't tell her mother that. So I appealed to her as a leader.

'I want justice. The criminal attacked the Sarmatian horses, and murdered your grooms, so he should be given to the Sarmatians for punishment,' I said. 'Your daughter needs to take on leadership responsibilities, so she should be in charge of the punishment.'

The last part was a feeble reason, and Amage regarded me suspiciously, but wasn't going to discuss her daughter's marital qualifications in front of anyone, so she agreed. She also gifted the Germanii cavalry with one of her superb horses, which pleased my centurion.

Melanipa executed the criminal personally, and sent his ears to Ganna for her temple. Surus got some food from his homeland from her, and Micipsa got some delicious apples. And me? She taught me how to ride, and ride like the Sarmatians, who are in the saddle before they can walk. It's a skill that has saved me many times.

13

Gods of War and Water

Next morning I was praying to the war gods as the rising sun's rays pierced the early mists, when Queen Boudicca summoned me to her tent. "Time for a test of your skills, Druid. There's a Roman fort where a bridge crosses the River Gwash. It's to the north of my lands, on the way to Lindum. There are hundreds of Romans holding the fort, and I have thousands of warriors besieging it, but they can't get in because the walls are too strong. If we can capture it, we will cut off any Roman reinforcements from the north. If we don't take it, my reputation will suffer, the tribes won't follow me, and this revolt will be in trouble. Go with Druid Caicer and advise him. He'll coordinate with my war leaders."

I checked around for Tenvantius. The war chief was standing in the shadows, saying nothing, but looking pleased with himself. It was a strange reaction to me getting a command job. I was suspicious that this was a trap.

Caicer and I rode north with four of my men. I ordered Lukon and the rest to recover the sunken ballista from the causeway ambush, and bring the three ballistas north on carts.

The Roman fort was a big one, large enough for an entire cavalry wing, with high walls surrounding not only the fort's buildings, but also enough area for a parade ground and a cavalry exercise field. Such forts are the same all over the empire, and I knew without looking what it would be like inside: where the stables, commander's house, bathhouse and granary were. They would have enough supplies to outlast a siege, and enough men and horses to raid the surrounding countryside. The only thing keeping them in was the size of Boudicca's army, but undisciplined siege armies don't last long: boredom and disease set in, food runs short, then deserters start sneaking away. We had to act quickly.

The fort guarded the river crossing, on the floodplain at the bottom of a shallow valley. The whole area was boggy and crossed by meandering rivers. Caicer and I rode around it with Boudicca's war leader Dervalon, a brown-eyed, stockily-built man with a plaited beard and an air of calm competence. He explained the position.

"Inside is part of the Ninth Spanish Legion," he said.

I knew the Ninth: they had been part of Claudius' invasion, fought Caratacus, and put down a revolt by the Brigantes tribe. Killing them was part of the mission given to me by the High Druid, long ago.

"The walls are twice the height of a man, wooden inside and out, with earth between. We tried hitting them with a ram, and it didn't work. The walls are also long. It takes about half a day to walk around them at a safe distance."

That reminded me of Camulodunum, and how it fell. "If the walls are so long, how can they defend it all?" I asked.

"Our men have fought their way to the top of the wall a couple of times," he replied. "The Romans use their cavalry reserve: they gallop up, and the riders run up steps inside. They can get more men on top of the wall faster than we can. They also have slingers and archers who can shoot our men when they get on the wall, because there's no protection on the inside."

"What happens when you attack in many places at the same time?" asked Caicer.

"Same problem. Getting up the siege ladders is slow. It only takes a few Romans to knock down the ladders. And they have towers from where they can shoot at our men as they climb."

"What about the gateways?" asked Caicer.

"Let's ride round and I'll show you," said Dervalon. "But don't get your hopes up."

We rode around to where the road to Lindum crossed the river on a wooden bridge. The gateways were high and strong.

Caicer scratched his chin. "What do you think, Caz?"

"My father taught me to search for the enemy's weakness, and exploit it. Amergin told me to find the enemy's strength and convert it into a weakness. Their walls are strong, but they depend on their cavalry reserve to defend them. We have to stop that reserve."

But how? I needed to consider it. "Give me some time to pray to the war gods. They will guide me."

I walked my horse away upstream, deep in thought. What did I have to fight with? I had thousands of Boudicca's warriors on my side. I had my years of experience. Memories of my battles came back to me. I remembered the death of my father, the loss of my brother, friends who had died, and the blood I had spilled. The High Druid's plan had brought me a lifetime of warfare and death. Could the present be any better? If so, it was up to me. The gods help those who help themselves. Gazing at the river, I sought inspiration. All was grey and damp.

I prayed to the gods of war, Toutatis, Belatucadros and Cocidius. For good measure I invoked Andraste, Boudicca's goddess of victory, and Baduhenna, Ganna's war goddess, too.

THE DRUID AND THE ELEPHANT

I asked for an omen, a sign to guide me to revenge and victory.

The river was swollen from the rains, nearly topping its banks. As I watched, a patch of vegetation floated downstream. A twig sticking up from the water snagged on an overhanging reed. A cold gust of wind blew, and I smelled rain on the way.

The gods speak to us in riddles. Only a fool expects the clouds to part and a deep voice to boom out precise instructions. The first raindrops fell, soon increasing to an icy downpour. Moisture seeped between my war crown and my forehead. In the river, drops created a multitude of rings, and in the middle of each, a splash would shoot a little drop up into the air again, only to fall back into the centre of the ring, washing everything away. I opened my mind in prayer, and it was then I understood the message of the gods. I went to tell Caicer and Dervalon.

The next day, we left a holding force surrounding the fort and took the rest of the army downstream. Thousands of men can move a huge amount of soil surprisingly quickly, and in a few days we built a ten-foot high earthwork across the valley. The final stage was to fill wicker baskets with stones, and throw them in the river, blocking it up. Gradually the water level rose, until by the next day it had overflowed its banks, and the floodplain was ankle deep. The Roman engineers had raised the fort above the normal flood level, but only just. Water was lapping at the walls.

Leaving a few work-teams to plug any holes that might open up in the dam, we took the army into the forests, and built hundreds of ladders, and the transport to get them to the fort.

My ballistas arrived, and we set them up on punts again, so that during the attack we could move them into range. Lukon was confident of hitting the towers, even in the dark.

"They'll be sky-lined," he said. "The sentries will be looking down at a black river, and I'll be looking up at the towers with the stars behind them. I can keep their archers' heads down so they won't be shooting our attackers off their ladders."

A couple of days later and the bridge to the fort had disappeared underwater. The wooden walls were like an island.

"How deep do you think it is inside?" Caicer asked me. His pine marten regarded the flood disapprovingly.

"Chest high, probably. They'll have moved food and vital equipment onto the walls."

"If the horses can't climb up, they won't survive for long up to their necks cold water. A waste of some good animals."

"They might have got some onto the roofs of buildings, but if so, they're stuck there. If they got some onto the tops of the walls, it will block their troop movements."

It was still raining, an incessant icy downpour. Life in the fort must have been pretty miserable.

That night we attacked. Caicer and I sat on our horses on the nearest dry land, and listened to the assault go in. His pine marten watched curiously as our warriors crowded onto large rafts with ladders fixed at one end, and under cover of darkness poled them downriver and around the fort.

As the rafts got near, the Romans saw them coming, and raised the alarm.

"Now," I said, and Caicer blew the attack signal.

Dervalon's men attacked in twenty places at once, leaping up the ladders. Defenders' ran around the walls, and bows twanged as archers shot at them. From the towers I heard the deeper thrum of ballistas, but in the blackness their shots missed. Lukon and his crews shot back, keeping the Roman's heads down. The defenders tried to knock over the ladders, but they were were fixed to the rafts, and did not fall. A horn rang out from one of the assault teams, signalling success, and Caicer used his horn to

THE DRUID AND THE ELEPHANT

signal other rafts to the same place to reinforce them.

With the battle in full swing, Caicer looked at me.

"Now?"

"Yes, send them in."

He signalled again, and the second wave of rafts poled downstream. The Romans were too busy fighting to see them all, and a fresh wave of warriors climbed the ladders onto undefended parts of the wall. They spread out and attacked the defenders from behind. Vicious and bloody fighting raged through the night, but by dawn it was over. We had won.

Caicer and I took a raft across to the fort and climbed a ladder onto the walls. Inside, Iceni bodies floated face down in the frigid water, but the Romans had sunk under the weight of their armour. A few Roman survivors stood on the barracks rooftops, using their shields as a protective barrier around them.

"How do we get to them?" asked Dervalon.

"We'll float my ballistas across on rafts, and hoist them up on top of the towers. Their bolts will go straight through those shields. Or we can order the Romans to surrender and take them back to Boudicca."

"She'll just kill them."

"Not if we find a use for them. Caicer, would the Queen would keep them alive for prisoner exchange?"

"It's worth a try, especially if there are some noble ones."

"Right, let's do a warning shot to make their negotiating position clear, and see what they have to say."

We rafted the ballistas across to the fort, hauled them up to the top of the towers, pointed them into the barracks, and loaded them up. I was at the heavy ballista, with an iron bolt as long as my arm, and when Lukon released the first shot, it thudded into the eaves of the commander's house, its vibration an unmistakable threat.

"Romans, surrender," I shouted in Latin. "Stay there, and you die by ballista, cold or starvation. Surrender, and I will ask the Queen to use you for prisoner exchange. If you stay, you die. If you surrender, you may live. Drop your weapons and armour into the water and swim over here. If any of you are slaves, I will set you free."

There was a brief silence, then arguments broke out. On one roof, a centurion was beating those who wanted to surrender with his vine rod. On another, a fight started, and bodies splashed into the water. But the roof that commanded my attention was the one with a glint of gold. Swords flashed, men died, until all that was left was a ring of figures in gold scale armour surrounding a tall warrior in a gold cavalry face mask, who shook a sword at me, and shouted, "Sarmatians never surrender! If you want my life, come and take it!" I recognised the mask and the voice. It was Melanipa.

I swore, loudly and profanely.

Caicer regarded me. "You know her?"

"Yes!"

"In a good way or a bad way?"

"Good!"

"Enough to want to keep her alive?"

"Definitely."

Dervalon grinned. "You've just helped us take the fort, and probably saved this revolt. I can allow you to take a few prisoners. But be careful: she looks dangerous."

I nodded, but I knew dealing with her wasn't going to be easy.

Before I could deal with her, I had lives to save, and lives to take to make it happen. Lukon put a ballista bolt through the centurion, and the others on his roof surrendered. A few on the other roofs fell on their own swords, but most gave up when they realised we were only shooting those with a death wish. At last there was only Melanipa's roof left.

"Melanipa," I called, "daughter of Amage, granddaughter of King Zorsines of the Sarmatians, I do not require your surrender. I respectfully request that you accompany me to pay a royal visit to Queen Boudicca, to set up cordial relationships between the future free island of Britannia and the Sarmatian people."

"Who are you, how do you know my name, and why should I trust you?" she demanded. Fortunately, she didn't use my name, and I hoped she hadn't recognised my voice. I didn't want my identity getting out: too many Roman and Iceni ears were listening. And I didn't know how Melanipa would react. Would she see me as a traitor, or an enemy? There was no way to explain my true mission to her. Druids meant nothing to her. Chances were, she would not be happy to see me leading an enemy army. Right now, I just wanted her off that roof, and I would handle the details later.

"I am the emissary of the High Druid. The fame of your people's martial prowess has reached us even here. I give you my word, you and your companions will not be harmed."

I nudged Caicer. "I am Queen Boudicca's Druid. I also give my word," he called.

I nodded to Dervalon, who shouted, "I am the war leader of the Iceni. I give my word."

"I accept."

"Swim over to the steps. We will escort you to the Queen."

So she and her companions plunged into the water, and I sent them away with an escort and orders to wait for me in the next village south. I had things to attend to first, such as thanking the gods for their gift, and asking what on earth they wanted me to do with her.

Next day we hooked the Roman corpses out of the water, and stripped them of their weapons and armour. We planted their heads on spikes along the Lindum road as a warning. The bodies we threw in the river. We broke the dam, and let the water wash the invaders away. Caicer and I led the ceremonies of sacrifice to the gods of war and victory. When all was over, I went to talk to Melanipa.

14

The Riot

Druid Caicer and I left Boudicca's war leader, Dervalon, and the Iceni army to destroy the fort, and my men to scavenge anything useful from the Roman equipment. We rode south to collect Melanipa and take her to Boudicca. Caicer's pine marten rode confidently on his horse's saddle horn, as if the steed was his own. When we arrived in the village where they were waiting for us, a farmer directed us to the headman's hall. He came out to greet us.

"Bad news, I'm afraid," he said. "We had a feast last night to celebrate your victory. When we woke up this morning, your Princess and her companions were gone, and they took the escort's horses. The escort are out with my hunters, trying to track them, but with a good head start and fresh mounts, they'll be far away by now."

Caicer nodded. "Call off the search, and when the escort return, send them back to Dervalon. We need to go to the Queen, and if we don't start now, we won't get there by nightfall."

As we rode off, Caicer laughed at my expression. "Don't look so disappointed! You knew she wouldn't want to take the risk of throwing herself on Boudicca's mercy, didn't you? What is this woman to you, anyway?"

"She saved my life."

"How did that happen?"

So I told him about the rabble, the riots and the rabbits.

After I finished basic training with the Germanii, they promoted me to Munifex, the lowest level Roman soldier. Ganna, Melanipa, and Surus took me out to celebrate. Druid Dubhtach wasn't there, because now that Claudius' victory parade was over, he had gone back home, along with the rest of the Atrebates delegation. Ganna, however, had decided to stay on in Rome to run her temple of Baduhenna.

Ganna had told the fortune of a food stall owner's wife, and her prediction had come true. The woman therefore owed her a favour, and she took us to her establishment for a strange meal. She led us into a round building, with a dirt floor that had lots of holes in it, each about a hand-width wide. The owner brought out an animal that looked like a stoat. I didn't think there was much meat on it, but then he asked me to choose a hole. I pointed to the biggest, and he dropped the stoat down it.

There was silence, a scuttling, then an animal like a small hare shot out of the hole. The owner had a net, and tried to catch it, but it jumped straight up into the air, over the stoat and the net, and back into the hole. The stoat followed it, and this time the owner put the net over the mouth of the hole. When the animal shot out, it got tangled in the net. The owner swung the net hard into the wall, and killed it.

'Take a seat, and have a drink,' he said. 'I'll start cooking these.'

We sat, and I felt confused. 'Why did he say "these", when there's only one?'

'Because, Munifex Decimus,' said Ganna, 'that rabbit was pregnant, and we're going to eat laurices.'

'Oh,' said Melanipa, 'I had one of those at Claudius' victory feast. They're very fashionable.'

When the dish came, I discovered that laurices were tiny unborn rabbits on skewers. It was a shame to kill and eat something that had never even had a chance to live, but I didn't want to seem ungrateful to Ganna, so I ate one and said it was delicious. Actually, it was vile, but I put enough sauce on it to hide the taste, and got through my share. I washed it down with wine, and noticed Melanipa doing the same. Looking back, it might have been another one of Ganna's tests, but of what? Manners, self-control, tolerance, friendship? All of these? Who knows? But some good did come out of it later.

As a Munifex, and still the shortest soldier in the guard, the Germanii didn't trust me with protecting the royal family, and instead I watched over the administrative staff in the palace, keeping an eye out for spies and intruders.

One morning, I found myself in the same room as the two most dangerous men in the empire. The first was the emperor's favourite freedman, Narcissus, who was in charge of administration. An elegantly dressed man, with dark curly hair, it was him who had blamed druid magic for causing the loss of the war elephants, and earlier, when Claudius' soldiers in Gaul had been too scared of the druids to invade, it had been he who had headed off a mutiny and persuaded them to attack. He was definitely one of those who the High Druid wanted revenge on.

The second was Rufrius Crispinus, Prefect of the Praetorian guard. Immaculate in gleaming parade armour, he had a nose like an eagle, and piercing eyes to match. He was leader of the most powerful unit in the Roman army, the one who had put

Claudius on the throne, and could probably take him off it. His was the only Roman army unit allowed to bear arms in the city. They were extravagantly paid, and got bonuses for every plot they foiled and rebellion they quelled, so they operated a network of spies. The Praetorians had been part of Claudius' invasion force, and were targets of the High Druid's revenge. Of all my enemies, they scared me the most. I rubbed my sweating palms on my tunic, and hoped they wouldn't notice me.

The two men were sharing wine and planning violence. I stood in the shadows and listened.

'You can expect a riot tonight,' said Narcissus.

'I've heard the rumours,' replied the Prefect. 'Is it serious? What's going on?'

'There are two factions among the Judeans. One faction thinks their God sent a messiah, a liberator, to set them free. The other faction disagrees, saying that this messiah never became king, never united their people, and never brought peace to the world.'

'Tall order, that. No-one becomes King of Judea without our blessing; they're obviously not united if they're arguing about this; and as for world peace, we've got to defeat the tribes of Britannia, Germania, and the Parthian empire first.'

'We're not taking sides in this. The Emperor told them to sort it out among themselves, and if they didn't, he'd have to get involved. He threatened to exile them from Rome.'

'That was restrained of him. I'd have made an example of a couple of them.' The Prefect smacked a fist loudly into his other palm. 'Why do you think they will riot?'

'I don't. They'll be the target of the rioters. They're involved in financing the property market. The Emperor's threat made their business more risky, which put up the price of borrowing money. The property owners who've borrowed from them put up the rents to pay for it, and the tenants blame the Judeans, and the Emperor.'

'Put more men on the streets, knock a few heads together, nip it in the bud before it starts.'

Narcissus shook his head. 'The other problem is the street gangs. They want a riot as cover for looting. If the tenants don't start a riot, they will.'

'Knowing you, I assume you have a plan, and me and my men are part of it?'

'One of the property owners has decided that renting to the poor doesn't give good enough returns to pay the higher price of borrowing. He's going to evict all the renters, demolish his old buildings, and rebuild a better class of housing for better-off renters. The eviction notices go up this afternoon.'

'So you know where the trouble will start. What do you want me to do?'

'Position your troops to protect the palace. No need for the Praetorians to sully their reputation by doing riot control. Leave it to the urban cohorts to arrest the riot leaders. As for the criminals, my informants have told me where they plan to loot. When the urban cohorts arrest the looters, the gang leaders will have lost most of their men, and the cohorts will move in on them, too.'

'Then what?'

'We'll keep them prisoner. The Emperor will tell the Judeans to put the price of borrowing back down, because the dangerous men are off the streets. If they won't, he'll release them, and he won't be responsible for their actions.'

'This is going to take a lot of men. Who'll be protecting the Emperor?'

'I'll put the Germanii on alert. The Emperor also kept the Sarmatian cavalry in town. He doesn't want to be seen attacking his own people, so if things get out of hand, and serious blood needs to be spilled, bring the barbarians in to do the dirty work.'

At the end of my shift I reported all this to Gamus, the Centurion of the Germanii. When I marched in and saluted, he did not seem pleased to see me.

'I already know,' he said, after I told him the news. 'I have received his alert. You once told me that your elephant could break up a mob in a riot. Get it ready. Full armour and a crew of archers. Listen for the Cornicen's signals. Keep the rioters away from the palace.'

'Yes, Sir.'

'And, in Hercules' name, next time don't wait until the end of your shift before reporting important information. Tell the Guard Commander when he does his rounds, and he'll relieve you.'

'Yes, Sir.'

'Right. Get to work. Dismissed.'

I went to find Lukon, Trenus, and Eppilus to be my archers, and we went down to the elephant lines. Surus and Ganna were there.

'There you are,' said Ganna. 'I had a nightmare about you last night.'

'Very funny nightmare,' said Surus with a grin.

'I dreamed you were a tiny laurice, inside a rabbit. A crowd of stoats ran into your mother's hole, forced you out into a net, and then roasted you on burning skewers.'

I glared at Surus. 'What's funny about that?'

'You, laurice!' He put his hands beside his head, like rabbit ears. 'Poor little Decimus.'

Lukon laughed. 'I bet he tastes awful.'

'Where did they put the skewer?' asked Eppilus.

'This is serious, you idiots,' said Ganna. She held up a loop of cord with a metal symbol on it. 'This is an amulet of the war goddess Baduhenna. Wear it. Wear it in every battle. It'll keep you safe.' As she hung it round my neck, she whispered to me. 'This is not the time to be a good man, Caz. If in doubt, kill. The blood is not on your hands, but mine and Baduhenna's.'

We armoured up Micipsa, and the lads climbed up onto the platform. Lukon was carrying something resembling a bow attached to the end of a three-foot plank.

'What's that?' I asked.

'Gastrophetes,' he grinned. 'Greek for "belly bow". Long range and accurate, but slow to load. Trenus and Eppilus can handle the short range, rapid fire stuff. I can pick off the leaders.'

'We want to capture the leaders alive.'

'Oh, really? All right, I'll just shoot them in the legs so they can't run away.'

I was worried about what Ganna had said about nets, so I took a billhook that we used to cut branches for Micipsa, and also took a barrel of water in case of fire. I was wearing my banded armour on my body, and cavalry scale on my legs, in case of attack from below. My shield I stowed behind me on the front of the platform, and my horn, gladius and dagger were slung by my sides. I laced up my helmet, and then checked Lukon's armour while he double-checked mine. Surus gave me the goad, and climbed down. All was ready. We just had to wait.

A guardsman's job is waiting, waiting, and more waiting. For every heartbeat of action, there are days of standing still, or marching back and forth. Some men can't stand it, and transfer out to the legions or the auxiliaries. Those who stay develop ways to cope. Some dream of girls, some of food, some of wine, and some, like Lukon, dream up new weapons. But dreaming is dangerous: fall asleep on guard and the sentence is death.

To keep alert, we swapped news. Lukon went first, showing us his new toy.

'I found it at the back of the armoury. They said no-one

used it because you can't shoot it from a horse, and on foot it's cumbersome. But nobody's tried it on an elephant.'

'How does it work?' asked Eppilus.

'Watch.' Lukon slid the middle part of the plank down, and clipped the bowstring to the top end of it. He stood, pressed the other end down onto the platform, and leaned on the top of the other part of the plank with all his bodyweight. The bowstring stretched, and clicked into place. He loaded a bolt, and shot it at the beam supporting the stable door. The bolt head buried itself into the wood. Surus tried in vain to pull it out. He had to get a tool from the workshop to pry it loose.

'Shooting is easy when Micipsa is standing still,' I commented, 'but how about loading and shooting on the move?'

So we tried it with Micipsa trotting up and down the yard. After a lot of trying, and nearly falling off, Lukon managed to reload it.

'Now shoot it!' I challenged him. He shot at the stable door, and hit one edge.

'Aim it first!' I teased him.

We practised for a while, and he got better, but Micipsa was getting tired from the weight of the armour, so we took a break. It was Trenus' opportunity to tell his story.

'I almost died today,' he told us. 'I was guarding the Emperor's son, Britannicus. It was just him, me, and a nursemaid. He was playing with some wooden blocks, trying to build a little aqueduct. But he was starting in the middle, and it kept falling over. The maid had no idea why. The kid burst into tears. Reminded me of my little brother. There was no-one else around, so I went over and showed him what to do.'

'How would you know?' asked Lukon.

'Remember on the march down we went past a half-built aqueduct? When we learned road building, I asked the foreman how it stood so tall without falling down. He said you need to lean the ends against hillsides, put the pillars in foundation holes, and use formwork to support it all until it's finished. So Britannicus and I started with one end against the wall, raised the ground level with wooden blocks, put in some foundations, and used more blocks as formwork.'

'Cut the architecture lesson. Get to the almost dying part,' said Eppilus.

'We were just taking the formwork away at the end, when I heard a noise and glanced up. Standing there was Eppilus, the Guard Commander, and the Emperor, come to visit his son. And I hadn't noticed them come in. I almost had a heart attack.'

'I tried to warn you,' said Eppilus. 'I was standing at the back, waving at you, but you were concentrating so hard on playing with your toys that if Micipsa walked in, you wouldn't have noticed!' He grinned at us. 'You should have seen his face. He went white. I thought he was going to throw up!'

Trenus grimaced. 'I was about to jump to my feet and salute, when the Emperor said "At ease. Continue. I want to see if it stands up." My hand was shaking like a leaf, so I got Britannicus to do it. It worked. He was so happy. He ran over to Claudius, going, "Look, Daddy, look what I built!" And Claudius promised to take him to see a real aqueduct.'

'How come the Guard Commander didn't skin you alive for dereliction of duty?' I asked.

'The Emperor told him to double the guard on Britannicus, and the kid wanted me to go with them to visit the aqueduct. The Guard Commander couldn't beat me because I would need to be in good shape for the visit, but he gave me extra guard duty to make up for doubling the guard on the kid.'

At that moment, I heard the Cornicen's signal summoning us.

'Right,' I said, 'here we go. Get ready. They wouldn't call for us unless there's trouble.' I nudged Micipsa into a swift walk. We emerged from the side of the palace into the open area in front of it. A crowd of rioters was pushing the Praetorians back towards the palace. The soldiers had linked arms to make a wall against the shoving of the crowd. Although the Praetorians were pushing back, the crowd was bigger, and slowly the soldiers were retreating. The Prefect, Rufrius Crispinus, and his officers were mounted in the middle, behind the wall. The Sarmatians were lined up along the front of the palace, their horses shifting restlessly. It was dusk now, and the crowd were carrying flaming torches. More and more rioters were pouring in from the main street facing the palace. I worried that the Praetorians were going to be shoved back so close to the Sarmatians that the horses wouldn't have space to get up speed to charge.

The Cornicen on the roof of the palace, and Centurion Gamus was with him. Gamus issued an order, and the Cornicen sounded the "Elephant Forward" signal. I raised my horn, blew the "Advancing" acknowledgement, and urged Micipsa on.

We went wide of the left end of the Praetorian line, and curved round in front of them, clearing a space between their wall and the crowd. Micipsa trumpeted, and the crowd nearest us fled. People started to trip, get trampled by the fleeing feet, and be crushed up against the crowds still surging in from the surrounding streets. I didn't want to kill people, so I slowed Micipsa and guided him towards the centre of the Praetorian line.

When we got there, I pivoted Micipsa to face the crowd, and blew a challenge. The Praetorian infantry moved up beside us and Rufrius Crispinus walked his horse in front.

'People of Rome,' he proclaimed, 'your Emperor loves you. He understands your grievances, and he will address them. But tomorrow, not tonight. For now, you need to go home. Leave the area.'

THE DRUID AND THE ELEPHANT

He dug his knees into his horse's flanks, and moved slowly forwards. I moved Micipsa to keep pace with him. The crowd started to move back.

From my vantage point high on Micipsa's back, I noticed movement in the crowd. Most were edging back, but from a building on the edge of the open area I saw a group of men with torches heading our way.

'Trouble,' I warned my crew. 'Lukon, aim for the leader over there. See him?'

'I see him.'

'Wait. Don't give them an excuse to get violent.'

'I don't think they need one.'

A rock came arching out of the crowd and hit Rufrius Crispinus's horse. It reared up, snorting, and a hail of stones flew our way. Lukon shot his gastrophetes just before the stones hit us. The bolt sped across the heads of the crowd into the riot leader's thigh, and the impact threw him backwards. The bolt went right through the flashy part and nailed his leg to the wall.

Stones thumped off our armour as the rioter's missiles hit us, and I heard the Germanii Cornicen sound the Charge. I slapped my heels into Micipsa's neck and we surged forwards, around the Praetorian Prefect, and charged at the stone throwers. People scattered screaming before us, and the stone throwers fled. That's where I messed up. We got too far ahead of the Praetorians and blundered into a trap. Burning torches appeared among the crowds, and hidden gangsters among the rioters formed a net of flames, herding us towards the buildings. I couldn't slow down, as my cavalry instructors had drilled into me that a slow rider is an easy target, so I aimed Micipsa for the main street, searching for somewhere to turn without it looking like a retreat.

As we entered the street, tiles started to drop on us from the buildings on either side, as rioters on the roofs sprung their ambush. My crew shot back. As the crowds fled out of our path into side alleys, the road forward cleared to reveal a wall of carts blocking our way. On top stood a man with a torch, shaking his fist at us and exhorting the crowd.

'Lukon, shoot him,' I yelled.

I heard a twang from behind me, and the man fell back into the crowd, who roared with anger. I wanted Micipsa to crash through the carts, but the crowd stood on top of them waving burning torches, and Micipsa halted in fear. We were trapped, and tiles and rocks pelted us. The net of fire was in front and behind us. To our left and right were buildings with colonnades of arches at the front, holding up a roof to protect Rome's shoppers from the sun. Now the rioters were hiding behind the arch pillars, popping out to throw stones, and standing on the roofs throwing tiles. Remembering Trenus' story about how the end of a line of arches in an aqueduct needed support, I charged Micipsa into the arch column at the corner of a building. The architect had designed it to take the weight of the roof above it, but not to be shoved sideways by an elephant. The column collapsed, and rioters ran as the roof fell all the way along the front of the building. I spun Micipsa around, and did the same to the building on the other side of the street. At least now our flanks were not under attack, and the hail of tiles from the roofs stopped.

I wheeled Micipsa back towards the palace, poured the water over his head to protect him from the flames, and charged back towards the line of torches. He became more reluctant as we approached the rioters, and when a flaming torch was thrown at us, he halted.

'Shoot a way through,' I yelled to my crew, but with just two bowmen, and Lukon struggling to reload, they couldn't make an impression. All seemed lost. I clutched Ganna's amulet of

THE DRUID AND THE ELEPHANT

Baduhenna and prayed.

That's when Melanipa saved me. She was in command of the Sarmatian reserve, and saw the trouble we were in. She led her cavalry round the backstreets, attacked the wall of carts from behind, jumped them, and surged past us, into the rioters in front. They fled before her lances, and we followed her back to the palace.

Melanipa's mother, Amage, saw the rioters in disarray, and charged into them, clearing the space in front of the palace. The Praetorians went into the buildings and dragged out the rioters. Before long it was all over, and we returned to the elephant lines, with our armour dented by tiles and stones, but otherwise undamaged. Poor Micipsa, though, was shaking, and it took Surus until dawn to soothe him.

Next day we were called in to see Centurion Gamus. 'By Hercules, you're lucky to be alive, you idiots,' he stormed at us. 'You fell into a trap and had to be rescued. I don't like it when other units have to save my men. It's embarrassing. You also destroyed the front of two buildings, injuring many citizens. What do you have to say for yourselves?'

'They were trying to kill us, Sir!' I protested.

'You shouldn't have gone down that street on your own, Decimus. You should have stayed with the Praetorians. They would have protected you, and you them.'

'Yes, Sir.'

'However, your charge when Rufrius Crispinus was being stoned probably saved him. The Emperor gave the Praetorians a reward for quelling the riot, and they sent over a share for you. But I'm fining you all of it, and sending it to the Sarmatians, because without them, you'd be dead. The cost of repairing those arches will come out of your future pay or rewards. Any objections?'

Easy come, easy go. The reward would go to Melanipa. She deserved it.

'No, Sir.'

'I still doubt that your elephant belongs in the guard. Twice it froze in combat. It needs to learn to charge through fire. Understand?'

'Yes, Sir.'

'Lukon, watching you trying to reload your gastrophetes on a moving elephant was a tragic comedy. Put it back in the armoury, and draw a small ballista, the swivel-mounted type with a crank for reloading. Get the armourers to make a fitting for it on the elephant's platform. Go to the archery ground and practice.'

'Yes, Sir.'

'Trenus, since you like aqueducts so much, I've arranged for you to go for surveyor training. If you do well, I'll put you with the engineers. You'll be in the immunes.'

'Thank you, Sir.'

'From last night's disaster, it's obvious that elephants need cavalry support. I'm transferring the rest of you to the cavalry. Eppilus, you're going to be in charge of the horsemen screening the elephant. I want you and Decimus to go and see Polybius, the emperor's historian. He'll teach you about elephant warfare tactics.'

'Yes, Sir.' My dreams of commanding an elephant unit were coming true.

'The Sarmatians and Praetorians speak highly of you, but this is my unit, and I make the decisions here. Despite your rashness and tactical failings, you showed leadership and fighting spirit. With more experience you may be useful, so I'm going to give you another chance. Don't make me regret it.'

'No, Sir,' we chorused.

THE DRUID AND THE ELEPHANT

'Dismissed.'

When I finished the story, Caicer nodded. "You know you're in trouble now, don't you?" the druid said. "You can't keep Melanipa's escape from Boudicca, and she's going to suspect you of aiding the enemy. And Melanipa will probably remember your voice, and from you knowing her parentage, she'll guess who you are. Then she'll come after you. If she thinks you're a traitor, she'll try to kill you."

He was right about Melanipa, and knew Boudicca well. "Any advice?" I asked him.

"Win more battles. Boudicca won't kill you if you're useful, and you'll reduce the number of Melanipa's allies."

I wished Micipsa and Surus were with me. I'd have felt far safer on the elephant's broad back. The setting sun broke through the clouds as we approached Boudicca's camp, painting the marsh water crimson, like a sea of blood. It was an omen from the gods. I held Ganna's amulet, and prayed that the blood would be my enemy's, not mine.

15

A Test of Loyalty

Queen Boudicca listened to Druid Caicer's full report. When she heard about Melanipa, her face, which had been elated at our victory, hardened.

"If you have to choose between me and her," she demanded. "Who would you choose?"

"My debt of honour to Melanipa is now satisfied. I would choose you."

"Let's see." She signalled to her guards. "Bring her in!"

Led by Tenvantius, with an evil expression on his face, the guards dragged in a woman dressed from head to toe in scale armour, and wearing a helmet with a cavalry mask.

"Only death proves true loyalty," stated Boudicca. "Kill her."

Tenvantius grabbed the woman by the helmet and pulled it back, stretching her neck. He drew his sword and, with the tip, lifted a scale on her neck, exposing her throat for a killing thrust. The war chief thrust the hilt in my direction.

"Here. Take it and show your loyalty. Refuse the Queen's command and you die."

His words took me back to Rome, long ago, and to another Queen who demanded death.

THE DRUID AND THE ELEPHANT

Melanipa used her reward money from the riot to invite us all out to eat. Fortunately, she disliked rabbit as much as I did, and we went for seafood.

'Did you hear about Celer?' asked Eppilus, his mouth full of fish.

'The guy who paid eight thousand sesterces for a red mullet?' I asked.

'For one fish? You're kidding!' said Ganna. 'That's a year's pay for all of you put together.'

'Yes, him. Well, he's been accused of plotting against the Emperor, and condemned to death.'

'But he was a consul, and he and the Emperor were friends. Who's powerful enough to do that?' asked Lukon.

'There's only one person in the empire that powerful," replied Eppilus. "The rumour is that Empress Messalina has got it in for his family. She accused his brother before. And he was a consul, too.'

'Watch out for Messalina,' said Ganna. 'the Emperor lets her do whatever she wants, and as Empress, no-one will refuse her. And if they try, they die.'

'She's just protecting her son, Britannicus,' said Melanipa. 'She had Julia Livia, Emperor Tiberius' granddaughter, killed, because she was worried that her son might rival Britannicus for the throne. And she had the Emperor Caligula's sister killed, too. They won't be having any more babies to challenge her son.'

'Good,' said Trenus. 'I like Britannicus. He's a nice kid. He'll make a good emperor.'

'If he survives,' said Lukon, stabbing an oyster between its shells and twisting it open with his knife. 'If he dies on our watch, Claudius and Messalina will have our heads.'

'What about you?' I asked Melanipa. 'One day you might have a son who can challenge for the throne of Sarmatia. That attack on the stables, was the killer after you?'

'Yes, and I made him suffer for it! My mother doubled the guard on me. The only reason I can come out with you tonight is that you are Germanii, and she thinks you can guard me. We stay in Rome because it's far from the politics at home, and this is where kings and princes come. She's searching for a husband with a big enough army to protect me.'

'Met anyone you like?' asked Ganna.

'They're all old and fat! Surrounded by jealous, murderous relatives, their mothers worst of all! To them I'm just a thing for making babies and alliances. But I don't need them. One day I will have my own army.'

A few months later I was on duty watching over Narcissus again, when an imperial messenger arrived with a summons from the Empress. 'Come,' he ordered me, and we hurried over to her suite. Outside the door were two of my veteran comrades. At the sight of him, they rapped on the door, and one of Messalina's ladies opened it.

'Stay here,' Narcissus told me. I was confused: I couldn't protect him if I wasn't with him. I glanced at my colleagues, and they nodded and signalled me to stop.

After Narcissus entered and the door closed, the senior soldier, Optio Hospes, took one look at my eyes and whispered, 'You're Decimus, aren't you?'

I nodded.

'Listen, kid, you're new at this, so you need to know how this works. Guarding these people is dangerous. If you see or hear too much, you end up dead. If they tell you to wait outside, don't hesitate, do it. Understand?'

I nodded again.

'Good. Messalina's got it in for someone, don't know who yet. If we don't make it back to barracks tonight, you tell Centurion Gamus. Now stand still, at attention, until you're summoned. If you go outside the palace with Narcissus, rub your sweat on things when he's not watching, so our dogs can track you and find your body. Give you a decent funeral.'

I noticed the other guard had a strange expression on his face. He was trying not to laugh. They were pulling my leg, trying to scare the new boy. I stared him in the face until he cracked up, and we all tried to laugh silently, for fear of disturbing the Empress.

After a while, Narcissus emerged, but instead of heading back to his office, he led me to the Germanii guard commander. The commander sprang to attention when we entered.

'I have a job for this guard,' Narcissus told the commander. 'Relieve him.'

'Yes, Sir.'

Narcissus addressed me. 'Get your elephant and crew ready. I'll meet you at the elephant stables.'

'Yes, Sir. What's the mission, Sir?'

'We're going on a raid. Expect violent opposition. Now hurry!'

'Yes, Sir.'

I ran off to prepare.

Surus was helping us armour Micipsa when Ganna arrived. She watched us silently, and as we climbed aboard, she said, 'You're going to need spears.'

'What kind of spears?' asked Lukon. 'Lances, javelins, pila?'

'I don't know!' she exclaimed. 'Something long and pointy for stabbing things!'

'What kind of things?'

'Animals. I dreamed they were trying to climb up Micipsa and eat you.'

Surus nodded. 'There are some lances in the stores. I'll get some.'

He was back soon with three long lances. Lukon, Trenus and I took one each. Lukon's ballista took up so much space on the platform that there was only room for him and Trenus. Eppilus was riding with the escort, and I was sitting on Micipsa's neck.

We heard a clatter of hooves in the yard, and Narcissus' voice. 'Follow me.'

Ganna and Surus waved us off. As we turned the corner, I looked back. Ganna was praying.

To my surprise, Narcissus led us to the Praetorian's barracks in the north-east of the city. Formed up and waiting were three *turma* of Praetorian cavalry, with thirty horsemen each. Narcissus rode forward and addressed them.

'Praetorians! Last night, an intruder was caught trying to kill the Empress. He is a follower of Marcus Vinicius, whose wife Julia Livia was recently executed on the Emperor's orders. Our mission is to bring Vinicius to justice. We will ride to his country estate, capture him, and I will carry out the Emperor's commands. As Praetorians, your duty is to protect the Empress, and you will be well rewarded.'

I had heard of Marcus Vinicius. He was one of Claudius' commanders in the invasion of Britannia. He was on the High Druid's list of those who should die.

Narcissus nodded to the Praetorian leader, Rufrius Crispinus. 'Prefect?'

Crispinus rode forward. 'The estate is large, and the villa is walled. The plan is to go in through the front gate, as befits messengers of the Emperor. However, Vinicius may be expecting trouble, as the lack of news of the death of the Empress will tell him that his killer failed. If our entrance is barred, the elephant will break in. The occupants are mostly civilians, so there shouldn't be much opposition, but Vinicius has guards, and if they want a fight, we'll give them one. He also breeds exotic animals for the amphitheatre. Don't let them spook the horses.'

He dug his knees into his mount's side, and stood up in the saddle, drawing his sword.

'We are the Praetorian Guard. We are the blades of the Emperor. No-one threatens our Empress and gets away with it! Ride for vengeance!'

'Vengeance!' boomed a hundred voices.

'Forward!' shouted Crispinus, and we rode out with a thunder of hooves.

We arrived at the estate at dusk. Crispinus deployed two of the turma around the walls to prevent escapes, and took the rest of us to the front gate. Lukon cocked the ballista, the ratchet clacking and the taut sinew creaking just behind my helmet. If those sinews broke, they'd take my head off. Crispinus pounded on the gate with the butt of his lance. 'Open, in the name of the Emperor,' cried Narcissus.

'Who's there?' came a voice from inside.

'I, Narcissus, demand an audience with the Consul.'

'The Consul is in mourning and is not to be disturbed. You'll need to make an appointment. He is not receiving unannounced visitors, especially freedmen. Come back tomorrow.'

Crispinus pounded on the gate again.

'I, Rufrius Crispinus, of equestrian rank, Prefect of the Praetorian Guard, demand immediate admission on the Emperor's business. Refuse me at your peril!'

'The Consul outranks you, Prefect. My orders are to admit no-one except the Emperor himself, and I don't see him with you.'

Crispinus shook his head in exasperation, and waved me forward. I touched Ganna's amulet for good luck, then moved Micipsa towards the gate. We were nearly there when Lukon, standing behind me at the ballista, pointed over the gate and yelled, 'Ambush!'

A flight of arrows curved over our heads and into the Praetorians behind us. Horses reared and snorted. I knew that my next act would be decisive. The standard response to an ambush is to charge it, to take the fight to the enemy, but I knew that was what they would expect, and they would have traps and defences ready. I kicked my heels and urged Micipsa along the wall for about thirty paces, then swerved him at it. We'd been practising fighting in a city, based on Polybius' advice, and I put one of his ideas into practice. I reared Micipsa up on his hind legs, and he brought his weight down on the wall with his front feet. The wall couldn't take the pressure and collapsed inwards. Micipsa smashed through, widening the gap. Turning, we charged the ambushers. Lukon shot his ballista, which was loaded with a mass of slingshot bullets, another of Polybius' ideas. The bullets sprayed the archers in the unshielded flank, and the survivors fled.

The Praetorian cavalry jumped over the collapsed wall and charged after them, impaling them with their lances. Their Cornicen sounded the 'Follow' signal, and they galloped up the road towards the villa, about a hundred paces away.

From beside the villa, shadowy shapes ran at the leading cavalrymen, leaping up and clamping their fangs into the horses' necks. I recognised them from palace mosaics. Lions! Horses reared and fled in terror, their riders unable to control them. Lions ripped at the steeds' hindquarters, bringing the animals crashing down. Behind me, Lukon and Trenus frantically cranked to re-load the ballista. Micipsa trumpeted, and I saw a lion streaking towards us. It sprang, and Micipsa impaled it on his tusk, shook it violently, and threw the corpse away. Another lion sprang at our flank, clawing its way up the armour. Its pale, soulless eyes stared into mine, its snarling fangs ripped links off Micipsa's chainmail, and it stank of death. I stabbed at it again and again with my lance, but it swatted away the blade. It seized the shaft in its jaws, wrenching it out of my grasp. I grabbed ballista bolts in both hands, and thrust again, faking at its eyes, then hitting its paws. Finally it lost its grip, fell, and Micipsa stamped on it. Bones crunched, and the beast was still.

I scanned the area for danger. The Praetorian cavalry had got themselves organised, and were hunting down lions with their lances. Eppilus and his men had got one trapped against a wall. Another lion had got Narcissus' horse by the throat, and he was lying on the ground, with a leg trapped under his mount.

'Hold still!' cried Lukon, and I leaned forwards and shushed Micipsa.

There was a twang, and a ballista bolt shot past my shoulder, straight into the lion's heart, killing it instantly.

'Good shot!' I exulted. 'Looks like that was the last of them.'

A Praetorian arrived, pulled Narcissus' leg out from under his horse, and helped him up.

'You alright, Sir?'

'Just a few bruises. Let's get on with it.' He was tough for a civilian, I'll give him that.

The two-storied villa had a main building, with wings projecting towards us on either side, balconied on the upper floor. A road led up the middle, an ideal ambush site. The same thought must have occurred to Crispinus, as he stopped his troops fifty paces short, and sent scouts forwards.

I moved Micipsa up, and when the scouts came under slingshot attack, I yelled down to Eppilus, 'I'll move Micipsa to the end of a wing. Use him as a ladder!' Eppilus nodded, and Lukon sprayed the length of the balcony with slingshot from his ballista.

We trotted up to the end of the building, where the balcony finished. Slingshot bullets from the opposite wing pinged ineffectively off our armour and shields, and I got Micipsa to kneel. Eppilus and his men dismounted, and using Micipsa's knees and back to climb, scrambled up and onto the balcony.

They ran along it from room to room, using their shields to protect themselves and driving the slingers before them. The Praetorians saw what was happening, and using a horse as a ladder on the other wing, did the same.

Before long the balconies were clear, and Crispinus walked his horse up to the main door. This time he didn't bother rapping on it, and just waved us forward. Micipsa put his back to the door, and gave it a mighty kick. The bar inside snapped, and the door flew open. The Praetorian scouts, waiting on either side, charged in with their shields raised, followed by their comrades. Resistance was short-lived.

Lukon, Trenus and I climbed off Micipsa's head onto the balcony of the main building, and Eppilus beckoned us through the room behind it, which led out to another balcony overlooking the atrium in the middle of the villa. A distinguished middle-aged man, wearing a full toga, was standing by the pool, holding a cup of wine. Narcissus limped up to him.

'Consul Marcus Vinicius, you stand accused of the attempted murder of the Empress Valeria Messalina.'

Vinicius looked down his nose at the freedman. 'Really? What is your evidence?'

'Your would-be killer was caught, and confessed.'

'A false confession, probably extracted under torture, from a dupe deceived by any one of the Empresses' many enemies.

It's his word against mine, and I am the grandson-in-law of the Emperor Tiberius, and have been twice a consul. Who will the Senate believe?'

'This isn't going to get to the Senate,' said Narcissus. 'The Empress gives you a choice: poison or the blade. Which do you prefer?'

To his credit, the man could think on his feet, and came up with an alternative.

'My wife was permitted exile. I claim the same privilege. It's in Messalina's interest. If I become a martyr, she will make many new enemies.' He pointed at the Praetorian Prefect. 'And you, Rufrius Crispinus, wouldn't be where you are today without me. I helped kill that madman Caligula, allowing you Praetorians to put your man Claudius up as emperor. You, Narcissus, have risen high in his shadow. Have you the sense of honour to admit your debt to me?'

'Exile is not an option,' replied Narcissus. 'Blame Seneca. He wrote to Polybius, campaigning to be recalled from exile. For a philosopher, he's not very subtle. The Empress wishes he'd been executed for his relationship with your wife. To her, exiles always present a threat of return, and if fortunes change, revenge. As for honour, I permit you to die by your own hand. Make your choice.'

'I will follow in the footsteps of the great Socrates. I am unjustly condemned, as he was. I will die as he did. Give me the poison.'

He held out his hand imperiously to Crispinus, who passed him a vial. Seating himself on a marble bench, he poured the poison into his wine, and drank it.

16

THE GREAT MAN'S GARDEN

The memory was over in a heartbeat, and I knew what to do. I grabbed Tenvantius's sword hilt. The woman that the war chief was holding made muffled noises, and he shook her. When you've known someone as long and well as I've known Melanipa, you recognise the way they move, and Melanipa moved like a warrior, with grace, control and precision. No way this woman was Melanipa. I saw why Tenvantius was so happy with himself about the order to kill. I was damned if I did and damned if I didn't. Refusing to kill her was not an option. Killing her would prove my loyalty, but was also a trap. If Boudicca knew that this wasn't Melanipa, and thought that I knew, killing would only show that I was trying to deceive her.

Centurion Gamus had told me to learn tactics, and one that I had learned from Marcus Vinicius was that when an enemy offers you two choices, come up with other options. So I went for one Tenvantius had not given me.

'This woman is not Melanipa,' I accused him. With his sword, I sliced the laces of her helmet and pulled it from her head. Under it was a stranger, gagged, shaking, and in tears. 'Caicer, you saw Melanipa at the fort. Is this her?'

'No,' said Caicer. 'That's not her. Not even close.'

I'd had enough of Tenvantius. It was pay-back time. I threw

the woman's helmet at his feet.

Tenvantius went red with rage. The war chief grabbed the woman by the hair and yelled, "If you won't kill her, I will! Give me that sword back." The noise frightened Caicer's pine marten, who burrowed into the druid's beard.

I knew Tenvantius wanted to destroy the evidence of his trick by killing the woman before she revealed that she was not Melanipa.

"No, Tenvantius," I snarled, "you gambled, you lost. This is my sword now." I pointed at him with my left hand and held the sword up behind me in my right. "If you want it, come and get it!"

Tenvantius thrust the woman aside and drew his dagger.

"Stop!" ordered Boudicca. "Put away your weapons. Now!"

Tenvantius dropped his arm, and I handed the sword to Caicer. The druid stepped forward and said, "There is a way to resolve this, and kill two birds with one stone. I have a plan to re-capture Melanipa and take more Roman forts. Melanipa probably went south towards Londinium, as the further south you go, the more Romans there are. The next important ford south of the Gwash is where the Lindum road crosses the River Nene. There are two forts there, one at Durobrivae and the other not far downstream, where the Ninth Legion's base is. Melanipa's probably in one of them. I suggest a competition between Tenvantius and Cassibelanus. Give them both equal parts of your army, let them choose a fort each, and see who can take it first."

I knew that Caicer was helping me out with his advice to win more battles, but Tenvantius was angry and hostile, so I had to trick him into agreeing.

"What will it take to convince you people?" I demanded. "I've already taken a fort for you. Now you want me to take a tougher one?"

"Scared, Druid?" challenged Tenvantius. "That first one was just luck. You won't take another!"

I went on the defensive, to suck him in. "It wasn't luck." I touched the war crown on my head. "The gods are on my side."

Boudicca cut us both off. "Silence! I decide how we fight this war. We are not here to play games. We need to head south towards Camulodunum, and take it while the legions are still divided. Durobrivae is on our way and controls a vital river crossing. We must defeat the Ninth Legion before Suetonius gets here with his legions and joins them. My armies are large enough to attack both forts."

She rounded on me. "The gods are not only on your side, Druid. We are on the same side and the gods are on our side. We will let them decide who takes which fort."

She stooped and picked up a straw from the floor. "Whoever draws the short straw takes Durobrivae." She broke the blade at a point a third along its length, hid her hands behind her back, and evened up the projecting ends. She offered them to Tenvantius.

He searched her face and hands for guidance, but she gave no hint, so he took the one nearest him. It was the long one.

"Yours is the honour of facing the Ninth," she declared. "Druid, Durobrivae is yours."

"Ha!" said Tenvantius. "I've seen Durobrivae. The land there is as flat as a sword blade. Your flooding trick won't work. You don't stand a chance." He grabbed his sword from Caicer and stalked out.

Seeing him go so quickly, I was worried that he would ambush me when I rode back to my men. I rubbed my temples, and my fingers touched the war crown. The wearer of a crown must both command and be protected. It was my duty to warn the Queen.

"Without Tenvantius or I here to protect you, you are in danger here. And Dervalon won't want to divide his forces. It is your army to deploy as you will. And if you are present at the taking of the forts, the victory will be yours. More tribes will follow your banners."

"Your warriors take heart when you are with them, my Queen," added Caicer.

She nodded and gave orders to her servants. "Break camp. We are going to the Nene."

A few days later, Dervalon, Lukon, Trenus, Eppilus and I scouted out Durobrivae and its fort. The road to Londinium ran right through the middle of the town, down to a wooden bridge across the river. To the west of the town, across a brook, was the fort. It was about a hundred paces wide and the same long, surrounded by a ditch and a rampart with wooden spikes. The Romans had cleared the ground for a bowshot around, so attackers would have no cover.

"The Romans first made the fort to protect the bridge builders," said Dervalon, lifting his plait-bearded chin in that direction. "When they finished the bridge, they left it, filled in the ditches and took away the defences to use elsewhere. But when the revolt started, they came back to protect the bridge and the town. They re-dug the ditches, and put in a bank with a wall on top. I saw it before the wall went up, and inside it's just tents, no buildings."

"How many soldiers?"

"About a cohort. Auxiliary cavalry, mostly."

"And the town?"

"About the same, maybe five hundred, including men, women and children."

"And what about Tenvantius' fort?"

"Half a legion of the Ninth. Maybe two thousand men. Big fort. He wants more men."

"Give him the chariots and the foolhardy young warriors ambitious to make a name for themselves. I want the archers, slingers, and solid men with sense and experience. I also need foresters, carpenters and hunters."

"Sounds like you've got a plan."

Lukon raised an eyebrow. "What are you thinking?"

"Remember searching for Asiaticus in the Gardens of Lucullus?"

"Yes. Can I use my ballistas? I want to try something new."

"I'm counting on them."

"Good. I found some more in the towers of that fort we took. Another eight. One on each tower. And a new type of bolt."

"I wondered why you were looking so pleased!"

"What," asked Dervalon, "are the Gardens of Lucullus? And who is Asiaticus? What's your plan with the ballistas?"

So I told him about the Empress Messalina and the suicide in the gardens.

This was years ago, at the same time as Ostorius replaced Plautius as governor of Britannia. There was trouble in Rome, caused, as usual, by Claudius' wife Messalina. A few weeks after the raid on Marcus Vinicius' villa, Optio Hospes came to find us.

'You're to report to Centurion Gamus tomorrow morning, after parade.'

'Yes, Optio.'

'I don't know what you've done, but he's not happy. Make sure you look your best. Lots of spit and polish.'

Gamus was never happy, and Hospes was probably just winding us up. But when you are called up in front of the

Centurion, you'd better be spotless, so we stayed up late, shining our armour and weapons until they gleamed.

Next morning, Optio Hospes marched us into Gamus' office. 'Left, right, left, right, left, right, left. Squad, halt! Left, turn. Squad, salute!' I smelt trouble, because behind Gamus was Rufrius Crispinus, Prefect of the Praetorians.

'You are going on an escort mission,' said Gamus. 'Empress Messalina wants to visit Senator Publius Suillius Rufus' wife in her villa, and you are going to take care of her. You need to be prepared for trouble. Marcus Vinicius' friends and supporters are not happy with our Empress. The Senate is in an uproar, because if Messalina can have Vinicius killed, none of them is safe. However, we must not give the impression that we are worried, so don't put obvious battle armour on the elephant. Prefect Crispinus will tell you the details.'

Crispinus stepped forwards. 'We leave tomorrow morning. I will lead one turma of cavalry in front. In the middle will be the Empress' coach, with curtains closed and full of Praetorians in case of an attack. It will be surrounded by another turma. Behind that will be you. The Empress wants to ride on the elephant, so get a suitable platform for her, with curtains so no-one can see her. At the back of the parade will be another turma as rearguard. We'll meet you at the elephant lines at mid-morning. Collect the Empress, take her to Rufus' villa, wait there, then bring her back via a different route. Understand?'

'Yes, Sir.'

'Also, I have a gift for you from Narcissus.' He opened a sack at his feet and pulled out four lion skins. 'This one is for you, Decimus. It was full of holes where you stabbed it, and ripped where the elephant stamped on it, but that just shows it died in battle. For Lukon, here's the one you shot, with a big hole where the ballista bolt went in. For Trenus, here's the one that the elephant killed with its tusk. Finally, for Eppilus, here's the one you killed with your lance.' He came round the desk, and put the lionskins on our shoulders, with the hollowed out heads on our helmets.

'Be careful,' he said. 'The skins have been tanned, but they still smell of lion. Get the horses and the elephant used to them.'

'Yes, Sir.'

'Anything you need for the mission?'

'Yes, Sir. The Empress needs a suitable platform. Her ladies know what she likes. One of her ladies knows Optio Hospes here. Request permission to bring the Optio along as liaison, Sir?'

Crispinus glanced at Gamus, who nodded. 'Granted. Anything else?'

'Yes, Sir. We need a platform fit for an Empress. We'll need the workshops to alter ours, and money for fitting it out.'

'See the Quartermaster,' said Gamus. 'Tell him I said to help you. Anything else?'

'No, Sir.'

'Right, get to it. Dismissed.'

Hospes marched us out, and waiting to congratulate us on our lion-skins were our comrades. I was so proud and happy to be one of them that I forgot all about the High Druid's mission. I was a member of the Imperial German Bodyguard, guardians of the most powerful man in the world, leader of the world's greatest empire. Cold, foggy, Britannia was in my past, but here was a promising future. Glory, honour and Roman citizenship were within my reach. But then the Empress went and spoiled it by showing me the greed and rot at Rome's heart.

When Surus heard about the parade, he pointed out that as it was not a military mission, but a civilian one, he would ride Micipsa. He saw me hesitate at this.

THE DRUID AND THE ELEPHANT

'Don't worry,' he said. 'Come and see this.'

In the storeroom he showed me a type of elephant platform I hadn't seen before. 'It's called a howdah,' he said. 'It means a camel bed, in my father's language. The Empress can recline inside with her lady, and you and Hospes can stand at the back to protect her. I'll sit at the front, on Micipsa's neck.'

Hospes soon arrived with Messalina's lady Julia, carrying armfuls of rugs and cushions. The Quartermaster sent over a team of workers, and by evening we had transport fit for an Empress, with hidden armour on the sides and roof. I didn't want one of her enemies dropping things onto us from tall buildings and hurting her. In case enemies attacked us, I took water for fire, and a pot of honey I could throw to attract bees away. We armoured Micipsa's body and forehead, covering them with the imperial purple cloth that Claudius had used in Camulodunum, and practised with Julia playing the Empress. It was magnificent.

Next morning the Praetorian escort arrived, and we went to pick up the Empress. She emerged from the palace with Julia and a man. He was young, confident, smiling, and fashionably dressed, with curly black ringlets and a gracious manner. Just being near him made me feel like an uncouth barbarian.

'Who's that?' I whispered to Hospes, who was standing beside me on the back of the howdah.

'That's Mnester, the actor. Claudius commanded him to obey her every wish.'

I'd heard of Mnester. It was said the previous emperor, Caligula, would personally whip anyone who made a noise during his performances, and Messalina had had a bronze statue made of him. The three of them climbed up Micipsa's boarding ladder and disappeared behind the curtains. I pulled up the ladder, stowed it, and off we went.

The journey to the villa was disturbing. Messalina's voice,

muffled by the curtains, was teasing and giggling, Mnester's like liquid gold. I understood why the women of Rome adored him. He was a charmer, and I hated him instantly. If I was an emperor, I would not have allowed him anywhere near my wife. But a guard's job is not to judge, only to protect and obey, so I tried to ignore them, and keep an eye out for danger.

The trouble started on the way back to the palace. Crispinus's route took us past a tall wall with pine trees on the other side. I heard Mnester's voice waxing lyrical, then Messalina's, giving instructions. The lady Julia stuck her head out of the curtains and said, 'Hold! The Empress wishes to enter the gardens.'

Surus brought Micipsa to a standstill, and I took out my horn and blew the halt signal. The whole parade stopped. The Romans have a signalling system for spelling out unusual orders letter by letter. They arrange the letters of the Roman alphabet into a five-by-five square, called a Polybius square, so each letter becomes two numbers, one for the row and the other for the column. To disguise the fact that I was giving the Empress' orders, I made it into a tune. In Latin, 'Visit the garden' is 'Hortum visita', so I blew 2,3 3,4 4,2 4,4 4,5 3,2. 5,1 2,4 4,3 2,4 4,4 1,1. As a musician, I was thinking it would be much quicker to use two notes from a musical scale for each letter, rather than up to ten blasts for each, but for tone-deaf legionaries, the long way is best.

Fortunately Crispinus comprehended my signal, cantered back from the head of the parade to the garden doors, and rapped on them with his lance butt. There was no reply from the gatehouse.

'Open these gates in the name of the Emperor!' Still no reply. He pointed at Surus, and signalled us forwards.

I didn't want Micipsa to kick the door down, as it would violently shake the Empress's platform. So I edged forwards along the howdah side, and told Surus to move us opposite the

THE DRUID AND THE ELEPHANT

gatehouse. I used Micipsa's boarding ladder to walk across to its roof. Pulling the ladder after me, I climbed down it to the ground. In the guardhouse, an old slave was snoring beside an empty wine flask. He awoke with my blade at his throat, which had an instant sobering effect, and I forced him to unbolt the gate.

The Praetorians walked their horses through and spread out to search the garden. Micipsa was too big to go through the gate, so when the search was over, we helped the Empress and Mnester down the ladder, then tried to stay out of their way as they strolled arm in arm.

How can I describe the wonder of those gardens? They were in Persian style, commemorating Lucullus' time conquering in the east, beyond the Tigris River. Broad gravel pathways lay alongside long pools, surrounded by flower beds with cypresses and poplars behind. Ornate mosaic-floored villas offered shade and respite from the heat. Sculptures adorned the lawns. One statue of the Goddess Diana shooting a stag was so realistic that when I first saw it, I took it for a real deer. The garden was like paradise on earth, the most beautiful place I had ever seen, and I wanted one of my own. Messalina and Mnester drifted around, examining the statues. Mnester was expounding on the surrounding delights, and comparing them to the woman beside him. She was lapping it up, and gazing around herself with a covetous eye.

It was sunset before she decided to leave, so I had plenty of time to daydream of bringing Ganna and Melanipa to wander the paths and swim in the pools. Unfortunately, I only got to visit the gardens again twice, and both times it was for bloodshed.

It wasn't long before Messalina's covetousness became action. Centurion Gamus called us in again.

'I read the report on the Empress' visit to the garden,' he said. 'You did well with the howdah, and she was pleased. However, I, by Hercules, am not. Lukon, you should have hidden a weapon on the howdah between the Empress and Decimus. When Decimus was off the elephant, you should have been on it, acting as sentry. Eppilus, you should have scouted the garden for a way for Micipsa to enter. Trenus, you should have gone with him and inspected the walls for weaknesses. Decimus, the whole neighbourhood heard your signalling. Go and see the Cornicen and learn how to signal with flags. Also, your elephant stood still for a long time. How many times do I have to tell you that cavalry's strength is in its mobility? It's a miracle you weren't attacked and caught napping. Any time when there's nothing to do and you're just standing around, you should be thinking of what to do if you are attacked, and taking action to make sure the attack will fail. Do you understand me?'

'Yes, Sir.'

'Right. Time to earn those lionskin cloaks of yours,' he said. 'You're going on another raid. Senator Rufus, whose wife you took the Empress to visit, accused the owner of the Gardens of Lucullus, Consul Asiaticus, of adultery. The Emperor has ordered Asiaticus' execution. He's very rich and powerful, so much so that he almost became emperor when Caligula died. He's also a soldier, who campaigned in Britannia. His men may put up a fight, like Marcus Vinicius's did. He's in his country villa in Baiae, and the Praetorians are going down there to arrest him. They want you to go along. They'll search the grounds, and you can break down any walls or kick open any doors. Get Micipsa ready, and at nightfall, make your way to the Praetorian barracks. Use your brains this time. Understand?'

'Yes, Sir.'

'And keep your mouths shut about this one. Asiaticus is

popular with the people. I don't want rumours getting out and a riot at our doors.'

'Yes, Sir.'

'Right, get to it. Dismissed.'

Midnight a week later found us at the back entrance of Asiaticus' estate on the coast. The Praetorians surrounded the walls on the outside, then scouts slipped over, killed the guard dogs, and opened the gates. The cavalry filed in, making a line all the way along the wall, and then walked forward together, followed by the infantry. They searched every hut, bush and villa, and nothing slipped between them. We followed them in, Micipsa's feet scrunching on the gravel paths.

The line halted when the centre reached the main villa. At the top of the main entrance steps stood Asiaticus.

Prefect Crispinus walked his horse forwards.

'Decimus Valerius Asiaticus, you have been found guilty by the Senate of adultery with Poppaea Sabina. The Emperor has ordered your arrest.'

'Tell Claudius I had nothing to do with Caligula's death. Request that my wife and son be spared. I have left provisions for them in my will.'

'Tell him yourself, you are coming with me to Rome. Take him!'

The Praetorians grabbed him, chained him, and he was dragged away.

Asiaticus was brought before Claudius, and condemned to die. His friends persuaded the Emperor that in view of his long and loyal service, he be allowed to choose the place and manner of his passing. He chose the gardens of Lucullus, and ordered his own funeral pyre to be built there. The Empress ordered us to take her there on Micipsa, so she could watch and know the instant the garden was hers.

Asiaticus was about to slit his own wrists, when the wind changed. He grabbed the opportunity to annoy his enemy and delay his own death. 'The smoke from the pyre will stain the trees,' he told his retainers. 'Move it to a better place.'

Consuls get pyres befitting their high rank, and it took a long time to take it apart, move it, and rebuild it. Messalina was fuming. Empresses demonstrate their power by making other people wait, and hate to be kept waiting themselves. 'Tell him to get on with it,' she demanded, 'or his son will join him!'

Asiaticus knew his time had come, and with a flourish, opened his veins. There was a man who knew how to die.

"What," demanded Druid Caicer, "does this have to do with taking the fort at Durobrivae? You don't have an elephant to kick down the walls."

"We are going to stain the grass of Durobrivae with fire and the blood of our enemies! The trees will come alive, and we will sweep from one end of their fort to the other. And we're going to take the time we need to prepare properly."

"And how are you going to manage that?"

"They have two strengths: the mobility of their cavalry, which we are going to rein in, and the protection of their walls, which we are going to turn into a cage. And we're going to practise until we can do it right."

I needed warriors. "Dervalon," I said, "how many men can you give me?"

"Our force has grown. Men from the other tribes have

seen your victory and joined us. They want to fight for you. They believe you can do magic." He stroked his plaited beard thoughtfully. "I can give you five thousand."

"Good. Call a council of the leaders. I'll explain the plan."

I took the army deep into Iceni territory, away from Boudicca's impatience. We built a copy of Durobrivae fort and practised attacking it again and again. Eppilus formed a group of horsemen to play the role of the enemy, attacking or escaping until we learned how to block his moves. When I was confident that every man knew his job, and could do it silently and in the dark, we were ready. I gave strict orders that any female Romans, especially cavalry, were to be captured alive and brought to me. Any women, children, and slaves were to be spared. Then we headed off to war.

In the Gardens of Lucullus the trees had hidden the walls from the inside. My army marched to the forests to the west of Durobrivae, and built portable wickerwork walls in ten-foot sections, which they carried using cross-members on the inside. They put leafy branches at the top of the walls, and bracken at the bottom. We made three hundred and sixty wall sections, which took over three thousand men to carry, but were enough to surround the entire fort. Other men carried parts of towers to put the ballistas on. Trenus helped them build sections of towers to fit together and raise in the time the wall carriers were crossing the open ground around the fort. Ballista-carrying elephants would have been faster and more mobile, and I was reminded again of Micipsa and Surus. But there's no point wishing for the impossible.

Lukon and his teams practised with some special creations of his. On the last day before the attack, I sent hunters out to scout the forest and set up markers to guide the wall carriers to the fort. They also caught game, fresh boar meat to feed our army and raise morale before the attack.

At midnight we picked up the wall sections and moved off. The scouts guided us along their trails to the edge of the cleared ground to the west of the fort. The men laid the walls flat on the ground, and, crawling forward, dragged them towards the Romans. At a hundred paces from the defences, we positioned our walls on all sides of the fort, leaving a narrow gap to the west. The crews with the parts of the towers crept forwards to just behind these walls, with the ballistas ready to go on top. I touched the war crown and prayed for the gods' blessings.

"Listen," whispered Lukon. "Hear that?"

In the distance sounded the baying of hounds. Closer and closer they came, the voices of my hunters urging them on. An alarm sounded from inside the fort. My army leaped to its feet and raised their sections of wall, surrounding the fort and preventing escape. Dark shapes flashed by: deer flushed by the hounds. They dashed through the western gap towards the fort. The dogs herded them on, pushing them to the defences. Deer in flight can jump twenty feet, and these cleared the fort walls with ease. Sentries cried out as stags leaped past them. To the defenders it must have seemed as if the forest had come alive, and risen up to attack them.

As the alarm sounded, Lukon and his crews shot their ballistas. Lukon had modified the special bolts that carried slingshots to carry burning coals instead, and these arced over the walls and sprayed fire onto the tents inside. One shot hit the fodder for the horses and started a blaze that lit up the fort.

I raised the aurochs horn that the High Druid had given me, called the Horn of Cernunnos, and signalled the attack. The wall carriers on the north and south sides picked up their sections and advanced. Arrows and slingstones from the fort flew at them, but in the dark and with the carriers shielded behind the walls,

THE DRUID AND THE ELEPHANT

there was no-one to aim at, and they did little damage. The tower crews in the east and west fitted the ballistas to the tower-top platforms and raised the towers. The ballista crews clambered up and frantically reloaded.

The wall carriers arrived at the defences. Some walls were tipped forwards to cover the ditch, and warriors carried the others across these and leaned them against the fort walls, providing ramps. Lukon's second volley soared over their heads, lighting up the fort. At this signal, thousands of roaring tribesmen flowed over the walls like a giant wave, and charged into the camp.

I joined Lukon on his tower. Flaming tents illuminated the chaos inside. Deer charged around, confused by the men and fire. Some of the Roman cavalry were in the saddle, trying to form up where the main streets crossed in the middle of the camp. Tribesmen were charging at them from all directions, so they took the clearest route, galloping north along the main street towards the entrance that led to the river bridge. Tribesmen jumped aside and hurled spears at them, felling several. When they got to the entrance, they found it blocked by our wall sections. They wheeled, and galloped towards the opposite entrance.

The practice against Eppilus' horsemen paid off. He had tried to escape this way, and we had devised a tactic against it. The tribesmen pulled up the pegs of the tents, and, holding the tents by the guy ropes, used them like giant nets to trip or catch the cavalry. Burning tents were also ripped from the ground, and used to block the streets. With spears and fire, the tribesmen herded the cavalry into a corner of the fort.

I couldn't see Melanipa among them. "Shoot them!" I ordered.

Lukon sprayed them with a third fire bolt, and the rest of the ballistas followed his cue. Our spearmen rushed into the herd of panicked and injured horses to finish them off.

One group of Romans on foot made a shield wall and attacked

the south entrance. Lukon reloaded with iron-tipped ballista bolts, which tore through the Roman shields and armour. The shield wall fractured, and our spearmen charged in for the kill.

As suddenly as the attack had begun, it was over. We made a line of a thousand men along the west wall, and swept across the fort, making sure nothing Roman lived. Most of the deer had escaped over the walls, but a few had broken their legs tripping on guy ropes or been killed by the Romans. When we were sure that none remained alive except us and a few prisoners, we hauled the wall sections into the fort and made shelters by leaning them together in pairs.

At dawn, Druid Caicer led our army in prayer to the war gods, and we had a victory feast of the Roman's supplies. Queen Boudicca arrived in her chariot, and we cheered our leader and our triumph.

Amid the celebrations, I slipped away to search the dead. To my great relief, Melanipa was not among them. Next morning the tribesmen cut the heads off the Romans and threw the corpses into the river. They floated away, a message for the rest of the Ninth legion in their fort downstream, and my message to Tenvantius. I stood on the ramparts, gazing east, wondering where Melanipa was, and if she was alive.

17

Death in the Garden

My thoughts of Melanipa were interrupted by a messenger. "Queen Boudicca wants to see you."

"Where is she?"

"By the south gate."

When I got there, Boudicca pointed to a line of figures on the road to Londinium, straggling south from Durobrivae town. "Why are they still alive?" she demanded.

I knew her thirst for Roman blood, her hatred for those traitors who served the Romans, and her desire for revenge. So I appealed to arguments that I hoped were stronger: her heart and her need for victory.

"Some of them are mothers, like you, trying to protect their children. Some of them are old people, who need to stay with their families, wherever they go. They will spread the word of your victory, sapping the morale of our enemies. The more that leave, the better."

"And what about the town? Why isn't it in flames?"

"It's an army town. Armies need smiths, carpenters, traders to bring them supplies. Your soldiers need them as much as the Romans do. They will strengthen your army. But there are also some who are hated, and if you punish them, the people will love you for it. Catch the tax collectors, tie them to a post in the middle of town, and let the people whip them for all the hardship they have caused. Also the idle rich, who live off the hard work of others. And the criminals, the bully boys who demand protection money. Have them all lashed. Strike the first blows yourself, and show how justice is done, show how the justice of Boudicca is better than that of the Romans!"

"You're a strange man, Druid. Last night you led an army and massacred an entire cavalry wing, leaving none alive. This morning you don't want to kill anyone. In a few days Tenvantius will win and we will go south. Why should I risk leaving living enemies behind me? Give me one good reason why I shouldn't kill them all!"

"I saw the Empress of Rome try to kill all those who might threaten her son, and she murdered so many that in the end her allies thought they were in danger and plotted against her."

"What made them think that?" asked the Queen. So I told her the story of Messalina and death in the garden.

One bright Roman morning, we formed up for parade before guard duty. Trouble was brewing because Centurion Gamus was there, which was unusual, and he took us into the guardhouse, away from prying ears.

'Prepare for bloodshed today, men,' he warned. 'It's started already. Polybius is dead. The Empress discovered that her enemy Seneca wrote to him, but Polybius didn't tell her about it. She accused him of treachery, and had Hospes kill him on the spot.'

I felt angry. Polybius had been good to me. He was an expert in elephant warfare, and taught me about tactics. He had taught me how to use Micipsa to break a wall, and taught Lukon about firing slingshot bullets from a ballista, as we did in Marcus Vinicius' garden. I owed a lot of my success to him.

Gamus went on. 'The Emperor is away in Ostia, inspecting the new harbour, so he wasn't around to protect Polybius. He's not back yet, so there's no-one to over-rule the Empress. Claudius' other freedmen, like Narcissus, are worried. They also knew about Seneca's letter, and worry that the Empress will find out.'

He was right. Narcissus had mentioned the letter to Marcus Vinicius. Lots of other people had heard him too, so his life was in danger.

'Now listen carefully. I know Narcissus has been good to some of you, like Decimus here. But we are the Imperial Bodyguard: we guard the Emperor and his family. Other people in the palace are secondary. If the Empress orders you to kill someone, you kill them. If someone orders you to kill the Empress, or you hear them plotting to kill her, that's treason, and you arrest them and bring them to me for interrogation. I'll rip the traitors apart for answers, by Hercules! Do you understand me?'

'Yes, Sir.'

'Right. Tonight is the festival of the grape harvest. The Empress has ordered a party to celebrate. Hopefully she will be busy preparing and it will take her mind off the letter. The party will be a feast in honour of the gods Venus and Jupiter. The Empress will go as Venus, and Senator Gaius Silius, who's going to be Consul next year, will stand in for the Emperor and play Jupiter. Everyone will get drunk. Don't be fooled, it's an ideal opportunity for an attack. Be ready.'

'Yes, Sir.'

'Any questions?'

'Sir?' I asked. He raised an eyebrow.

'Where's Narcissus, Sir?'

'In Ostia with the Emperor. One less target for us to worry about. If he's out of the palace, he's not our responsibility. Let the Praetorians handle it.'

'Yes, Sir.'

Gamus was right about one thing: everyone got drunk at the party. A priest of Dionysus opened the proceedings with a prayer, explaining that his god would enter the bodies of the party-goers, and they were to drink deep and surrender to the gods' whims. Until dawn they were no longer mere humans, they were the vessels of the god, and the god wanted to play in his worshippers' bodies. It turned out that the god's whim was for an orgy, and all ideals of proper conduct were gleefully abandoned. The Empress portrayed Venus, the patron of wine fit for humans, and Silius acted as Jupiter, patron of the wine for sacrificing to the gods.

At the height of the orgy, the priest decided that Venus and Jupiter should be joined in marriage. Silius was an attractive man, and Messalina drunkenly grabbed him, and pulled him forward to the priest. The party-goers, looking forward to the happy occasion, cheered them on, and the priest carried out a debauched ceremony, which ended, not with a kiss, but with an instruction to consummate their nuptials. The onlookers gave raucous cries of encouragement, and Venus and Jupiter disappeared hand-in-hand towards the Empress' quarters. I was Silius' personal guard for the night, so I followed, as did Hospes, who was Messalina's.

Venus and Jupiter ran giggling down the marble corridors to her quarters, with us hurrying to keep up. As we got there, the door slammed in our faces. We stood outside uncertainly. It was obvious that she didn't want us in there, but we couldn't protect her from outside. After a few moments, a small hatch in the door opened, and Hospes' friend, Julia, said, 'Wait here. She'll be alright with him.' She chuckled. 'More than alright.'

Hospes nodded, and indicated me to a spot on the other side of the doorway. We waited.

Part of the guard commander's job is to do the rounds, and before long Centurion Gamus came striding down the corridor with a squad at his back.

'Report!' he commanded Hospes.

'Empress is inside with Senator Silius, Sir. The lady Julia ordered us to wait here.'

'If either of them leave, you send word to me immediately, understand?'

'Yes, Sir.'

He left two men with us to act as messengers, and took the rest of the squad with him on his patrol. We waited all night, but no-one came out, and at dawn the relief shift arrived, and we were dismissed.

As we were working nights, we went back to barracks and got our heads down until the late afternoon, got up, polished our kit, ate, and paraded for duty again. Gamus arrived, face strained with exhaustion.

'To the stables,' he ordered. As we hurried towards them, he briefed us. 'Here's the current situation. The Emperor is back in the palace. This morning the Empress and her children went to meet him on his way back from Ostia, and she claimed that the marriage to Silius was just a performance at a party, and the god Dionysus had possessed her. The Emperor sent them back to the palace and went to Silius' home to question him. There he found lots of heirlooms of his own ancestors, stolen from the palace. Narcissus convinced him that this is a plot, that Silius is trying to overthrow him. The Empress tried to visit Claudius, but

Narcissus refused to let her in, and accused her of treachery. She fled to the elephant lines, and ordered Surus to help her escape on Micipsa. They broke through the guards and made a run for it. The Praetorians have tracked them down to the Gardens of Lucullus. But they can't get her off the elephant. Surus is obeying her orders, and Micipsa attacks anyone who goes near. By Hercules, they want to shoot the animal, and they've sent for a ballista! We need to get there first. Move it!'

'Yes, Sir.'

We leaped onto our mounts and galloped to the garden. On the way, we passed a fruit stall, and I grabbed a bag of apples as we passed. I touched Ganna's amulet and prayed we'd be on time. When we got to the garden, Micipsa was standing in one of the pools. His ears were back, his trunk was curled out of harm's way for battle, blood dripped from one of his tusks, and at his feet, two dead horses were crushed into the ground. A ring of Praetorian cavalry surrounded him at a respectful distance, and when the horses moved nervously, Micipsa would turn towards them and trumpet a threat. Fortunately, the ballista had not yet arrived.

Gamus and I picked out the Praetorian commander. It wasn't Crispinus; it was a tribune I didn't know. With him was a colleague of Narcissus called Evodus, and an older woman, well-dressed, noble, and with vaguely familiar features, who I didn't recognise.

'Greetings, Gamus,' said Evodus. 'This is the Empress' mother, the lady Domitia Lepida. I will draw back my men, and your elephant rider will calm the beast, then escort the lady to it, where she will talk to her daughter.'

I looked at Gamus, who nodded. Evodus gave the command to pull back, and the cavalry retreated. I removed my helmet so Surus and Micipsa would know it was me, then the lady and I walked slowly towards Micipsa.

'Surus,' I called, 'this is the Empress' mother. She wants to talk to her daughter. Come out of the water and let down the ladder. Micipsa, I have apples for you.'

I lobbed an apple gently into the pool in front of him, and he sniffed it cautiously, picked it up, and ate it. I threw another, to the edge of the pool, and a third onto the path next to it. Slowly I enticed Micipsa out of the water and onto the gravel, and he calmed down.

When he was contentedly chomping away, the lady Julia stuck her head out of the howdah curtains, and spoke to Surus. He climbed back to the howdah and let down the ladder. Lady Julia descended, and then tried to assist the old lady over to the ladder.

'I can't climb that at my age, don't be ridiculous, girl! Messalina, come down here at once!'

'But I'm scared, Mother.'

'You are the Empress of Rome. An Empress has no fear. People fear her. You are the most powerful woman in the Empire. Come down here and take command of the situation.'

'What if I don't?'

'If you don't, the soldiers will shoot you with their bows, and you'll die slowly and painfully, full of arrows. I want to protect you from that. Come down now, and I won't let it happen. Show some propriety.'

The curtains moved aside, and Messalina slowly descended the ladder into her mother's arms. I gently nudged Micipsa, and Surus guided him step-by-step away from them.

Evodus stepped forwards, with Gamus and the Tribune. 'Empress Valeria Messalina,' he said, 'you have entered into a bigamous marriage with Senator Gaius Silius, committed adultery, and betrayed your emperor. You are condemned to death. In view of your rank, you are permitted to take your own life.' He drew his dagger and held it out to her.

She made no move to take it, but regarded him with hatred. Her mother took the knife and pressed it into her hand. She tried to slash her wrists, but snatched her arm away at the pain every time she tried. Bursting into sobs, she clung to her mother.

Lepida rounded on me. 'Help her!' she snapped.

But I couldn't kill her. I am a druid. I don't murder people. And I was an Imperial Guard, sworn to protect the Emperor and his family, not harm them. I could not break my vows. But as a druid, I could help her face death.

'We will pray together,' I said to Messalina. 'Give me your hand.'

She dropped the knife, and clutched my palm with one hand, and her mother's with the other.

'Stand up straight, close your eyes, and pray with me,' I told her. She nodded.

'Almighty gods,' I intoned. She shut her eyes.

'Take this woman into your embrace.' I nodded to the tribune, who drew his blade.

'Protect and guide her son, Britannicus, and her daughter, Octavia.' The tribune advanced silently.

'Guide them to the throne.' The tribune rammed his blade into her body, and she collapsed into my arms.

'Let them live full and happy lives, to the honour of their mother.'

The breath went out of her. I laid her carefully on the ground and crossed her arms over the wound. In death her face relaxed, and she seemed serene. Such a waste. Such a loss for her children.

Evodus displayed no sign of sympathy. 'Put her in the Lady Lepida's carriage,' he commanded. 'Everyone back to the palace.'

Gamus and I mounted our horses and followed the

Praetorians and the carriage out of the gate. As we left, I realised I had changed my mind about wanting a garden.

When Claudius was told of the death of his wife, his only reaction was to call for more wine. He wandered around the palace in a daze, unmoved even by the mourning of his children. The Senate, relieved that the woman who had caused death of so many of their number was gone, took revenge by ordering Messalina's statues to be torn down, coins with her image to be defaced, and her name removed from the annals of Rome. It was to be as if she had never existed. She had converted her allies, men like Narcissus, into enemies, and obliteration was her reward.

Boudicca nodded. "I see her mistake. She didn't kill fast enough. If she had had Claudius killed by her new husband, Silius, or that Praetorian commander, Crispinus, she might still be alive. And she should have got rid of Narcissus when she killed Polybius. Killing your enemies one by one is too slow. I want the gates of Durobrivae closed, and the entire town put to the torch."

I was horrified. "But their relatives in the villages and farms around will want revenge!"

"My armies can protect me, and can quell any revolt."

"They are Catuvellauni. They are our allies. Their entire tribe will rise against you. This war will change from a war against the Romans into a tribal war, and the Romans will let the Catuvellauni and Iceni tear each other apart, then swoop in to crush the victor."

She glared at me. "Why is it that every time you win me a victory, you immediately throw away the trust you've earned by arguing with me? No! I want that town in flames, I want the traitors in it dead, and I want it without a revolt. You're a druid. Work your magic. Make it happen."

She mounted her chariot and galloped away.

18

MESSENGERS OF THE GODS

As the hoof beats of Boudicca's chariot faded, I heard footsteps behind me, and rounded to see Lukon approaching.

"What's up?" he asked.

"Boudicca wants me to burn Durobrivae to the ground and butcher everyone in it."

"Orders are orders. Not your fault. If you don't obey, she'll kill you, us, and all our lads. You know what Queens are like, remember Messalina and Agrippina? You don't have much choice."

"It's a Catuvellauni town. They're our allies. If they turn against us, this revolt will fail."

"Have you seen the size of this army? As long as we can keep the legions separate, the Iceni have got a fighting chance, even on their own. We just beat the Romans twice."

"They failed before, a dozen years ago. When Ostorius took over as governor, they rebelled and he beat them, and the Brigantes, too. Then he disarmed them. This army is ill-equipped and untrained. Tenvantius vastly outnumbers them, but he still can't beat just half of the Ninth Legion."

"Because he's an idiot. You're not. Do what you always do, think back over the years we have fought together, pray to your gods, and they will show you the way. All the druids on this island are praying for the High Druid's plan to succeed. And pray to Vulcan, he's the god of ballistas and fire. The men believe that you can perform magic. The Gods will show you how to do it again."

I nodded. "You're right. I need to pray. While I do that, you deploy the men to hold the bridge, guard the fort and surround the town. I don't want any nasty surprises before I figure out what to do. The Ninth might decide to break out and head for Camulodunum, which would bring them here. The bridge is the choke-point, so site your ballistas overlooking it."

"Yes, Sir!"

"Get Trenus to work on rebuilding the fort's defences, and send Eppilus on patrol. I want to know what's delaying Tenvantius, and what's happening up and down the road. Keep the men too busy to cause trouble. I don't want anyone wandering around with nothing to do, and going into Durobrivae."

"Yes, Sir."

"Good. See you later."

Lukon was right. I needed to think back to my time guarding Messalina and Agrippina. Messalina had failed because she alienated her allies, the freedmen who served Claudius. Agrippina had risen to power by making allies. Somewhere in her gory history I might find a message from the gods about how to disobey a Queen's bloodthirsty demands and get away with it.

To talk to the gods, and open myself up to them, I wandered upstream along the Nene. Before long, I left the pastures behind and found an oak grove in the forest. I sat down on a fallen log, touched Ganna's amulet, the war crown, the Horn of Cernunnos, and prayed.

As I finished the bird song changed, and a dog trotted into the grove with a stick in its mouth. I like dogs and dogs like me. This

THE DRUID AND THE ELEPHANT

was no wild cur, scrawny and worm-ridden, so I got it to come to me, patted it, and threw the stick for it to fetch. As it ran to get it, I scanned the edge of the grove, and saw a shadow where someone was standing behind the trunk of an oak.

When the dog brought the stick back, I threw it past the tree, and as the dog went to get it, he ran around like his owner was there.

"You can come out," I called. "I'm a druid. I won't hurt you."

Two children stuck their heads out from behind the oak, a boy and a girl of about seven, dark-skinned, with curly brown hair and brown eyes. I recognised them as forest people, a tribe who never farmed, but hunted and fished in the wilds, avoiding civilisation. I had known a few before, among the boys when I was training to be a druid, and had learned their language.

I spoke to them in their tongue. "Come sit with me in the sun. I have some cheese. You want some?"

The forest people don't have cows or goats, so cheese is a rare luxury for them. I took out a piece and held it up. The smell made them curious, and they came cautiously towards me. They were dressed in leather and furs, with bare feet, and were shorter than farm children. They were carrying staffs as long as they were tall, and slings with bags of stones on their belts. I broke off two small lumps of cheese and tossed them to them.

"I'm Caz. What are your names?"

"Sego," said the boy.

"Dia," said the girl. She nodded at the dog. "He's Duro."

"Where are your family?"

"By the river, fishing," said the boy, Sego.

"What are you doing here?" asked Dia.

"Praying. Thinking about when I was young. You?"

"We're hunting," said Sago.

"Caught anything?"

"Not yet."

"I saw deer tracks by the river."

"We saw them too, a doe and a fawn. No good for hunting. It's naughty to hunt mothers and children," said Dia.

"Quite right."

"You don't look like a druid," said Sego. "Your beard isn't long enough. And you've got scars. You look more like a warrior. What's that on your head?"

"It's a druid war crown. I was learning to be a druid when I was a boy like you, but then I was sent away to be a warrior. Now I'm both."

"Why were you sent away?"

"To learn about the Romans."

"I've seen Romans," said Sego. "They come into the forest sometimes. They smell of fish."

"That's because they like to eat a sauce made of rotted fish."

"They're strange," said Dia. "A druid came to our camp last year and told us stories about them, full of strange people and places. Do you know any stories?"

"I know a story about how the King of Rome chose a new Queen. Would you like to hear it?"

"Does it have love?" asked Dia.

"Yes."

"Does it have warriors?" asked Sego.

"Yes."

"Tell us."

"Once there was a king of Rome, and his wife died. He was very sad, and so were his son, Britannicus, and his daughter Octavia. They were a bit older than you are now. After a while, the elders told him that it was time to find a new Queen. Three women were suitable, the elders said. One had been wife to the previous King. Her name was Paulina. She was beautiful, and she loved to wear pearls. But she had a son already, called Regulus, and the elders were worried that she would try to make him king instead of Britannicus."

"That wouldn't be fair," said Sego.

"The second woman was called Paetina. She had been married to the King before, but she was cruel to him, and they split up. She had a daughter by the King, called Antonia. One of the elders said they should get back together again and be a family, but the other elders said she would be cruel again. So the King asked about the third woman."

"Poor Antonia," said Dia.

"The third woman's name was Agrippina. She was young, beautiful, clever and ambitious. She was the King's niece, sister of the previous King, and had been married before, to a very bad man, and had his son, Nero. She had two canine teeth on the top right side, a sign of good luck. Again, the elders were worried that she would try to make her son the next King. But since she was the King's niece, and because Britannicus was too young to be King, they hoped she would be nice to them."

"No-one else?" asked Dia.

"No-one else," I said. "So, which one would you choose?"

"Choose the mother of the strongest son," said Sego. "The son who will lead the tribe best. If Britannicus is strongest, choose the mother with no son."

Dia shook her head. "Choose the mother whose son Octavia can marry. Not the second woman. She had no son. Not Nero. He had a bad father, and his mother was the King's niece. You can't marry someone so close: my mother says the babies will be no good. That leaves the first one, Regulus, whose mother liked pearls. Marry her."

"You are wise, children. I wish that was what had happened."

"So, who did he marry?" asked Dia.

"He married the cleverest one. Agrippina didn't wait to be chosen. She knew the elders were worried, because the King's dead wife had tried to kill them before. So she became friendly with one of the elders, and they told the King that she would be best."

"If it was our tribe, the people wouldn't like the King marrying his niece."

"Some people didn't, but Agrippina and Nero were popular with the people because her father was a famous warrior. They thought Nero would be a good leader. And he married Octavia."

"Were they happy?" asked Dia.

"As far as I know, they are still married."

"Have they got any children?" said Sego.

"No, not yet."

At that moment, a duck quacked from the river.

"That's Dad," said Sego. "We've got to go. Bye, Druid Caz."

"Bye Sego, bye Dia. Stay away from the Romans." They ran off into the trees, the dog Duro leading the way.

My prayers answered, I walked back to camp, and found Eppilus. "Take me to Druid Caicer," I ordered, and he gave me my horse and led the way. We found Caicer playing with his pine marten and chatting to Dervalon, at the Iceni camp outside the fortress of the Ninth.

"I hear you took Durobrivae fort," the war leader said. "What about the town?"

"Boudicca wants it burned down, and the people killed. But they are Catuvellauni. It would break our alliance with them."

"So, what are you going to do?"

"Use our allies. Dervalon told me that men from other tribes have joined us. How many Catuvellauni do we have?"

"A few hundred chariots, and the same in foot soldiers."

"Good. Take me to their leader. I need to talk to him."

"He's called Teuhant. His part of the camp is over there. I'll introduce you."

We rode over to the Catuvellauni camp, and Caicer made the introductions. Teuhant was a tall, well-built warrior, younger than me, with black hair and piercing blue eyes. He wore a golden torc around his neck.

"I've taken the fort next to Durobrivae," I told him. "Boudicca wants me to take the town next. The people there are from your tribe. Some are collaborators, some are innocent. You should decide their fate. How many men do you lead?"

"More than enough, Druid."

He addressed his warriors. "Take a message to Tenvantius. We're going on a raid. We'll be back. Charioteers, come with me. Carry an extra warrior each. No more banging our heads against a wall! We're going to do some real fighting!"

With a cheer, they mounted up and swept out of the camp with us in front. Leading the chariots reminded me of my father and brother. I was a warrior again, and the blood sang in my veins to the thunder of hooves.

That night, my men carried Trenus' portable walls from the fort and used them to climb Durobrivae's defences. At the sound of the Horn of Cernunnos, the Catuvellauni warriors led the assault, opened the east gate from the inside, and Teuhant and his chariots charged in. A small force of Romans tried to escape out of the west gate and cross the river, but Lukon's men shot them with the ballistas. I personally set fire to the Roman message station in the middle of town, and then we went to the temple, smashed the statues of the Roman gods, and gave sanctuary to those people of Durobrivae in need of protection. I left Teuhant to mete out justice as he saw fit.

Next day I was summoned to see Dervalon. He was twisting

the plaits of his beard worriedly. "Tenvantius is injured, he was leading a raid last night and took a slingshot to the head. Luckily, it just creased him, but he's out of action and I'm in command now. We've got to take that fort quickly. We've been here too long. Men will get sick or desert soon. I want you to come up with a plan. Oh, and your friend Melanipa's in there."

19

THE EMPEROR'S WEDDING

Boudicca's war chief Dervalon wanted a plan for attacking the fort, but there's no point in trying to think when you're tired, hungry, and need a clear mind to understand the god's portents. So I got some sleep, then went in search of food. I found Boudicca's druid, Caicer, in her command tent, feeding his pine marten on morsels of meat. While I ate, he commented on the distinctive timbre of the Horn of Cernunnos. He asked if I had played in Rome, so I told him the story of the greatest musical performance ever.

After Empress Messalina's death, they promoted me to the rank of Cornicen, which meant I marched at the front of the cohort and signalled the Centurion's commands to the unit by blowing a Roman horn called a cornu. It was a big circular metal pipe that went from my mouth down to my waist, curled up behind my back and shoulder, ending in a bell-shaped mouth above my right ear. It was loud enough to hear in battle. The sound it makes is epic: perfect for signalling a charge, or to announce gladiator fights in the arena.

To celebrate my promotion, Surus, Ganna, Melanipa and

I went to the amphitheatre for a night out. Melanipa, being a Queen's daughter, got good seats, and we sat near the front, next to the musicians. There were a couple of cornu players, a drummer, and an organ.

'They're playing well today,' I commented. 'Putting their hearts into it.'

'Rumour has it that the Emperor is going to re-marry,' replied Melanipa. 'The band's putting on their best show, trying to get invited to audition for the marriage entertainment.'

The fight I remember best was a beast fight. A herd of huge wild cows called aurochs were herded into the arena by men with dogs. A bull with shoulders as high as I am tall led a dozen cows and calves. He must have weighed as much as six men, and his hide was as black as a tax collector's heart. He didn't like being herded, and left one dog that got too close gored to death on the sand.

The herdsmen beat a hurried retreat, and the bull snorted. At the other end of the arena, a horn sounded, a door opened, and a pack of wolves entered. The blares of the cornus were matched by the bellow of the bull. The wolves stayed silent.

'Why aren't the wolves howling?' asked Surus.

'Wolves don't howl until after the kill, it would warn the prey,' replied Melanipa.

The wolves loped forwards. The arena walls meant this wasn't a chase. Backing away to the other end of the arena, the aurochs put their backs to the wall, with the calves behind them. The bull bellowed a challenge and pawed the ground.

Wolves don't communicate like humans, with lots of noise and back-and-forth. The pack watched the leader, and from his actions they took their cue. While he faced off with the bull, keeping eye-contact and darting in and out, the other wolves surrounded the flanks of the herd, searching for an opening. As the cows backed away on both sides, calves bleated in protest as they were crowded in the middle. The wolves tested each of their prey, looking for weaknesses. Which animal was slow, which aggressive or impulsive? The drummers beat faster and faster, and the organ matched their pace, building to a crescendo. The crowd chanted, matching the rhythm, 'Kill, kill, kill, kill!'

The attack was sudden and frightening. A young wolf split away from the pack, ran behind the leader and around the herd, gaining pace. It curved towards the wall, and at full speed leaped at the wall above the cows' heads, bounded along the stones, then jumped off into the centre of the herd, landing among the calves and grabbing one by the throat. Chaos struck the herd. Some cows tried to kick the wolf, but it was under a calf, with its teeth in its neck. Other cows panicked at the predator in their midst and ran. The herd split left and right, leaving the bull. It turned to help the bleating calves, and the wolf pack leader jumped on him from behind. The bull span round, and while more wolves attacked its flank, others attacked the calves and dragged them away. The bull whirled and tried to get to the calves, but the wolves leaped at him from all sides. He gave up, and ran off to rejoin the surviving cows, while the wolves ripped into juicy young calf flesh. The cornus blared the victory. Wolves are the symbols of Rome, and the aurochs represented the weak whom the Romans prey upon with their teamwork and intelligence. Ganna and Melanipa were on their feet cheering with me, and only Surus was more reserved.

'Don't worry,' I told him. 'Even a pack of wolves couldn't take down Micipsa. Aurochs don't have armour and weapons, and you to guide them.' He nodded and cheered up a bit, and we went to get a snack before the next event.

As Cornicen, I was in charge of signalling, and to make it more fun, I announced that I was forming a band, and invited the guards to audition. There were some men with a good sense of rhythm, who I trained to signal with drums, and a few who played the horn, so I gave them the cornets and trumpets. We practised signalling by sending rude jokes in code, and played the popular songs of the day, but changed the lyrics into comic versions in the Germanii language. On feast days, we hired an organist and put on concerts. The guards would clash the flats of their sword blades on their shields in time with the rhythm, and sometimes Ganna would come and lead us in war hymns to her battle gods. If there's one thing I miss about Rome, it's the music. The best bands from across the Empire all wanted to play in Rome, and I got to see them, and play their songs with my musicians. It was a bard's dream.

On New Year's Day I was on duty for the Emperor's wedding banquet. When I arrived, the slaves were setting up, and in the middle of the room a noisy argument was going on. I went over to the man I was replacing on duty.

'Report', I commanded.

'Hail, Cornicen. You know the chief steward, Halotus, on the left?'

I nodded.

'On the right is the manager of the band, the famous Homopolon. The cornu player has got cold feet and disappeared. They can't play without him. The singer is crying in a corner. The Emperor's wedding party will be without music. Someone's going to get executed for this.'

Homopolon was infamous. As manager of the best band in the Empire, he thought too much of himself, and was arrogant, difficult, and snobbish. He was famous for his bad moods, and for taking offence at any lack of deference to his status. Even his name was fake, being the ancient Greek form of Apollo, God of

THE DRUID AND THE ELEPHANT

Music, but he refused to respond to any other.

The singer crying in the corner was called Euterpe, after the muse of music. The poets worshipped her as "giver of delight". She brought strong men to tears with the beauty of her singing, and had to be guarded day and night by a team of ex-gladiators to fend off the advances of love-sick suitors.

I listened to the dispute. The steward Halotus I knew, and it was his head on the block if the party wasn't perfect. I also knew that he wasn't the type to cover for a subordinates' error, and if this kept up, heads would roll. As the senior guard in the room, it was probably going to be my job to remove the offending heads, something I'd prefer to avoid.

Then it hit me. I was a musician. and as the Cornicen of the Germanii had played the tunes when we sang rude lyrics in barracks.

In the middle of the room, Homopolon was ranting and calling on Apollo. Halotus was yelling at him. I strode over, grabbed both of them by the front of their tunics and gave them a good shake. I'd reached adult height by then, and was a head taller than both of them. 'Who am I?' I demanded.

'Cornicen Decimus,' replied the Halotus, in confusion.

'And what instrument do I play?'

Realisation dawned on his face. 'The cornu!'

I gave Homopolon a little shake. 'I am Apollo's answer to your prayers. I know the songs. I've played in front of thousands in parades, including the Emperor.'

'A Cornicen! A mere signaller?' he replied in horror, staring up at me. 'A barbarian? No, not in Homopolon's ensemble! Over my dead body!'

I gave him a harder shake and hissed into his face. 'It's not just your dead body. This is the Emperor's wedding. Let him down and he will kill not only you, but your whole band.'

Euterpe gave a little scream and started sobbing again. But it made no difference to her idiot of a manager.

'No, no, no! Homopolon is answerable only to Apollo, the God of Music himself. Homopolon will never sacrifice artistic integrity!'

I decided to try a different strategy. I let go of his tunic and punched him in the jaw. He collapsed unconscious to the floor, where I placed my hob-nailed sandal on his face.

'Anyone else want to argue?'

No-one did.

'Good. It's rehearsal time.'

"It's a mystery to my men," I told Druid Caicer, "how I keep my spirits up sometimes, when we're cold, wet, and tired. The secret is, I remember that night. I played in the greatest performance ever: the wedding of the most powerful man in the world, with the best musicians in history, and it was like Apollo himself possessed us. Music poured from our souls, Euterpe's voice made my heart quiver, and the audience wept or cheered at our command. So when all seems lost, and people wonder why I have a smile on my face, I am remembering that night."

"Why?" asked Caicer. "Did the Emperor reward you?"

"No, the opposite. Homopolon had powerful friends, so I got in a heap of trouble. I had technically deserted my post, but since I was in the room with the Emperor all the time, and saved the evening's entertainment, they only busted me to Decanus, in charge of one squad of men. But Homopolon also had enemies among those he had slighted, and a badge of a golden cornu appeared on the Cornicen's parade uniform. It's handed down from Cornicen to Cornicen of the Germanii, along with the story. Every Cornicen learns not only to signal, but also to play well, in case more musical ass-kicking is required."

"I'd like to have seen that," said Caicer. "The demotion seems a bit rough, though."

"I have no regrets about it: even if they had sentenced me to death, I'd have gone to the gods a happy man. And not just because, at the end of the night, Euterpe kissed me. Don't tell Melanipa."

"I doubt she'll raise the issue."

"I was in a good mood for weeks. I can't say the same for Claudius. The new groom's happiness didn't last long. Agrippina was now Empress, and quickly proved herself as troublesome as Messalina, but in a whole new way."

Dervalon entered, looking harassed. "Boudicca's on her way. I need a plan. Tell me you've come up with something!"

"Yes," I said, "talking to Caicer here has given me an idea. Listen." And I told him how to use wolf tactics against the Romans. I had just finished when I heard Boudicca's voice outside, so I hid in the shadows beside the doorway. I didn't want Boudicca's lack of trust in me scuppering the plan.

She strode in, accompanied by her bodyguard and tribal war leaders. "Well?" she demanded to Dervalon.

"The plan is ready," he said.

"Out with it," she replied.

Dervalon stroked the plaits of his beard into place and addressed the gathered leaders. "Our situation is this: for too long we have been stuck here, trying to get into this fort. All the while, Suetonius and his legions are approaching, and every day the momentum of our revolt slips away from us. The commander of the Ninth legion, Cerialis, knows he only needs to hold out until Suetonius arrives and catches us between them. If we stay here, it's only a matter of time until they trap us. We need to strike south and take Camulodunum. But we can't leave and let them attack us from behind."

"So here's how we are going to outwit them. Our armies just took the fort at Durobrivae by surrounding it with walls to trap the cavalry inside. We will do the same here. We will bring the wooden walls from Durobrivae and build them around the fort. The only problem is the river next to the fort, so we will dig a ditch to divert the river around the outside of our wall, cutting off the Romans' access to the water. We will dam the old river course and build the wall on top of the dam. We'll rip the town Durobrivae apart and use its stones and the earth from the river ditch to strengthen the walls. That way, we will trap the Romans inside."

"Then our cavalry and chariots will strike south. The Queen and I will lead the Iceni, Teuhant will lead the Catuvellauni. The Trinovantes, the Coritani and the Dobunni horsemen will come too. Our infantry will stay here to keep the Ninth from following us. They will build a second wall outside the first, and camp between the walls, so if Suetonius comes they will be safe. Tenvantius is recovering well from his wound, and he will take charge here."

"Communication will be vital. We need to know if Suetonius comes here, and if the Ninth try to escape. Send any druids and musicians who know how to read and write to Druid Caicer here, and he will teach them to send messages."

"The chariots and cavalry will strike for Camulodunum first, and then on to Londinium. We will destroy the Romans' towns, kill their people, and throw them back into the sea."

He drew his sword and waved it in the air. "Victory will be ours. Freedom will be ours. The riches of the Romans will be ours."

The war chiefs cheered him.

THE DRUID AND THE ELEPHANT

Boudicca stepped forward. "Three generations ago, the Roman Emperor, Julius Caesar, came here and our grandfathers threw him out. We've done it once, and we can do it again. The Romans bring riches, they bring silks, slaves and wine. But these soften our people. I know what it's like. I have worn silks, been served by slaves, and drunk their wine. But it was a trap, and when my husband died, they took it all from me. Better to live a life hard but free than be enslaved by luxury. The Romans tried to take my lands. The Roman veterans took the Trinovantes lands around Camulodunum. The Romans will take this entire island if we don't fight back. Dervalon has shown us how. We will sweep the Romans from our shores with fire and blood. Have no mercy on those who collaborate with the enemy. Make our victory so horrific that Romans will weep in terror, and their armies will never set foot upon these lands again. We will teach them a lesson they will never forget."

She drew her blade and thrust it in the air and called on her goddess. "To victory! To freedom! For the glory of Andraste!"

They cheered her hoarse, and then Dervalon gathered the commanders and gave them their missions. When all was arranged, I slipped out and went to give Lukon, Trenus, and Eppilus their secret orders. Boudicca would have killed me if she knew what I had planned.

20

THE EMPEROR AND THE WHALE

My plan was to break Melanipa free without Boudicca knowing anything about it. I took Lukon, Trenus and Eppilus into the beech woods outside Durobrivae where no-one would overhear us, and gave them my orders. "Trenus, show the infantry how to build walls. Move your mobile walls here and reinforce them with earth from the ditch. But build a secret gateway. If anyone asks, it's for attacking the fort when they are starving and weak. But really, it's for Melanipa. She's our comrade. She's fought beside us in battle, and we have to give her a fighting chance. If her Sarmatians come out of the fort, signal her by name, and open the gate. Behind the gate put a tunnel leading to the outer wall, and a secret gate there. Don't worry if the other Romans escape, just send a signal and we can ambush them."

"Yes, Sir."

"Lukon, Trenus will build you some towers on the wall opposite the fort's gates. Put some of your ballistas there, and shoot at the infantry if they come out. I'm going south to Camulodunum and Londinium, and I might need ballistas there. So try putting them on carts, or adding wheels, so that they can move. If the ballistas in the fort shoot at you, you can change position. Use some of those fire bolts to keep the fort sentries sleepless, and make Tenvantius think you're useful."

"Yes, Sir."

"Eppilus, you're coming south as a scout and messenger. Boudicca's plan is to massacre her way to Londinium. I want you to scare the villagers into hiding before Boudicca's cavalry gets there. At each village, ride in, set a few shed roofs on fire, steal any good horses, grab any handy food, then ride out. No need to kill anyone unless they try to trap you. If you see Roman units, avoid them and send me a message. Understand?"

"Yes, Sir."

"Any questions?"

"What if Suetonius comes here?"

"Get the Roman heads from Durobrivae fort. Put them on stakes around the outer walls. Try to convince Suetonius that we have already taken the Ninth's fort. He may give it up as a lost cause, and move on. If not, you need to make it hard for him to take the walls. Trenus, divide the gap between the walls into sections, with gates between them. Make him fight for each one. Delay him for as long as you can. Send a messenger to me, and we'll bring the cavalry and hit him from behind. If we don't come, and all looks lost, pull out and head south. Meet me and the cavalry, and we'll give him a battle he won't forget. We outnumber him ten to one, and he doesn't have enough men to defend all the Roman towns. We can still wear him down. And, Gods forbid, if everything goes wrong, meet me at our old camp in the fens from when we did the ambush on the causeway."

"Yes, Sir."

"Anything else?"

"How long will we be staying here, Sir?"

"Suetonius is marching towards us from the Holy Isle with the Fourteenth and the Twentieth legions, and auxiliaries. That gives him about ten thousand men. Boudicca hasn't got enough chariots and cavalry to defeat him, so we'll need the infantry from here. Right now, her cavalry can move faster than his infantry, so I think she'll take Camulodunum and Londinium before he can catch up. Then she'll want to defeat him in battle, and she'll need her infantry. He'll want to crush the rebellion, and his best option is a fight where he can use battle strategies that tribes have never seen before. I predict a titanic battle in less than a month, and at most, a small holding force will stay here."

"Can we beat him?" asked Lukon.

"My plan is to use masses of spearmen to fend off his cavalry, and thirty ballistas to punch holes in his heavy infantry. We outnumber him so much that we can outflank him even through the toughest terrain. Barbarian armies led by Roman-trained officers have defeated the legions before: remember the story of Hermann? He defeated three legions in the forests of Germania. We can do the same. Even the most dangerous enemy has weak points. Remember the day Claudius killed the whale?"

"We weren't there, we only heard about it" said Eppilus. "What really happened?"

So I told them.

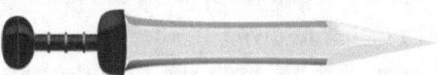

One sunny morning in Rome, Surus and I were training new cavalry to get the horses used to Micipsa, and learn how to charge in formation with him, when a messenger came running.

'The Emperor wants to go to Ostia on the elephant, and he wants to go now! Meet him at the front gate. The Praetorians are waiting there for you.'

Stopping only to mount the throne on the platform, off we went. Surus was on Micipsa's neck, and I was behind the throne.

We found the Praetorians, led by Prefect Crispinus, who I had worked with before. The Emperor emerged from the palace with his bodyguard and two boys wearing miniature uniforms. Surus made Micipsa kneel with his belly on the ground. The Emperor climbed up onto the platform, followed by a bodyguard, Gamo, who I knew because he was Optio Hospes' brother. He came to stand beside me, behind the Emperor. The two boys were given horses and rode with the Praetorians. They were the Emperor's son Britannicus, who was about nine, and Agrippina's son Nero, thirteen. Crispinus gave the order to march, and we moved out.

'What's going on?' I whispered to Gamo.

'There's a whale trapped in the new harbour at Ostia,' he replied. 'The Emperor is going to demonstrate the might of Rome by killing it. Narcissus suggested he ride the elephant to show his power over gigantic beasts.'

The fishermen at Rutupiae had told me about whales. They were a blessing and a curse. If they got caught in the nets, they might smash or capsize a boat. But if they beached, they provided meat and oil for a village for months. Some were placid, and only ate fish, but others were dangerous, had long sharp teeth, and ate seals and dolphins. I hoped Micipsa would just be the transport for today, and not be involved in the whale hunting. We had a couple of lances with us from the cavalry drills, and one of Lukon's small ballistas on the back of the platform, but those would only sting a whale, not kill it. The fishermen had told me of whale hunters who speared the mighty beasts, fighting with them for days. In the tales, men died, drowned in smashed boats, or dragged down into the depths, tangled in nets and ropes.

It took all morning to get to Ostia, and I spent the time as Centurion Gamus had taught me, thinking of tactics to kill a whale. 'Can you swim?' I whispered to Gamo.

'Don't even think about it!' he hissed back. 'Don't involve

me in your crazy plans. I guard the Emperor, and he's not going swimming! Concentrate on this escort mission and keep an eye out for danger around us. Stop daydreaming about whales.'

When we got to Ostia, we found that a ship had wrecked in the new harbour, and its cargo of untanned leather had fallen into the water. A toothed whale, attracted by the smell of meat, had come to eat it, and had made a channel for itself in the sand, where it had got stuck. The incoming waves had lifted it towards the shore, the tide had gone out, and it was beached in shallow water. Its black back and tall curving fin were sticking up above the surface, and its eyes and white belly patches were below. All around, crowds of sailors and dock workers had come to see the Emperor kill the monster from the deep, lining the docks and the surrounding boats.

Claudius climbed down off Micipsa and boarded a boat full of Praetorians. They rowed out to the whale, and on the Emperor's command, they thrust their lances into the beast. It thrashed around in agony, and managed to roll and turn. It raised its giant tail and smashed it into the Praetorian boat. Everyone staggered, and Gamo only just grabbed the Emperor as he almost went overboard. The oarsmen backed them off.

The whale had a dozen lances sticking out of it, but was still very alive and very angry. It thrashed the blood-stained water, churning up the sand. One of the Praetorians, a gigantic man, swept off his helmet, grabbed a lance, and jumped in. The water came up to his chest. He waded towards the whale's head, and the monster twisted away. The Praetorian raised his lance to thrust, and the whale twisted back. The rush of water from the movement knocked the Praetorian off his feet, and the whale grabbed him by the legs with its jaws and thrashed violently, whipping the man's body from side to side. It threw him against the boat, and he sank. His comrades fished his limp body from the water and took him below decks. The crowd groaned. Things were looking bad. The Emperor needed to make a decisive killing blow, and he needed to do it fast.

Gamo talking to one of the Praetorian officers, and they were staring in our direction. I was worried that they were thinking of ordering Micipsa to fight the whale. That might be spectacular for the crowd, but it was potentially fatal for Micipsa, Surus and I. Time to think quickly.

I touched Ganna's amulet, and gazed around the port. All kinds of ships were tied to the docks: giant corn transports from Egypt that kept Rome supplied with bread lay next to war galleys that protected Rome's shipping lanes from pirates. All the big ships were too deep-keeled to get into the shallows close to the whale. Only the barges, designed for canals where the water depth was just a few feet, might get anywhere near it. Then I noticed one of the barges, a flat-bottomed raft with a crane on top. It had been hammering in the logs that supported the jetties, but had stopped for the crew to watch the whale. On deck was a stack of piles, their ends sharpened to penetrate the mud and sand on the harbour bottom.

I pulled out the signal flags that Centurion Gamus had ordered me to carry on Micipsa. Using my Cornicen training, I waved the signal to attract attention, and after what seemed an age, Prefect Crispinus' signaller noticed me.

He waved the 'Send message' signal, and I flagged across my idea. The signaller spoke to Crispinus, who examined the vessel, then went to the Emperor. Claudius nodded, and the signaller waved 'Do it' to me.

I had expected them to take command, but if my idea failed, no-one else would want the responsibility. So now it was up to me. I climbed forward and explained to Surus.

'We'll wade out to the raft,' he said. 'There are too many

people on the docks to get through.' He urged Micipsa forwards, and staying well clear of the whale, we walked into the water and made our way to the raft. The water was deep, but Micipsa kept his feet on the bottom and his trunk above the water, while Surus and I stood on the platform to keep our heads in the air. Fortunately, the harbour wasn't as deep by the raft, and I clambered aboard. The captain came to meet me, and I told him what I had in mind.

He nodded, and yelled orders at this crew. They attached a pile to the crane and started hoisting it into the air. Meanwhile, a hawser was passed to Surus, who attached it to Micipsa's harness, and we dragged the barge across the harbour. Micipsa waded ashore as close to the whale as possible without being in danger, and pulled the raft into position next to it. The whale tried to escape, but was stuck in the sand and only thrashed around. After a few moments it tired, and lay still. The Emperor raised his arm, looked around as if he were about to start a gladiator fight, and the crowd went silent.

Claudius dropped his arm. The barge crew let go the rope holding the pile, and it dropped like an arrow into the hole on the top of the whale's head. The sharpened log drove deep into the beast, a fountain of blood shot up, it gave a convulsive heave, and collapsed. Cheers erupted from the crowd. Britannicus and Nero were jumping up and down, and the Emperor applauded.

Crispinus' signaller waved his flags at us. 'Surus,' I said, 'They want us to tow the whale onto the beach.'

He waded Micipsa through the scarlet water around to the whale's tail, the elephant grabbed the narrow part above the fins with his trunk, and hauled the beast ashore. The Emperor climbed up onto its head and waved to the crowds, who cheered him again.

When all was done, he beckoned us over, climbed back onto

Micipsa's platform, and Gamo swung up beside me. 'Well done, lads,' said Claudius. 'Now, back to Rome.'

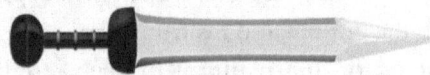

"That's why they promoted me back up to Cornicen again," I told Lukon, Trenus, and Eppilus. "But why it's important for us today is that even the deadliest enemy can be trapped and killed by forces who signal each other well. As long as we stay in touch, we can take down Suetonius. But Caicer's signallers are new at this, so you need to make sure they do it right, because Suetonius surprises us, we're in trouble. Understand?"

"Yes, Sir."

Their expressions told me that had their doubts, and they were right.

21

THE CHIEFTAIN IN CHAINS

We left Lukon and Trenus fortifying the walls around the Ninth's stronghold, and raided south with Boudicca's chariots and cavalry. The Queen had a thirst for revenge and was not happy unless the smoke of burning villages filled the skies. Teuhant, the Catuvellauni war chief, led his forces into each village, and took revenge on all those who had sided with the Romans. These were his tribal homelands, and his vengeance on collaborators slaked even Boudicca's bloodlust.

Eppilus and I did all in our power to save the innocent. We raided villages along with Teuhant's men, and while they picked out the guilty, destroyed their homes and executed their occupants, I used my druidic authority to free the slaves, and move the women and children to safety before the warriors turned on them. As soon as the executions were over, I hurried the warriors on to the next village, claiming that we needed to keep moving to stay ahead of Suetonius' forces. There were rumours that his scouts had been sighted, and we were in a race to reach Camulodunum before he got there and fortified it. I knew that soon we must meet him in battle, and that we needed a better plan to beat him. My ballistas were all with Lukon, and without them, Suetonius' heavy infantry were unstoppable. I prayed to the gods of war for a message, and they delivered.

THE DRUID AND THE ELEPHANT

One evening, after a day of bloody slaughter, Boudicca commandeered a headman's hall, hung him and his entire family from the rafters, and held a victory feast beneath their dangling corpses. When our bellies were full, it was time for entertainment.

"Teuhant," she called, "tell us of your battles. What drives your desire for revenge?"

"For seven years I followed Prince Caratacus," replied the war chief, "from the Medway to the Thames, to Camulodunum, before escaping west, where he led the Ordovician tribe in constant raids against the Romans. We fought in the forests and the mountains, but raiding never gave us a decisive victory, and the Romans kept pushing us towards the sea. Unless we defeated them in battle, we were doomed."

"Caratacus found an ideal battleground. It was a steep-sloped hill, with a river in front, and we built stone walls to slow down their soldiers. On the morning of battle I went from rank to rank of my warriors, lauding my veterans, encouraging the recruits, promising eternal glory for turning the tide against the Romans, praising the valour they had shown in raids, and vowing that the bards would sing of our deeds forever."

"Caratacus came to us. I still remember his words: 'Today is the first day of our freedom if we win, or the first day of slavery and death if the gods are against us. But I know the gods are on our side. The gods were on our forefathers' side when they defeated Caesar. Now the gods are on the side of the Ordovici, the Iceni, and the Catuvellauni. We are still free men, with free wives and free children, and no-one can take that away from us while our hearts still beat and hot blood runs in our veins. We will not shrink from weapons or wounds. We will not lose heart or hope. We will not tremble or turn. For we are warriors. We are swordsmen of the gods, spearmen who shrivel souls, axemen who need no armour but their ardour for Roman blood. Victory will be ours!' The warriors cheered him and swore death and destruction."

"A pretty speech," said Boudicca. "What happened next?"

"The Romans forded the river and advanced up to the stone walls under a hail of our arrows and javelins. We killed scores. But they hid under their shields, and ripped the wall apart, then pushed us back to the hilltop. They assaulted us from all sides, their swordsmen hacking at our front line, and their auxiliaries raining spears on us. At last there were only a few of us left on the summit, surrounded by the bodies of the brave who had given their lives. We had to get Caratacus to safety. On the hilltop was a grave of standing stones, built in the dawn of time, its earthen covering worn away by the ages. We threw our weight behind a boulder and rolled it down the hill. It smashed through the Roman lines, and we charged through in its wake. The Romans in their heavy armour were too slow to catch us, and we escaped."

"How many got out?"

"Not enough to keep him safe. We went north, to the Brigantes, to raise a new army. But their Queen, Cartimandua, betrayed us. She put Caratacus in chains and sold him to the Roman General, Ostorius. Gods curse them both. Her treachery was so abhorrent that her own husband raised a rebellion. She only survived with the help of the Ninth Legion. After we drive them and the other Romans into the sea, I will turn north and take my revenge on her." His warriors pounded their fists on the tables.

"How did you escape?" the Queen asked.

"Caratacus appealed not only to the Brigantes for help. Between the Ordovices and the Brigantes live the Cornovii tribe, and he sent me there to raise an army. But after Cartimandua handed him to the Romans, the heart went out of them. So I came back here, and bided my time, training my people to fight. And now we will."

"What happened to Caratacus?"

"The rumours say that he was taken to Rome and paraded through the streets, and that he made a fine speech, and the Emperor forgave him. I don't know what to believe. He always did have a golden tongue, but I doubt Claudius would forgive years of warfare and the deaths of thousands of legionaries. He's probably long dead."

Here was the answer to my prayers, a god-given opportunity to restore my reputation in Boudicca's eyes, convince her to restrain her blood-thirsty policies, and persuade them of my battle plans.

"No!" I cried. "Caratacus lives, and I have seen him. I was at that parade, I saw him speak to the Senate, and I heard Claudius' words."

There was uproar in the hall. Teuhant and his men leaped to their feet, relief and hope transforming their battle-weary faces. "What!" he yelled. "He lives? Tell us!" So I did.

As the Romans had promoted me back to Cornicen and I was thus a junior officer, I was guard commander for the morning shift. I was called into Centurion Gamus' office for a briefing.

'I smell blood,' he warned me. 'The Empress Agrippina is killing anyone she thinks was loyal to Messalina, and anyone who might threaten her or her son. There are a lot of panicking people who may try to kill her before she kills them. Be extra vigilant, and if anything seems off, even if you're not sure, sound the alarm.'

'Second, she's replaced the head of the Praetorian Guard,

Rufrius Crispinus, with Sextus Afranius Burrus. He's steady and reliable, but he doesn't know us like Crispinus did, so we need to gain his confidence.'

'Next, the rebel prince Caratacus arrives today. He, his wife and daughter will be held here in the palace until the victory parade. Caratacus is famous far and wide, and the parade is important for the Emperor's reputation. Make sure Caratacus is safe from those who would embarrass the Emperor, and make sure he doesn't kill himself first.'

'Yes, Sir.'

'Finally, your friend Ganna has been arrested, and is also being held here. The Empress has charged Messalina's mother, Lepida, with attempting to take her life by magic, magic provided by Ganna. She's a priestess of Baduhenna, and her acolytes might try to break her out. I know you sacrifice to her god sometimes. If she escapes, you're going to be the prime suspect. You will be tortured, you will confess, you will be executed. By Hercules, don't even think about it. Understand?'

'Yes, Sir.'

'Don't do anything stupid, Decimus. You're also a known associate of Crispinus, and were good to Messalina and Lepida in the Garden. Don't attract the Empress's attention. I have to build her confidence in the Germanii, and I'm not going to stick my neck out for you if you get into trouble. If you do, I will have no choice but to make an example of you, to show the iron discipline of the Germanii. I will put you on a cross and hammer the nails in myself. Do I make myself clear?'

'Yes, Sir.'

'Right. Dismissed.'

Of course, it wasn't long before I was in deep trouble. But with good reason. I fell in love.

THE DRUID AND THE ELEPHANT

I went down to the cells to check they were secure, and that there was nothing there that Caratacus might use to kill himself, and no tricks like snakes in the air vents. The guards there were experts, used to all kinds of threats and madness, but you have to check these things yourself, because it's human nature for men to try to cover up any problems so they don't get into trouble. All was in order, so I went to see Ganna.

'Don't worry about me,' she said. 'Worry about yourself. It's far from my time to see the gods, but I dreamed of you being in terrible danger. You were fighting for your life. I saw you give your knife to the youngest among you. Now get away from me before the guards wonder why we're talking for so long.' It was time to go and receive Caratacus, so I left.

Caratacus arrived at the palace with his wife and daughter, escorted by Praetorians. I had met him years before, at the battle of the Thames, and I didn't want him to recognise me. Some men will do anything to save their own lives, or those of their wives and children, and I didn't want him to try to bargain my identity for their safety. I was wearing my cavalry helmet, with the steel face mask to hide my features. As guard commander, it was highly unlikely anyone was going to question my choice of equipment, and if they did, I would cite Gamus' warning.

In the past, people have tried to trick the guard by handing over stand-ins for the real prisoners, so we always match their appearance to a written description. Caratacus was as I remembered him, tall, confident, commanding, but with more lines on his face from years of cares and sorrow. The written description of his battle wounds matched with his scars.

His wife held herself like a queen. The written description of her was less detailed, but there was no trace of hair dye, her age was right, her height was correct, and so was her eye colour. By the way she stood near Caratacus, they were a couple. I got one of the palace slave girls to check her clothes and hair for pins or other weapons, but there was nothing.

The daughter was next. The description said 'Eyes: green'. Her head was bowed, so I lifted her chin with my finger to check, looked into her eyes, and fell in love. It was the strangest thing. One moment I was myself, alone, the next I was something new, something different, I was at once myself, but part of me was someone else, someone I would willingly lay down my life for. That realisation reminded me of Ganna's warning, and a wave of foreboding swept over me.

I glanced down at my list, but barely noticed the rest of the description. To cover my disquiet, I signed for them, and led the prisoners and escort to the cells. On the way there, one of my guards kept flicking his eyes from the slave girl to the daughter. I realised I had forgotten to have her checked, so we did it when we got to the cells. I placed her in the cell next to her mother, made sure everything was in order, and left to write it up in the duty officer's log. It was only then that I noticed her name for the first time: Irgaine.

"He tells the truth!" exclaimed Teuhant. "Irgaine of the green eyes was with us all those years of fighting, and I watched her grow from a girl to a young woman. Many loved her, but none dared ask for the hand of Caratacus' daughter. A princess' fate is to marry a prince from another tribe, to cement an alliance, not to be wasted on a common soldier."

"I knew her, too," broke in Boudicca. "I met her at the court of King Cunobeline, Caratacus' father, before the invasion. The seers prophesied she would travel to a far-off land, and meet a man from home. We never imagined it might be Rome, or you! What happened to her?"

The prisoners secured, it was time to make the rounds. I collected my squad from the guardhouse, and, bearing in mind Ganna's warning, we kitted up in full battle gear. We didn't normally wear armour, to avoid alarming the civilians, but I trusted in Ganna's dreams. We patrolled the palace, including the cells, where, remembering Centurion Gamus' counsel, I left a couple of extra guards from my squad.

The final stop on the patrol was Nero's classroom. Agrippina had brought the philosopher Seneca back from exile to be his tutor, and curious to see the famous man, I halted the squad outside the room, and took in the new guard to replace the man who had been watching over them. The room was large, high-ceilinged, with ornate desks, and cupboards full of parchment scrolls lined the walls. Also in the room was Optio Hospes' brother, Gamo, who was Nero's personal bodyguard.

'Stay here for a minute, will you?' he said. 'I need to relieve myself.'

I nodded, and he left. Seneca was talking to young Nero, so I listened in to see what he had to say.

'What is the difference between a good ruler and a tyrant?' asked Seneca. I rolled my eyes. Of course, there are lots of differences. And it wasn't a fair question to put to a young man. Seneca had obviously been thinking about it for years while in exile, but was now asking his pupil to come up with an answer in a few heartbeats. It was also a dangerous question, because

Claudius was a tyrant to some, especially to those who had lost relatives and friends when Claudius' wives had persuaded him to order their executions. I knew, I had been there when some of them died. Seneca himself had only avoided execution because his death sentence had been commuted to exile as Claudius thought he was so ill he would die soon.

Nero, though, gave his best answer. 'A tyrant is a bad ruler, like the Dictator Sulla. A good ruler is someone like my great-great-grandfather, Augustus.'

Seneca nodded. 'Yes, but how can we tell if they are good or bad?'

'If they make the Empire bigger or smaller?'

'Yes, but how about on a more personal level?'

'If they're nice to people?'

'Exactly. The difference between a king and a tyrant is mercy. A tyrant kills when it is not necessary. He kills out of fear that his enemies will kill him. A good king converts his enemies to allies by showing mercy, and gaining them as faithful servants. Take me as an example, the Emperor Claudius rescued me from death, and I will be eternally grateful to him. One day, you will be a powerful man. You can show that you are not a tyrant by showing mercy to your enemies. Will you do that for me?'

'Yes, I will. I promise I won't be a tyrant.'

'You're a good man, young Nero. I'm sure you will make me proud.'

Gamo had been gone for a long time. I stuck my head out of the door and asked my squad if they had seen him. They hadn't. That was strange. I sent two of them off to find him and ordered the others into the room to protect Nero and Seneca.

'Don't worry,' I told them, 'just a precaution.'

We waited. Seneca was telling Nero about when to show mercy, and when not. My guards still did not return. I considered going to check myself, but I'd be on my own if there was trouble, and Nero would have one less guard. There would also be no one in command if raiders killed me. Time passed. I touched Ganna's amulet, but nothing happened. It was too long: I had to act. If I was wrong, Gamo and my guards would be in trouble, but if I didn't act, far more important people would be in danger.

As duty guard officer, I couldn't carry my large cornu around with me, but I did have a smaller signaller's horn, so I went to the window, leaned out, and sounded the alarm. Just as I finished the first notes, an arrow smashed into the horn, ripping it from my grasp and slamming it into my face mask. Fortunately it didn't penetrate the steel, but it did knock me back inside.

'Surround the civilians,' I ordered, and my men made a ring of shields around Nero and Seneca. I heard running feet outside, and I ran to the door. Every room in the palace is equipped in case of trouble, including door bolts and wedges, and I quickly bolted us in.

'Open this door, in the name of the Emperor!' ordered a voice outside.

'Password?' I demanded.

'Alpha omega,' said the voice. The words were right, but he pronounced it 'o-mega' instead of 'om-ega', which was wrong.

I backed away from the door and drew my sword.

The door rocked from a thunderous blow. Someone with an axe was outside, and wanted in. I needed a plan to delay them until reinforcements arrived. I scanned the classroom for anything useful, and ordered two of my men to help me shove a scroll cupboard and desks up against the door.

The wooden door panels started to splinter. I moved my men into the far corner of the room.

'Plumbata ready,' I ordered, and my men drew their heavy throwing darts. Remembering Ganna's words, I drew my dagger and gave it to Nero.

'Don't be scared,' I told him. 'We are the best fighters in the world. You're going to see the Germanii kill your enemies. More exciting than gladiators!'

The door broke apart, revealing the helmeted faces of the men outside.

'Throw!' I ordered, and the plumbata whipped across the room. We Germanii practise our aim every day, and the darts smashed into the faces of our enemies, barbs puncturing eyes and knocking out teeth. The helmets disappeared.

Someone outside was giving orders, and a shield appeared in the doorway.

'Front rank, ready spears!' I ordered. 'Throw!'

The spears arced across the short space and smashed through the shields. There were cries of pain, and the shields dropped to reveal the enemy.

'Second rank, spears ready, throw!' I ordered, and our second volley sailed across the room. The enemy were in ring mail, and the spearheads ripped the links apart, sinking into the bodies behind, who dropped to the floor, screaming in agony.

More enemies appeared and started thrusting the furniture aside.

'Front rank, charge!' I ordered, and three of my men ran forward, stabbing the assaulters while they were busy with the furniture. The rest of my men closed up around Nero and Seneca. Alarms rang out, and we heard the pounding of many heavy-sandaled feet running from the direction of the Germanii quarters.

I put my hand on Nero's shoulder. 'Don't worry, help is on its way.'

My front rank were doing well, and bodies littered the doorway. The enemy were still floundering in the furniture, trying to both fight and clear a path. From outside the window came the clash of sword upon shield.

Suddenly the commanding voice outside the door yelled 'Down!', and a large flask of oil flew through the door and smashed on the floor, followed by a flaming torch. The oil burst into flames, and the parchment scrolls and wooden furniture quickly ignited.

'Retreat', ordered the voice outside. The enemies at the furniture fled, leaving us trapped in the burning room, unable to get to the door because of the flames. The window was too narrow for a body to get through. Smoke was fast filling the room, making us cough. I checked around for inspiration. Front, back, left, right, up and down. Down! Under our feet was the hypocaust heating system. Each room has a maintenance hatch, so that slaves can clear out things that shouldn't be in there, like ants' nests and dead rats.

'Find the hypocaust hatch,' I ordered. 'Tap on the floor tiles until you find a place that sounds hollow.' Seneca was the first to find it, and we tapped around to find the edges, cunningly hidden in the pattern of the tile-work. Levering up the hatch with the tips of our blades revealed a crawl space below. Fortunately, the weather was warm, so the fires were unlit. I sent one of my smaller men in with a burning chair leg to light his way. He slithered to the hatch in the next room and lifted it.

'Clear,' he called, and we sent Nero and Seneca through while we stripped off our armour so we would fit. Then the rest of us wriggled along the crawl space and into the next room.

The palace has special underground rooms to protect the royal family in case of emergency, so we crawled along the smoke-filled corridors to the nearest one. We ran down the stairs, squeezed in, and locked the metal door.

'We're safe here,' I told Nero. 'We just wait until someone

comes who I know, and gives the right password.'

It took what seemed like forever, but eventually Centurion Gamus arrived. I recognised his voice, and he gave the correct password, so I opened the door. We escorted Nero to his mother and her husband. Agrippina was in tears, and hugged him tight. Claudius and Britannicus embraced him, too.

'See, Uncle Claudius,' said Nero. 'The guard gave me a dagger. I wasn't scared, was I, teacher?'

'No,' said Seneca, 'you were very brave.'

'And there was fighting,' continued Nero. 'The guards killed lots of enemies, and they ran away.'

'So you should reward them,' said Claudius. 'Ask them what they want.'

Nero raised his eyes to my masked face. 'What would you like?'

'Do you remember your teacher's lesson today?'

'Yes. He said I should show mercy, and turn enemies into friends.'

'That's right. This is your chance to do that. In the palace now are four prisoners. One is a prophetess. She had a dream and warned me there would be trouble today. That's why my squad were here to protect you. The others are the rebel prince Caratacus, with his wife and daughter. Show them mercy, and maybe their people will be as friendly to Rome as the Germanii who just saved your life. Oh, and do this for me, and you can keep that dagger to remember your first real fight.'

Nero grinned at that, and appealed to his family. 'Please, Uncle Claudius, please, mother, have mercy on them!'

Claudius nodded. 'I can free the priestess, the wife, and the daughter. But Caratacus is a dangerous enemy. I cannot let him go unless the people agree. What I can do is let him speak before the Senate. If they approve, I can grant him mercy.'

'Oh, thank you, Uncle Claudius.' He smiled at Seneca. 'See, I did what I promised.'

'That you did. You learned your lesson well.'

Centurion Gamus stepped forward. 'If you're ready, Emperor, I will escort you to the Praetorian barracks while we clean up here. You'll be safe there.'

'Lead on.'

A few days later, Caratacus was paraded through the streets of Rome. Thousands came to see the famous rebel prince. Nero's bodyguard Gamo, injured in the raid on the palace, was still recovering, so Nero asked that I take his place. Surus rode Micipsa, with Claudius on his throne, and Agrippina beside him. Lukon was behind them on the platform. Trenus and I rode behind, him guarding Britannicus and me guarding Nero. After us, and surrounded by Praetorians, were Caratacus, his wife, and Irgaine, followed by a group of prisoners taken by Ostorius in the wars. Word had spread that Caratacus would speak to the Senate, and an immense crowd trailed behind the parade, eager to hear his words, wondering if he would beg for his life, or go to his death with his head held high.

Claudius wanted everyone to see Caratacus, and judge from their reaction whether to spare him or not. The parade ended outside the Praetorian barracks, and their cohorts formed up to keep order. The prisoners were led forward, and the booty of war displayed. Next were Caratacus' family, and finally the man himself. All but he knelt to the Emperor and Empress, and the Senators behind them. He alone stood, proud and determined, and addressed the multitude.

'Had my luck matched my rank and wealth, I would have come to Rome as a prince rather than as a prisoner, and you would have welcomed me with a peace treaty as befits the monarch of many tribes. But this time, fortune is in your favour. Warhorses, warriors, weapons, and wealth were mine. Can you blame me for fighting to keep them? If Rome wishes to rule an Empire, should the whole world surrender without a fight? Where would be the glory in that, for you or for me? If I capitulated, no-one would remember the name Caratacus. But having fought and found fame, if you show clemency, it will be an everlasting memorial to your mercy.'

The crowd cheered his words, and the Senators applauded politely. Claudius looked around him, then rose to his feet.

'The power of Rome,' he declared, 'is proven by our victories over powerful enemies. Without men such as this to struggle against, how would we display our dominance? This prince is a living reminder of the might of our empire. Let him walk our streets, so that all who see him will be reminded of the glory of Rome. Prince Caratacus of the Catuvellauni, I, Tiberius Claudius Caesar Augustus Germanicus, Emperor of Rome, do hereby grant your plea for mercy. Guards, set him free.'

At my final words, Teuhant and his men burst into cheers, pounded me on the shoulders, and toasted my good health. But Boudicca sat silent. My words about the power of mercy, far from persuading her, had not gone down well. My sixth sense for trouble was warning me. I would have to watch my back.

22

THE TEMPLE OF THE WAR GODDESS

That night, a sentry shook me roughly awake. "There's a messenger here from Dervalon. You're to go with him for a council of war with Boudicca. The Ninth have broken out."

I climbed groggily to my feet. "Wake Eppilus, get the men ready to ride."

Following the messenger, I entered the council. Dervalon, Caicer, and Teuhant were standing in a group, so I joined them.

"What's going on?" I asked.

"The signals say that the Ninth have escaped, and they're on their way here," replied Dervalon, plaiting his beard as if to prepare for battle.

"Our goal is to take Camulodunum, not defeat the Ninth," I reminded them. "We need to get there as fast as we can. Raiding villages is just slowing us down. We can send forces to delay the Ninth, skirmishers to slow them down and ambushers to hold them up. We'll do it by tribes. Teuhant and the Catuvellauni can head for Camulodunum, with the Iceni and the Trinovantes. The Coritani and the Dobunni can delay the Ninth."

"What will you be doing?" asked Druid Caicer, scratching his pine marten under the chin.

"There are thirty thousand people in the town, and a detachment of auxiliaries, who know how to organise the defences. I'm going to put fear into their hearts. Then you can take the town, destroy it, and have time to turn to meet the Ninth, so they don't hit you from the rear while you are fighting in the town."

I strode from the hall. I had no idea how I was going to do it, but that was what needed to be done.

Outside the tent, Eppilus was waiting with my horse. To my surprise, Trenus was there too.

"Good to see you. You alright?" I asked him.

"Fine."

"Let's go." We walked our horses through the darkness, out of the camp.

"Where's Lukon?" I enquired.

"Coming south with the ballistas, but it's slow because there's a whole convoy of them, and they need an escort."

"What happened? How did the Ninth escape?"

"Tenvantius recovered, and was annoyed that you'd taken Durobrivae. Someone told him about the secret doors, and he ordered an assault on the south gate. The Ninth came out of the east and west gates, and their infantry caught him in a pincer movement. While they trapped him at the fort walls, their cavalry attacked our doors. They held them open long enough for the infantry to follow them, then shut them with him inside."

"Ha! How did Lukon do?"

"The ballistas wrought havoc in their ranks, but out of the two thousand in there, about fifteen hundred escaped, including Melanipa. They're on their way to Camulodunum, but they're being slowed down by the walking pace of their infantry, and the tribesmen are harrying them. If their commander decides that it's more important to save Camulodunum than to protect his infantry, he might leave them to fend for themselves and race down here."

"Let's hope he tries. We've got enough of a head start. If we can get to the town, and scare the inhabitants enough to make them flee, we can destroy the buildings before he gets there. Then we can use our infantry to surround him. As long as we can keep the Romans separate, we can beat them. How many cavalry has he got?"

"About five hundred."

"Good. With you, me and Eppilus, and the rest of the lads, there's only about a dozen of us. We can take a shortcut cross-country. With five hundred, he'll have to go by road, from Durobrivae south to the crossing of the Ouse at Durovigutum, and southeast to Camulodunum. With a bit of luck, he'll get ambushed, or blocked at the river. We can get there before him."

"How are we going to make thirty thousand people flee, when there's so few of us?"

"Like my old teacher Amergin said, magic is between men's ears. We're going to make omens of doom, and fake that we are the main army."

"What omens?"

"Ah, we need allies who are good with omens, and can raise an army. I know just the right people." And I told him my plan.

I took them deep into the forests north of Camulodunum, to the sacred oak grove where the High Druid had given me my mission many years before. It was night when we arrived.

"We wait here until dawn," I said. "I will go into the grove and perform a ceremony, and allies will come."

We set up camp and sat around the fire, eating and telling stories.

"You told Teuhant about Caratacus' daughter, Irgaine," said Eppilus. "What happened to her?"

"She was a Princess, and I was just a soldier. And I couldn't marry her until after I got my discharge from the guard, which was many years away. It was hopeless, so I gave up the idea."

None of which was a lie, but the truth was something I didn't want anyone else to know.

After Claudius freed Caratacus to walk the streets of Rome as a symbol of Roman mercy, I went to Ganna's temple to sacrifice to her war goddess and to give thanks for her warning. In the seven years that we had been in Rome, Ganna's shrine had grown from a glorified tent on a cart to a stone temple, with a sisterhood of priestesses and a stream of worshippers bringing offerings of war booty.

A white-clad sister met me at the gate. She took one look at my eyes, and said, 'The High-Priestess is expecting you. This way.'

She led me into the building, through the hall and behind the main altar, to a small door that I had never been through before.

'This is the inner sanctum. Be of brave heart. Enter.'

I opened the door, parted the curtains behind them, and stepped through. I was in a small circular room, lit only by a skylight in the dome above. Weaponry and trophies adorned the walls, and in the centre was an altar, about six feet long and covered with black and white leather. I recognised it as the skin of the whale that we had killed in Ostia.

Kneeling in front of the altar, with her back to me, was a woman dressed in the soft flowing robes of a high-class Roman lady, with elaborately coiffed black hair tumbling to her waist. She finished her prayer, and rose, turning to face me. It took me a few heartbeats to recognise her. It was Ganna. The black and white makeup of the High Priestess of the War Goddess

Baduhenna was gone, replaced by big dark eyes, with rosy lips and cheeks. The scent of flowers perfumed the surrounding air.

'Caz.'

She saw my expression of surprise.

'It's a disguise. They set me free, thanks to you, but Agrippina's got it in for me, and I'm not waiting around for her killers. I've sold everything, and I'm sneaking out of the city tonight. I'm going back to Dubhtach to finish my druid training. You'll have to carry out the High Druid's plan without me.'

My heart fell. 'Oh.' Not a response that did justice my feelings. More was called for. 'Well, as long as you'll be safe. Do you want me to escort you out of the city? Will you write to me and let me know how you are?'

'Stop worrying, I'll be fine.' She nodded at the sacrifices I had brought: the horn that the arrow had smashed, and a sword from a raider we had killed. 'Are those for the goddess?'

I nodded.

'Bring them here,' she said, and guided me over to the wall behind the altar. She hung the horn from a hook, and added the sword to a display below it.

'Recognise these?' she asked, pointing to other weapons on the wall.

'That's the lance I used to kill the lion, and that,' I said, pointing out a knife on a shelf in pride of place in the centre of the display, 'is the dagger that Messalina tried to kill herself with.'

'This is your wall, Caz. These are all the spoils of victory you've given me over the years to reward the goddess for her counsel. Until now I've been able to warn you and guide you, but after tonight you'll be on your own, and I need you to listen carefully. All right?'

'Go on.'

'When I was imprisoned under the palace, Irgaine was in the

next cell, and asked about you. She saw the eyes behind your mask and felt something pass between you. She asked me what her fate would be. So I prayed to the goddess, and she sent me a dream. I saw Agrippina deciding to marry her off to some petty princeling, and her embarking on a ship bound for far-off shores. There's no future for the two of you, Caz.'

I couldn't hide my disappointment.

'Oh, Caz. Sit down, and look into my eyes.'

I sat on the altar, and she took my hands and stared into my face.

'You've got it bad. But I knew this might happen, and I've got just the thing.' She fetched a pair of wine goblets and poured us both a drink. From her robes she took a small vial, and poured it into mine.

'Drink,' she ordered.

'What is it?'

'A potion to alter your fate, to take history by the horns, and bend fortune to our favour. No more questions.'

I drank.

She sat on the altar beside me and chatted about the arrangements she had made. I was to tell Surus and the lads about her departure, and apologise that she couldn't say farewell in person. After a few minutes, she reached up and took my cheeks between her palms.

'How do you feel?'

I was a bit light-headed, but nothing serious.

'Fine.'

'What are you going to do about Irgaine?'

'Dunno yet. I'll work something out.'

'Oh, Goddess, it hasn't worked!' She slipped down from the altar and stood directly in front of me. She put her hands on my shoulders, gazed up at the ceiling, and prayed. 'Baduhenna, give me a sign!'

Through the skylight the sun came out and bathed us both in rays of gold. Our shadows merged into one. Ganna lifted my face, put her lips to mine, and enamoured me with a magic that made me forget all about Irgaine.

In the pre-dawn light I blew the Horn of Cernunnos, entered the High Druid's sacred oak grove and performed the rite to welcome the day. As the sun rose, I saw I was not alone. A young girl of about nine or ten years stood on the edge of the grove, the morning light framing her head in gold. To my surprise, I noticed that her eyes were like mine: one green, one blue. Obviously, she was a message from the gods. She beckoned, and disappeared into the forest. I followed, trying to catch up, but she was nimble and this was her neck of the woods, so she stayed ahead until we reached a cleft in a low cliff, hidden by holly trees.

She slipped between the trees and the rock-face, and I followed, trying not to get stabbed by the sharp leaves. We emerged into a gorge and walked along a small brook until it widened into a dell. A turf-roofed hut, surrounded by a grassy clearing containing a few sheep and goats, was our destination. The girl ran to an ancient man with a white beard, sitting beside the hut door. As I approached, he used a staff to stand up, and I saw that it was my old master, Dubhtach. He recognised my eyes and smiled.

"You've grown, Caz," he said. "Romans feeding you well?"

"Is your nose getting bigger, old man, or is the rest of your head shrinking?"

We laughed and embraced, then he introduced me to the

girl. "This is my god-daughter, Cassie. Cassie, this is my old apprentice, Caz."

We chatted for a while, until Cassie went off to play with the goats, and then he asked me, "What brings you here?"

"Boudicca wants to attack Camulodunum and massacre everyone in it, then sweep on south, destroying everything Roman in her path. I'm helping her to fulfil the High Druid's orders to drive the Romans off this island, but if she has her way, she will wash them out with the blood of thousands of innocents. We have a couple of days until she gets here with her army, and in that time I've got to get the townspeople to flee."

"Well," said Dubhtach, "they're already worried, and some are leaving. It shouldn't take much to turn the trickle into a flood, but the more we can do, the more will go. What do you have in mind?"

"I need omens, portents of impending doom. And I need an approaching army to convince those who are not superstitious. For the omens, I want to destroy the symbols of Rome, maybe the Temple of Claudius, the Statue of Victory, the council chamber, or the theatre. For the army, I was hoping you knew people."

"I do. You know Ganna's in town? Don't look so surprised. It's the biggest city, and after living in Rome, she wasn't going to become a hermit, was she? When she finished her druid training she set up a temple to her war goddess. She has hundreds of followers. From her dreams she foretold you would come, so she sent me and Cassie here to meet you. She can't leave town now, as it's not good if the High-Priestess of the Baduhenna departs on the eve of battle, but I'll take you to her tonight."

"Good. I left Trenus, Eppilus and a few other lads at the oak grove. We'll need to get them. They have horses, so we can ride around and come in from the west. It will seem less suspicious."

"Come, Cassie," he called. "Help me to the grove. We're going to visit your mother."

That evening, we slipped into the city. Dubhtach knew the guards on the gate, and a simple, "They're friends of mine," got us in with no questions asked. He took us to Ganna's temple, and Cassie ran inside, calling, "Mummy, I'm back." Ganna came to greet us, and there were hugs all round. It had been ten years since we had seen her, and she had grown into her role as high priestess. She directed her staff to take care of the horses, and led us inside for a meal. The lamplight revealed fine lines that the years had etched around her eyes, and her position of command had made her expression stern, but her face softened whenever she spoke to Cassie.

When the meal was over, she sent Cassie to bed, and I set the men to check the horses and prepare for the night. Ganna led Dubhtach, Trenus, Eppilus and me to another room, along with a man who Ganna introduced as Bitucus, a foreman of one of the local construction gangs. I explained that I wanted to attack a symbol of Roman rule.

"The Statue of Victory is your best bet," he said. "It's in the town square, in front of the Temple of Claudius. The Temple itself is guarded, and the theatre across the square is too big to do much damage to. But for a frightening omen, you need to make it seem like the gods overthrew it. You can't just get a gang of men to tie a rope to it."

I raised an eyebrow at Trenus. "Any ideas?"

"Describe the area in detail," Trenus requested Bitucus.

"The statue is in the middle of the square. It's a figure of a woman with wings, holding a laurel wreath. It stands on a stone block, and the whole thing is three times my height. On the east of the square is the temple, behind which is the waterworks that bring in the drinking water from the aqueduct. To the west is the theatre, north and south are shops."

I raised my eyebrows in Trenus' direction, but he shook his head.

Eppilus cleared his throat.

"Out with it," I told him.

"Well, usually at this point you go off and pray. Then you come back with a plan. We're in a temple. If there's anywhere the gods will hear your prayers, it's here."

"Come with me, Caz," said Ganna. She led me down a corridor and into the inner sanctum. The walls were more sparsely decorated with weapons and trophies than those in her temple in Rome. There were also musical instruments of war: drums, and a traditional war horn, called a carnyx, of the type I had carried when I first met Ganna before the Battle of the Medway. Above the altar hung a dagger, and Ganna took it down and gave it to me. "Recognise it?"

"It's a pugio. Standard Roman army dagger." I examined it. Carved into the hilt was my initial. "Is this mine? Where did you get it?"

"That's the dagger you used to bribe Nero into setting me free. I heard the story after my release, and had one of my friends among the palace servants swap it for an identical one. Nero never knew the difference."

"Your advice saved me, and the lads, lots of times. I wish I'd kept something."

"There is something I want you to keep safe, but you must keep it a secret. Promise me."

"I promise."

"My daughter. I'm going to send her and Dubhtach back to the hut near the grove. Life around here is about to get dangerous, battle is coming, and I want them out of harm's way. No-one else should know where they are. When all this is over, you go and check on them. Make sure they're all right. Promise me."

"I swear it."

"Good." She pointed to a back corner floor of the sanctum. "Now help me bury the dagger in the box under that flagstone. If I don't make it through this, you give it to Cassie."

We levered up the floor stone, put the dagger in the box, and buried it. When we put the stone back on top, it was well-hidden.

"We should get back," said Ganna. "Have you still got Baduhenna's amulet?"

I tapped my chest. "Here. I've got the amulet of Baduhenna, the war crown of Toutatis, Belatucadros and Cocidius, and the Horn of Cernunnos. I am well protected."

She nodded. "I hope it's enough. This is the Roman capital, their temples are all around, and their gods are strong here. But if you're sure, let's go."

We returned to the others. "We forgot one thing," I told them. "When you look around for answers, you don't just look left and right, front and back. You also look up and down. Trenus, you've told us many times how important foundations are. We need to find a way to undermine the statue. Maybe we can park a cart there on market day, and go down through the bottom of it, or maybe Bitucus can do some maintenance work in the area, with a tent for storing tools, and we can dig down from that."

"No need," said Bitucus. "The square has got large drains under the surface to take away the run-off when it rains. They're huge, as they used to be trenches for the defence of the old fort. When the fort was knocked down, we just roofed them over. They lead out to the river."

"There's undefended access to the town?" I asked in disbelief.

"The entrance has a barred and locked gate." Bitucus grinned. "And as foreman, guess who has a key?"

"You do."

"Right. We can go in there, walk up until we find the small drainpipe that comes off the statue, and dig sideways off the drain until we hit the foundation stone. The problem is that we don't want to be there when it falls, because the drain roof will probably collapse."

"I know," said Trenus. "In siege warfare, when you undermine a city wall, you prop the wall up with logs, and when you want the wall to fall, you set fire to the logs. It takes a while, but it gives the miners time to get out."

"We can burn a softwood, like spruce or pine. It will burn faster," I said.

"What about the smoke?" asked Eppilus.

"It will come out by the river, outside the walls. If we do it at night, no-one will notice, or if they do, they won't link it to the statue," said Bitucus.

"Where else do the drains come from?" asked Trenus.

"There's one from the theatre, and one from the council chamber, but they aren't big enough for a man to get into."

"I saw a carnyx in the temple," I said. "The sound will carry along the pipes. I doubt if anyone has heard one since Caratacus fought here. The sound will scare anyone who hears it. They'll think the ghosts of that battle have come back to haunt them. If we beat the drums and clash swords and shields, it will sound like a ghost battle."

"We can plant some of my followers in the crowd," said Ganna, "and have them scream. It will start a panic. Add some people in the streets fleeing with their belongings, and others will follow their example."

"Talking of your followers," I said, "we need to seize the bridges outside the north and west gates so Boudicca's army can get in fast, before the Ninth catches up with them. Worshippers of the war goddess should be ideal for that."

THE DRUID AND THE ELEPHANT

"Good," said Ganna. "You lads get some sleep. Bitucus and I will put some teams together and prepare the things we need. We'll wake you when they're ready, and you can sneak into the drains." She beckoned me. "Come, we need to talk."

23

THE RIVER OF BLOOD

While Bitucus and Dubhtach went to organise Ganna's followers, she and I went to her quarters to check on Cassie, who was fast asleep. We sat by the coals of the dying fire and held a whispered conversation.

"What are you going to do when this is all over?" she asked me.

"We'll fight the Ninth legion, then go south to Londinium and take that. The other tribes will rally to our cause, and we'll have enough to take on Suetonius."

"I mean after that. When you've driven the Romans off this island. What then?"

"Suetonius destroyed the sacred groves on the holy island. The druids need to replant. I'll be needed there."

"What if the Romans won't accept defeat? They never do: Agrippina's father took revenge for Hermann's victory in Germania. They'll invade again."

"If they do, we'll be ready for them. What about you? What's your plan?"

"This temple will probably be destroyed in the next few days. I'll help you in the battle, then take Cassie and leave. I'll go back to my home tribe, east of the Germanii lands. Set up a new temple, fight the Romans from there."

My heart fell. I had only just found her again, and she planned to leave. What would persuade her otherwise? I appealed to the highest authority in her life.

"What do your dreams say?"

"Baduhenna is euphoric. She sends me dreams of an enormous battle, the biggest ever seen in these lands. Rivers of blood. I see Melanipa on one side, and Boudicca on the other. I'm searching for you among the corpses, but I can't find you."

"What happens next?"

"The dream changes. I see you in a city on fire, but it's Rome, not here."

"That's strange. I have no plan to go back there."

"You don't, but Baduhenna does. Remember the High Druid's plan, after Camulodunum? She spoke through me. She declared you the doom of Rome, and that's where the High Druid sent you. Do you know the meaning of the amulet I gave you before the riot?"

I felt it beneath my tunic. "What?"

"That amulet binds you to her. She has guided you from one battle to another. Your victories are her victories. The spoils of war you've brought to my temple have been tributes to her. You wear the druid war crown, but you are also a champion of the War Goddess. The battle is not just here. It's a battle between Baduhenna and Mars. She won't be satisfied, and your mission won't be complete, until she is victorious. Others can regrow the druid groves on the Holy Isle. Come with me across the sea. We have an empire to destroy."

Cassie stirred. In her excitement, Ganna's voice had risen.

"Hush, little one," said Ganna. "Mamma's here. Go back to sleep."

While Ganna tucked Cassie in and stroked her hair, I thought about what she had said, and I realised that the gods had sent me another message.

When Cassie went back to sleep and Ganna came back to me, I whispered. "You and I are going to create a river of blood. Let me tell you how." And I told her the story of Nero and the killer.

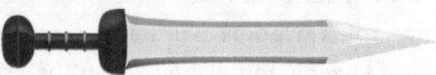

One scorching summer morning in Rome, Centurion Gamus called Trenus and me into his office.

'I've got a job for you,' he said. 'On the first day of August the Emperor is holding the official opening of his new aqueduct. Before he opens it, there will be a ceremonial inspection by his son and heir Britannicus, and the Empress's son, Nero. You will accompany them to where the aqueduct comes out of the hills, get into boats, and float the seven miles to Rome. Three canoes have been built specially. Micipsa will carry them to the aqueduct. The architect who's in charge will take the first one, rowed by one of his men. Trenus, Britannicus wants you to guard him in the second, and Decimus will guard Nero in the third. An escort of Praetorian cavalry will accompany you. Nero's bodyguard Gamo will go with you, but he's too big for a canoe, so he'll stay with the horses. You will do a full dress rehearsal the day after tomorrow. Decimus, you're in charge. Work out the potential ambush sites, and I'll have them guarded.'

'Yes, Sir.'

'We'll keep the plans as quiet as we can, but with so many people involved, including us, the Praetorians, the aqueduct staff and the ceremonial organisers, it's going to be hard to keep this a secret. What I'm now going to tell you now must not be repeated to anyone outside this room. Is that clear?'

'Yes, Sir.'

THE DRUID AND THE ELEPHANT

'Our spies tell us of whisperings among possible traitors, family members of people Agrippina has had killed. They believe she wants to put Nero on the throne after Claudius, and Britannicus is in her way. The traitors may go after Nero, too, like they did in the palace raid last year. You have to keep him safe, by Hercules, or Agrippina will never forgive us. Take the lightest, strongest shields and armour from the armoury. Also, miles of the aqueduct are high in the air on arches. Take some rope so you can get down quickly. Any other kit you want, get it from the stores. Questions?'

'No, Sir.'

'Dismissed.'

The rehearsal went off without a hitch, and three days later, we trotted up the Via Latina to its seventh milestone, where the aqueduct arches started. Nero and I climbed into the third canoe, and I stowed my round cavalry shield behind me, with a small hand-held ballista that Lukon had given me in the bottom of the boat. We pushed off, and floated along, propelled by the current, and by me pushing a paddle against the bottom of the channel, which was only shoulder-width wide, and two feet deep.

The architect was in the front canoe, sitting facing backwards to talk to us.

'This is the Aqua Claudia,' he proudly told us. 'Over forty miles long, from the hills east of Rome. From here, the arches carry the water almost in a straight line to the Prenestina Gate in the city walls. As we get closer to the city, the ground level drops, but to keep the water surface level, the arches are higher, and we will be a hundred feet in the air. The flow of water is enough to fill eighty amphora every second.'

'It's magnificent,' said Britannicus. 'When I'm Emperor, I want to build an aqueduct too.'

I saw the muscles in Nero's shoulders tense.

The architect's eyes lit up. 'You can build a wonderful aqueduct, bringing water from Lake Bracciano in the north. It would never run dry, and it carry as much water as all the other aqueducts put together. I can design it for you.'

'I don't see why we need aqueducts,' said Nero. 'What's wrong with river water and wells? Rome was here for hundreds of years before the first aqueduct.'

'Now we have a million people in Rome,' replied the architect. 'A million! The biggest city in the world. We need water for the baths, industry and public drinking fountains. People like the spring water from the hills. It's cleaner and tastes better.'

'How do you keep it clean?' asked Britannicus.

'You see these wooden planks on the sides of the aqueduct walls? They're covers. After we've finished our inspection, my men will put them back on to stop things falling in the water. And later on you'll see the sedimentation tanks, which are deep tanks where the water slows down and any mud or sand falls to the bottom.'

The water current was pulling us along at a fair pace. Below us, I heard the hooves of the Praetorian cavalry trotting to keep up. Britannicus and the architect were chatting away, and Nero was sitting silently in front of me, taking no notice.

'Observe,' said the architect, 'we're coming up to a sedimentation tank now. It's wide and deep to slow the water down. There's an iron bar gate as a filter to catch floating debris, but it's been lifted out of the way now for us to go through. You'll also see a bypass channel for the water to flow through whenever we want to empty the tanks and send the slaves in to clean the bottom.'

As I gazed forward to see the gate, the architect's rower twisted round for the first time. He glanced at Nero, then saw me watching him, and snapped his head back forwards. Was it nervousness from being seen looking at the Empress's son, or something more sinister? I quietly reached down and cocked the ballista, clipping the string into the notch on the back of the bolt.

The current washed the lead canoe into the tank, and drifted it across to the far wall. Britannicus' boat followed, then ours approached the gate. The architect's rower leaned out to steady his boat against the wall, then yanked on a rope. I jumped forwards to shield Nero. The iron filter gate dropped and hit my back plates, knocking me sideways. The canoe rolled, and we went overboard, into the tank.

I was in full armour, with helmet, chest and back plates, so I sank like a stone. Nero was swimming above me, and below me the ballista sank bolt-first to the bottom. My feet hit the floor of the tank. In the dim light, I spotted a ladder of handholds carved into the side of the tank. Grabbing the ballista, I half-walked, half-swam to the ladder, and hauled myself up. My lungs were bursting, but I knew that if I opened my mouth, I would drown. Two things saved me, my horn player's lungs and my druid training in self-control. I made it to the surface, and gulped in great breaths as I looked around. Trenus and Britannicus were throwing plumbata darts at the rower, but it's hard to throw from a rocking boat, and the darts missed him. He was rowing towards where Nero was swimming behind our overturned canoe. I lifted the ballista, took careful aim at his head, and pulled the trigger. The string was wet, so the bolt, instead of hitting him in the head, barely cleared the side of the canoe, hitting him in the waist. He screamed and grabbed at the protruding shaft. The architect dived off the canoe, rolling it, and the rower fell in the water. He tried to swim away, but Trenus' canoe was faster, and Trenus smashed him on the head with his paddle.

Nero and the architect swam over to the wall and climbed out.

The architect was shaking like a leaf, but Nero wasn't frightened, he was angry.

'I'll find out who's responsible for this and I'll crucify them!' he yelled.

I went over to the wall and shouted down to the Praetorians. They climbed the outside ladders and surrounded the tank, protecting the boys.

I went over to their commander, a junior officer who I had only met that morning. Fortunately, I outranked him. 'We need to get moving. The Emperor is waiting for us to start his ceremony. Give us one of your men as a rower for the architect. We'll take the boys in the canoes. You can leave some men here to sort things out, and the rest can escort us onwards, in case of more trouble.'

'Yes, Cornicen,' he said, and started giving orders.

The corpse of the architect's rower was fished out, blood from his side and head staining the water and flowing out towards the city he would never see again. We pulled the capsized canoes over to the tank outlet, righted them, and set off for the city. The rest of the journey was uneventful, and the August sun soon dried our clothes. We used the paddles to push ourselves along, and made it on time for the Emperor's ceremony. Britannicus and Nero reported to their father that the aqueduct had passed their inspection, and the Emperor opened the new fountains to the cheers of the crowds. No-one noticed the bit of blood in the water, which was lucky, as it would have been a terrible omen.

THE DRUID AND THE ELEPHANT

"Oh," said Ganna, stirring the coals of her fire to keep us warm, "that's what you're thinking. Put blood in the aqueduct here to scare the people into fleeing. But we'll need huge amounts, or it will get so diluted that no-one will notice. Where will you get it?"

"I'm not going to use real blood. In the marshes by the sea around here are the remains of salt pans, where people once made salt. There's so much broken red pottery, from clay trays used to boil off the water, that the places are called Red Hills. The sea has ground it into sand, and if it gets into water, the water turns red. We can load up some cartfuls, take them to the aqueduct, and drop it in through the inspection covers. The sedimentation tanks have bypass ducts for when they are being cleaned. We can open them, so the red water will flow here, and come out of the fountains in the square."

She put her fists on her hips and faced me. "I thought you meant that the river here would flow with Roman blood. That river!" She pointed to where the River Colne flowed in the moonlight. "Those Romans!" she stabbed her hand north. "That you and me would fight the Romans together, and begin our revenge on Rome! Not make some muddy water!"

"We will," I assured her. "When Boudicca's army gets here and the Ninth catches up. Thousands will die. The river will turn red. Baduhenna will be satisfied. But the Goddess doesn't want civilian blood, so we have to get them out of here first. Just like you want to get Cassie out of here."

"Don't tell me what Baduhenna wants! Don't bring our daughter into this!"

"What?! Our daughter?"

"Yes, you idiot! Can't you count the years? Why do you think I named her 'Cassie'? You saw her eyes! Don't you realise how much she looks like you?"

24

THE DEATH OF AN EMPEROR

There was a tap at the door. Ganna threw me a withering glance, and strode over to it. Dubhtach's voice came from outside.

"We're ready!" the druid called.

Ganna let him in. "Take Cassie to the farm by the grove when it gets light. I'll come when I can." She jerked her chin in my direction. "He knows." She stalked out.

Dubhtach shut the door. "She's had a hard time of it," he told me. "Crossing Gaul while pregnant, giving birth, bringing up Cassie while doing the training, then building this place. When Boudicca gets here, she'll sack the city, and years of work will go up in smoke. It's hard for her to help you do it. What did she say to you?"

"She wants me to be champion of Baduhenna, to be the doom of Rome and bring it down in rivers of blood. With her and Cassie."

He tilted his head sympathetically. "What do you want?"

"I'm a druid. I swore to carry out the High Druid's mission. What I want is for the Romans to leave, and I will wear this war crown until they do, but then it's over. I don't want to be the doom of Rome. I've got friends and comrades there. There are a million people in Rome, and millions more around the empire. They've done nothing to me. I don't want to doom them. Why is

THE DRUID AND THE ELEPHANT

my life full of people who want me to massacre others?"

"Because you're the chosen of the war gods. Do you remember the words of the High Druid?"

"Yes, he said the targets are the Emperor, all his followers who have violated our lands, and to draw away the Roman legions. I've done that: Claudius is dead, a usurper rules in his stead, and I am defeating his followers now. In a few months the mission will be over."

"What do you mean by 'I've done that'? Did you kill Claudius? Did you put Nero on the throne?" So I told him the tale of the death of the Emperor.

Nero told his parents how I had saved him in the fight at the sedimentation tank, so Agrippina rewarded the Germanii, and Centurion Gamus promoted me to Aquilifer, battle standard bearer of the cohort. Trenus got promoted too, and was put in charge of the physical defences of the palace. He loved it, and had secret doors and passages installed for guards to race through the palace and fight off any danger.

Surus and Micipsa helped move stones for the building work, and I explained Trenus' designs to them. Surus wiped the perspiration from his forehead, and from around Micipsa's toenails, which is where elephants sweat from.

'Why's he putting these in?' Surus asked me. 'Are we in danger?'

I checked around to make sure no-one else was listening.

'Yes,' I replied. 'Claudius' marriage to Agrippina is getting worse. He's much older than her, in his sixties, and not a well man. She's young, not yet forty, and full of ambition.'

'Of course!' said Surus. 'But now she's Empress. What more does she want?'

'Power. She demands to be treated like an emperor. He's put her head on coins, lets her sign government documents, and he married his daughter Octavia to her son Nero.'

'So what's the problem?'

'The more powerful she gets, the more the people of Rome are divided. Some think that Britannicus should be the next emperor. Others believe Nero would be better. He's older, well-liked by the military, and speaks well in politics. He was brave during the palace raid and on the aqueduct.'

'You're saying it's a choice between Claudius' son or Agrippina's son?'

'That's right. And you know what palace politics are like. Only one will survive. That's why Trenus is preparing for trouble.'

'Who would be better for Micipsa and me?'

'You don't have to worry, both of them like you.'

What I didn't tell him was that my real reason for preferring Nero was that Claudius was the Emperor who had invaded my homeland, whose soldiers had killed my father and brother, and who had named his son Britannicus to celebrate that campaign. The High Druid had sent me to kill him. If Nero took the throne, it would be the end of Claudius' line.

It was all just speculation and rumours until Nero's teacher, the philosopher Seneca, got involved. He was in a difficult position. He owed his job to Agrippina, who had brought him back from exile, but he owed his life to Claudius, who had commuted his death sentence to that exile. Being a philosopher, his conscience was plaguing him, so he decided to warn Claudius. However, he couldn't do it in an obvious way, so what he did was write a play, and rely on the fact that Claudius was a highly educated man, capable of reading between the lines.

Seneca was famous, so they gave his new play a royal-command opening-night performance in the palace, and since I was the guard commander, I was there to guard the Imperial family. A blood-soaked tragedy of murder, lust and betrayal, the play was called 'Agamemnon'.

The story starts with the ghost of the King of Olympia, who demands that his son, Aegisthus, take revenge on King Agamemnon, who is returning home after leading the Greeks to victory in the Trojan War. Aegisthus is sleeping with the Agamemnon's wife, Queen Clytemnestra. She is angry with her husband because he sacrificed her daughter, and is bringing home a new woman, the Trojan princess Cassandra. She also doesn't want to get caught sleeping with Aegisthus, so she decides to kill the king. Cassandra is a prophetess, and tries to warn Agamemnon, but over-confident from his victories, he dismisses her fears. Clytemnestra murders her own husband with an axe, then orders Cassandra's execution. Aegisthus becomes king.

Claudius saw the parallels between himself and Agamemnon, Agrippina and Clytemnestra, and Aegisthus with Nero. What tipped him over the edge and into action was his daughter Octavia. She was only thirteen when she married Nero. They were too young to wed, and their personalities were totally unsuited for each other. She was an aristocratic and proper young princess. He was the son of a disgraced politician who loved chariot-racing. Her unhappiness was obvious to her father, and it caused him to turn against Nero.

Claudius had previously made Nero his joint heir, along with Britannicus, who was underage. However, now he was nearly an adult, and Claudius considered divorcing Agrippina. He told the Senate that Britannicus and Nero were equals. Agrippina knew that when Britannicus was declared an adult, she and Nero would no longer be needed, so she had to act first. A real blood-soaked tragedy of murder, lust and betrayal was about to begin, and it didn't take the foresight of Cassandra to see it coming.

In early autumn I was sitting in the guard commander's office, when Pallas, Claudius' treasurer, and the man who had recommended Agrippina as the Emperor's new wife, came to see me. Rumour had it that he and Agrippina were secret lovers, a dangerous risk to take while Claudius still lived.

'I've come about the security arrangements for tomorrow's feast,' he said. 'Narcissus is out of town and I'm running it.'

I shut the door. 'What's up?'

'The Emperor is not in good health. The Empress is worried about him, and has ordered some special nourishing dishes for the feast. But it may not be enough. If the Emperor's health should fail him, a smooth succession would prevent any trouble. We don't want a repeat of the chaos when Caligula died, and Claudius was cowering behind a curtain for fear of his life. Everyone must remain calm and in their rooms until things settle down. I'm sure the palace guard recognises that Nero is the only adult son, and the only man qualified to take up the imperial purple. You have saved his life twice and risen high in the guard because of it. You have a promising career in front of you.'

What this meant was they were going to poison Claudius, and wanted me to imprison Britannicus until they had declared Nero emperor. If I did, I would be rewarded.

'We are Germanii,' I replied. 'Our loyalty is absolute. The purple must go to the legitimate heir. I look forward to continuing to serve him.'

He nodded. 'I knew I could rely on you. Others weren't so sure. They wondered why you asked for mercy for Caratacus and his family. Some said you were so taken by the beauty of his green-eyed daughter that you forgot to search her. He's a young man, they said. He likes her, they said. It's natural, they said. But others were more suspicious and started asking questions about your past. Then you saved Nero in the aqueduct and proved your loyalty. There's no need for further investigation, I told them. And thinking to the future, a new Emperor will want a parade, with his elephant. Maybe Irgaine will be there, and would like to meet Micipsa, his rider and her saviour.'

His meaning was clear: he knew where I was from, and if I didn't help him, I was a dead man. If I did what he wanted, Irgaine might be mine.

'I will do my duty,' I told him.

'A pleasure working with you.' He smiled, but not with his eyes. 'See you at the feast.'

Next morning, I went to the Germanii senior officers' meeting. As Aquilifer, I had the right to be there. It was my job to protect the battle standard, so I had to know what was afoot.

Gamus was worried. 'I'm suspicious that something is going to happen at the feast,' he told us. 'Narcissus isn't here to keep a lid on things. The Emperor's doctor, Xenophon, reports that Claudius is not well. Depending on when he dies, either Nero or Britannicus will take over. That gives some people a reason to wish him ill. From now until Britannicus becomes an adult, I'm doubling the guard. Tonight, I'll be Guard Commander, and attend the feast. Optio Hospes, you watch the food taster, Halotus, closely, and make sure he tries everything. If he's hesitating over a dish, he may be looking for a marked piece, so force him to eat a bit that you choose. Aquilifer Decimus, Gamo is guarding Nero tonight, so I want you in the kitchens and the corridors, making sure there are no strangers. No mysterious deliverymen, no new substitutes for sick slaves. Anyone you don't recognise, arrest them and bring them to me.'

'Yes, Sir.'

He went on, giving us our assignments. He'd covered the food, and the Emperor's health. Pallas had told me nothing substantial, so I had nothing to add.

'If things do go wrong,' he continued. 'I want a total lock-down. No-one except us moves around the palace, no-one goes in or out unless I say so. The Praetorians stay outside. I'm not having them choose the Emperor again, by Hercules! Is that clear?'

'Yes, Sir.'

'Right. Dismissed.'

The lock-down was what Pallas wanted as well. Was it a coincidence, or had Pallas talked to Gamus, too? Whose side was he on?

That afternoon I patrolled the palace kitchens and corridors, both inspecting and praying for inspiration from the gods. I touched Ganna's amulet, then noticed the food taster, Halotus, who was also the chief steward, going through the floral decorations, and moving them away from where Claudius would recline on his eating bench. I knew from Amergin's trick so long ago in Camulodunum that the Emperor sneezed near flowers. Halotus recognised me, since I had played the cornu at the Emperor's wedding, and had saved him from Homopolon's stupidity.

'Halotus,' I greeted him.

'Cornicen, I mean Aquilifer. Congratulations on your promotion!'

I nodded. 'Something wrong with the flowers?'

'The Emperor reacts badly to marigolds and daisies, so I always check for them.'

'Find any?'

'Not so far.'
'Let me know if you do.'
I walked away. The gods had spoken.

The feast went off without a hitch. Claudius enjoyed himself tremendously, and pigged himself on his favourite foods, including an orange-headed mushroom with a pale yellow stalk, called Caesar's mushroom. Halotus tasted all the dishes, and rejected several. I stared around to see if there were any disappointed poisoners, but no-one gave themselves away. Claudius over-ate, drank too much, and passed out, snoring. His doctor, Xenophon, had him carried away. Then I put my plan into action.

I went down to the kitchen and made myself a snack of mushroom stalks soaked in olive oil and honey. Delicious. By the time I got to the last stalk, its colour had changed to a pale olive. I rinsed off the oil and honey, leaving a discoloured stalk, then slipped into the secret passages and went to see Xenophon. The Emperor was fast asleep in his chambers.

'How is he?' I asked.

'Resting. He'll be alright, he just over-indulged.'

'I found this in the kitchen,' I said, showing him the mushroom stalk. 'It doesn't seem right to me. What do you make of it?'

Xenophon took it and smelled it. 'It smells like honey. It's the wrong colour for Caesar's mushroom.'

'Yes, I'm worried that it's a death cap mushroom. They smell like honey, and they're greenish like this one.'

'You may be right. Or it may be honey. Hard to tell.'

'Can you give him something just in case? Our sources say that people want to get rid of him before Britannicus comes of age, and I don't want him dying on our watch. Is there anything that won't do any harm, but will help if it is?'

'Well, there's always blessed milk thistle sap. It's good for the liver, too. He keeps drinking too much, and his liver worries me.'

'Sounds like just the thing. Well, I need to report to Gamus. Let us know if you need us.'

Druid Dubhtach wagged a wizened finger at me. "Amergin taught you well, Caz. You knew people who react badly to marigolds and daisies also react badly to milk thistle. You got the doctor to kill his own patient using medicine instead of poison! Why didn't he realise?"

"He probably thought flowers have pretty petals and thistles are ugly weeds, and didn't link the two. Also, he wasn't a druid, so maybe he didn't know. He was tired and stressed, and I put him under pressure about Claudius dying on our watch."

"What happened next?"

"Claudius died early the next morning. Gamus put the entire palace into lock-down. Agrippina introduced Nero as emperor, first to the Germanii and the Praetorians, and then to the senators, and they approved his succession. The reign of the emperor who invaded these shores was over, and the High Druid had his revenge. Nero was now in charge. It wasn't long before he went after Britannicus."

"You can tell me that one tomorrow. Go to sleep. Battle is coming, and you need to be alert."

25

THE THEATRE OF TERROR

Eppilus woke me next morning. Dubhtach and Cassie had left Ganna's temple, but with him was a chubby man with a big nose and expansive gestures.

"This is Roscius," said Eppilus. "He's the theatre manager, and he's on our side."

"Druid," said Roscius, "I'm told you want to scare people during the performance tonight. What do you have in mind?"

"What play are you performing?"

"We have a repertoire. Tell me what you'd like, and I'll tell you if we know it."

"It'd better be a tragedy." I remembered Seneca's play 'Agamemnon'. "Do you know anything with ghosts in it?"

"How about 'Apocolocyntosis'?"

"Perfect! I'll play the carnyx just after Pompeius' line to Caesar."

"I'll tell the actors to scream and flee. Some of Baduhenna's worshippers will be in the audience, and they'll run for the exits." He clapped his hands. "I love it: a synthesis of mimesis and anti-mimesis!"

"Good. I'll go into the drains when it gets dark tonight."

"I'll send one of the drummers to play with you, and show you where to go." He rubbed his hands together and gave an evil grin. "Oh, this is going to be the performance of a lifetime! I can't wait!" He strode to the door.

Eppilus furrowed his brow. "What," he asked, "is Apoco-whatever? And those other words: 'sin' and 'mim'-something?" So I told him how Pallas and Seneca conspired to keep Britannicus off the throne.

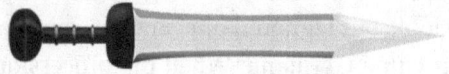

Three men kept young Nero in power as the Emperor of Rome: Seneca the philosopher was the brains, Pallas, who had threatened me, was the money man, and the new Praetorian Prefect, Burrus, was the muscle. It wasn't an easy job. Agrippina was trying to rule from behind the throne, and wanted to be in control. She held the official title of Augusta, which made her equal to an emperor. The first event that she demanded be done her way was Claudius' funeral. Members of the imperial family are cremated, then interred in the most frightening building in Rome, the Mausoleum of Augustus, which the god-emperors' ghosts are said to haunt. Unearthly noises have been heard there at night. I think it's the mating calls of amorous toads echoing in the drains, but why spoil a good story?

The day before the funeral, Agrippina suddenly took it into her head that she wanted a rehearsal, so that she would know what to do and where to go on the following day. As Augusta, she could not be refused.

I was guarding Nero during one of his lessons with Seneca, when a messenger ran in, and told the boy Emperor that his mother wanted him. We marched down towards her wing, and found her waiting in a special ornate carriage for priests and vestal virgins. It was surrounded by a guard of Praetorian cavalry. Nero climbed in, the guard closed the door and took his place beside the driver. From a second carriage Pallas beckoned Seneca. I closed the door for them, and, not having a horse, climbed up beside the driver. Protection outside the palace was officially the Praetorian's job, but Gamus would want a report, and I was curious to know what was going on. The driver gave me a strange look, but I ignored him, and he wasn't about to start an argument with a Germanii. When the procession started off, he had no choice but to follow.

Arriving at the Mausoleum on the Campus Martius, I saw a huge round marble building, surrounded by a park of cypress trees, topped by a colossal bronze statue of Augustus. Twin pink granite obelisks stood on either side of the arched entryway, where the head priest of the Imperial Cult was waiting for us. The Senate had declared Claudius a god, and the priest was in charge of making sure he had a fitting resting place.

'Welcome, Caesar, and welcome, Augusta, to the Mausoleum of Augustus,' he declared. 'Here lie the ashes of the Divine Emperors. If you would like to come this way, I will explain tomorrow's ceremony.' Nero and Agrippina descended from their carriage and followed him towards the entrance. I expected Seneca and Pallas to do the same, but the carriage door remained tightly shut, which was strange.

Wanting to know what was going on, I used an old soldier's trick. The back of a Roman helmet has a neck guard extending a palm-width back at ear level. From my seat beside the driver I leaned back and rested it against the body of the carriage. The vibrations from someone talking inside travelled up the neck guard to my head, and now that the noise of the wheels had ceased, I could hear what they were saying.

Pallas was talking. 'Once Narcissus is out of the way, we can control him. You, me and Burrus can run this empire, with him as a figure-head. We can distract him with things he loves, chariot racing, music, girls. The only problem is her. She wants to control him. He's growing up, and like any young man, he won't want to be a mother's boy. He will rebel. We can encourage him. She knows the value of Octavia for his legitimacy, but we can find an unsuitable woman to seduce him away, which will cause a rift between them. We can suggest exile for her.'

'In that case, we will need to make sure he has the support of the Senate and the people,' replied Seneca. 'We need him to be a good emperor, a contrast to his predecessor. I'll write his first speech to the Senate, promising to follow the ideals of Augustus and respect the privileges of the Senate and the position of the Senators. No more secret trials, no more corruption. That should get them on-side. If we can stop his mother murdering them, even better. As for the people, prepare to spend some money on bread and circuses. And what would be popular is you reining in the tax collectors.'

'That will boost his reputation, but how about the contrast part? We need to be careful about criticising Claudius when we've just declared him a god.'

'I'm thinking of writing a play about how ridiculous it is to claim that he deserves to be a god. Claudius killed enough people, and violated enough of Augustus' principles of good government, that I can mock the whole idea. By the time I've finished writing it, people will accept it.'

'What about building a temple for him in the meantime? He is a god, you know!'

'When Nero wants something, like an expensive inauguration parade, we can tell him that the only available money is being used for the temple, and he'll want it, so we can slow the construction to a halt. He's already got a temple in Britannia. There's no hurry for another one.'

'That reminds me. Britannicus. What are we going to do with him?'

'With Narcissus out of the way, he'll be vulnerable. Once Nero's accepted as Emperor, he can be pushed out of the way. Make him governor of Britannia: those troublesome tribesmen would keep him occupied for a lifetime.'

'Right, that's settled. Let's go and see where the divine ashes will go.'

I sat still and tried not to draw attention to myself. They walked straight past me without noticing I was there.

As I finished my memory of that day, Eppilus' confused expression brought me back to the present. "What does that have to do with the play?" he asked.

"Seneca's play is the one Roscius is putting on tonight. It's called Apocolocyntosis, and it's about how murderous Claudius' rule was. Mimesis is an actor's idea of whether life follows art, or art follows life. In this case, the play is based on a true story, and the play also is part of real life because it will get people to flee. Actors who fancy themselves as intellectuals love this kind of stuff."

"Oh. Well, if it keeps them happy, and it gets them to do what we want, so be it. I'm hungry, let's find some food."

That evening I carried my carnyx down to the river and found where the drains emerged. Trenus was waiting there, along with a small boy carrying a large thin drum.

"We're ready," said Trenus. "This is Cassius."

I smiled. Cassius means hollow, like a drum. "Is that your stage name?" I asked him.

"Yes, when I joined the theatre, Master Roscius said it was a new life, and he gave me a new name."

"It's a good name. I'm Cassibelanus. It means bronze and strength. This carnyx is made of bronze, and its sound is so strong you can hear it all over a battlefield. Together, you and I are going to help win a battle. Are you ready?"

"Yes."

I handed the Horn of Cernunnos to Trenus. "Take care of this for me until I get back. I can't carry two horns. Lead on." I should have kept it: I was going to need the gods' protection.

Trenus guided us into the black mouth of the drain. It was like entering the underworld. We blindly followed the splashing of his feet until a glow appeared in the distance. It was Bitucus and his workers, gathered around a small fire for warmth. Behind them, a narrow tunnel led towards the statue. I smelled the pine inside.

"All set," he told me.

"Light the props. By the time they burn through, the play should be nearly over."

"Good luck," he said, and we continued up the drain. Trenus had taken a log from the fire, and Cassius and I copied him, to see where we were going. It wasn't long before we got to a side entrance, and he led us into a smaller hole. Soon it split into several pipes, too small for us to go on.

"This is it," he whispered. "I'll meet you at the river exit later."

After he left, Cassius and I leaned against the wall and waited. Smoke from Bitucus' fire wafted through the tunnel. In the silence, noises from the theatre echoed down the drains.

"Do you know the play?" I asked Cassius, quietly.

"I know the music, and I've seen the play before, but I didn't understand what was going on."

Trumpets blared, and the opening lines echoed down the pipes.

"That's the god Mercury, who guides souls to the underworld," I whispered. "He is persuading Clotho, the fate who decides when mortals should die, to kill the Roman emperor Claudius."

"Why?"

"He's old, sick, and has many enemies."

"Does he deserve to die?"

"It was his legions that invaded Britannia. He's the reason my father and brother are dead. But I met him, and he was good to me. And he pardoned Caratacus. Only the gods can really know if someone deserves to die. Clotho decided it was time to end his life. She does it for us all. We can only pray to the gods to ask her not to take us just yet. But don't worry, lad, it will be years before she notices you."

Slow footsteps and the tapping of a walking stick sounded from above.

"What's happening now?"

"Claudius is walking to Mount Olympus. He wants to be a god, so he needs to ask the other gods' permission."

"But he's just a man. How can he become a god?"

"Some people believe that if enough people worship a man, he becomes a god. The Roman Senate decided he was a god, and set up temples to him, so people went there to worship. You've seen people worshipping at Claudius' temple here, haven't you?"

"Yes. But he's not a real god, like Dionysus."

"Why Dionysus?"

"Master Roscius prays to him. He says Dionysus answers our prayers and protects us."

I remembered Messalina and Silius being married by a priest

of Dionysus. He definitely did not protect them, but I didn't want to question the boy's faith. The gods aren't perfect. A deep voice boomed down the pipes.

"Who's that?" whispered Cassius.

"That's Hercules, son of Jupiter. Claudius claims that he's an emperor, and people worship him, so he should get the chance to appeal to the other gods, and let him join them."

"Hercules, is he the strong one who did the twelve labours? I've heard the stories."

"That's right."

Muffled voices came from above.

"What's happening now?"

"Claudius is talking to the gods about how powerful he was as emperor, and how well he ruled."

"Do you think he's a god?"

"I hope not. I was in the palace the night he died. He might want revenge on me." That was a massive understatement. Claudius' doctor Xenophon had died soon after his patient, and if Claudius was a god, and found out from Xenophon's spirit who had suggested the medicine that killed him, I was doomed.

From above, trumpets sounded again.

"What's going on?"

"This is where the Emperor Augustus comes in. He was the first emperor who became a god."

"What's he saying?"

"He's listing Claudius' crimes, like killing his wife."

"That's horrible."

"He didn't do it. His servant Narcissus claimed he ordered it, and the soldiers believed him, so they killed her."

"So why does Augustus say he did?"

"The play is a lie, to condemn Claudius and commend Nero."

"But that's wrong! People will watch the play and believe it!

THE DRUID AND THE ELEPHANT

Why did the play's writer tell lies? If I tell lies, I get beaten."

"The Emperor's wife hated the playwright, Seneca, and had him exiled. She thought Seneca was plotting against her. This is his revenge."

From above, the voices of a dozen actors boomed, "No!"

"That's the gods rejecting Claudius. So Mercury takes him to Hades."

"When do I play my drum?"

"Soon. Wait until he meets the ghosts."

The smell of smoke was getting stronger. From above a voice cried "Welcome, my Emperor!"

"Who's that?"

"Narcissus. He's introducing the ghosts of all the people Claudius killed."

"Tell me when to start drumming."

"In a bit, the list of victims is long."

Above, Narcissus was naming the ghosts. People I had known, waiting in the underworld for their killer. Messalina, Silius her lover, Mnester the actor, the garden owner Asiaticus, and many more, ending with Pompeius. I shivered. Would I end up in the underworld like Claudius? How many ghosts were waiting for me there? Hundreds? Thousands? How many more would I kill? Camulodunum was about to fall, and battle with Suetonius was inevitable. Blood would run like a river. If I died, would Baduhenna or the druid gods come to the underworld to save me from the ghosts of my victims?

Claudius spoke from above, "Friends everywhere, upon my word! How did you all get here?"

To this Pompeius answered, "What, cruel man? How did we get here? You sent us. You! The murderer of all the friends you ever had!"

"Now!" I told Cassius, and blew my carnyx with all my might.

The haunting wail of the carnyx and the thunder of Cassius' drum roll echoed through the pipes. From above I heard screams and the sound of running feet. I drew breath and sounded the war-horn again, raising the note to a petrifying squeal I hadn't heard since the last Battle of the Camulodunum, when Caratacus fought Claudius. If I'd been in the theatre, I'd have fled, too.

From behind us came a loud cracking, followed by an enormous thud. The Statue of Victory must have fallen. Then there was a roar, and we were hit, first by a blast of smoke, then by a wall of water as the roof of the main drain collapsed. Our flaming logs went out, and we were plunged into darkness and churning icy water. Liquid blasted up the pipes to the theatre, and then washed back, sucking us towards the main drain. It tumbled me through the blackness, like plummeting to the underworld. Was this Claudius' divine revenge?

I grabbed Cassius and held him tight until we came to where the drains joined. The water was blocked there and sloshed around. I found my feet and lifted our heads out. Cassius was coughing and sobbing.

"Sssh," I calmed him. "It's all right. We're still alive. We can get out of this. Are you hurt?" I felt him shake his head. He was clinging to me with his legs tight around my waist.

"We're going to walk back up the drain and find my carnyx. I'm going to blow a signal for help. My friends will come and get us out. Alright?"

Again I felt him nod.

"Climb round onto my back, so I can use my hands." I helped him move, and then we waded back up the drain, feeling with my feet for the sunken horn. I found it near the pipes, and felt it over. It was a bit dented, but not badly. I put it to my lips and sent out the emergency request for help in Roman signaller's code. Eppilus and Trenus would recognise it if they heard it.

We waited. Nothing.

I counted a hundred heartbeats, and blew again.

Nothing.

For ages I blew, waited for an answer, then blew again.

No reply. Cassius was shaking with cold. I held him tight to share my warmth, and blew again. I touched the amulet and the war crown, and blew once more.

It felt like forever, but eventually Trenus' voice echoed down the pipes.

"Caz, you down there?"

"Yes, with Cassius."

"Are you alright?"

"The boy's cold. Drop some hot food down."

"Will do. I'll organise a digging party."

Romans still patrolled the streets and the square, so Trenus had to get a wagon for cover, take it to the square, position it over our drain, and dig down to us. Fortunately, with half the population trying to flee, the Romans had other things on their minds, and they ignored the broken vehicle. It took all night, but Trenus and Bitucus' men dug us out as dawn was breaking, and Cassius flew into Roscius' arms. Ganna was there. She hugged me, then beat her fists on my chest and ordered me not to do such a stupid thing ever again. I was only saved from a severe bruising by alarms from the north of the square, and a shout of "Boudicca is coming! Run for your lives!"

"Quick," I ordered Roscius, "show us to the temple roof. We need to see what's happening."

He led us into the theatre, up past the highest seating, and onto the roof. From there we had a good view of the city. In the early morning light, Boudicca's horsemen and chariots emerged from the trees across the river to the north of the town. Horns were sounding the alarm, and in the city, soldiers were hastening to the walls.

"Who are they?" I asked Ganna.

"The Procurator's guard."

"Catus Decianus' men? Where is he?"

"Londinium. He's too scared of Boudicca to come himself. This revolt is his fault. If Boudicca captures him, she'll skin him alive."

I watched as their commander deployed his forces. One century ran through the north gate and down to the bridge, where they formed up to block Boudicca's forces from crossing the river. The second century took up position spread along the walls, and the rest of the troops, the wing of cavalry, formed up in the square next to the Temple of Claudius as a mobile reserve. Although from their round shields and chainmail they appeared to be auxiliaries, it seemed that their commander knew his business.

"Boudicca's going to attack," I warned. "We need to be ready to seize the gates and open them for her."

"All's ready," replied Eppilus. "While you were in that hole, our scouts told us Boudicca was coming. Ganna's forces are hiding in the buildings by the walls. We just need to time our attack right. If Boudicca can't get across that bridge, this may turn into a siege."

On the bridge, the Romans had formed up, blocking the crossing with a hedge of spears. They were about a hundred paces from the town, well within range of protective archers on the walls. Boudicca's army had halted further up the road. As I watched, dozens of chariots emerged from the flanks and took up positions about sixty paces from the bridge, just out of pila-throwing range of the soldiers there, and too far from the walls for the archers. They stopped. That was odd. Normal tactics were for the chariots to charge forwards and the warriors to jump off into combat. But the chariots wheeled away from the bridge. The warriors were just standing in them, wearing big cloaks, with their hands on their hips. What was going on?

A horn sounded, and Boudicca's cavalry charged. I couldn't believe what I was seeing. This was tactical insanity. The bridge was too narrow, the ranks of Romans too deep to penetrate, and the Roman spears would scare the horses to a halt!

As the cavalry built up speed, the warriors in the chariots suddenly moved. They whipped aside their cloaks to reveal ballistas mounted in the chariots. As the cavalry thundered onto the bridge, the ballistas shot. The heavy bolts ripped into the Roman infantry, driving through shields and chainmail. Men were knocked to the ground, spears fell, and the formation disintegrated. Boudicca's cavalry trampled the corpses and charged up the road towards the city walls.

"Signal the attack," I cried. Ganna grabbed the Horn of Cernunnos from Trenus and blew the opening notes of Baduhenna's war chant. Figures burst from the building by the walls and assaulted the gate. Taken by surprise, the auxiliaries there were outnumbered and overwhelmed. The gates were thrown open, and Boudicca's cavalry charged in. Seeing this, the rest of her forces flooded across the bridge and followed. The Romans on the walls couldn't get to the gate in enough numbers to re-take it, and their commander blew the retreat signal. They clambered down and ran to the Temple of Claudius. The Roman cavalry reserve galloped forwards to protect them. Boudicca's forces outnumbered them, but they managed to cover the retreat to give the infantry time to run. Boudicca's cavalry chased them, cutting down the stragglers, but most made it to the protection of the stone building, and slammed the door. The Roman cavalry galloped off towards the east gate.

It wasn't long before Boudicca herself drove into the square, surrounded by cheering warriors. Following her was another chariot with two men I recognised, Dervalon and Caicer. I gave them a blast with my horn, and they beckoned me down.

As we walked from the theatre, Boudicca's horsemen parted to make a path to her. The Queen waited in her chariot, her long red hair streaming in the wind, face elated in victory.

"My Queen," I said, "this is Ganna, High Priestess of the War Goddess Baduhenna. It was her people who opened the gates."

"You have done well, Priestess. You have my gratitude."

"Thank you, my Queen. I ask only that you spare Baduhenna's temple, my people, and their homes. Each is marked with the symbol of the club of Hercules."

"So be it. Pass the word," ordered Boudicca.

Ganna nodded and stepped back.

"Now, destroy every Roman thing in the city," ordered Boudicca. She pointed at a bronze statue of the emperor Nero, which stood in front of the temple. "Start with that. Rip it down and cut its head off. Caicer, sacrifice it to Andraste. Dervalon, surround the temple and work out how to kill all those inside." She addressed me. "Druid, the Ninth legion will be here tomorrow or the day after. Devise a plan to beat them." She mounted her chariot and galloped off.

I nodded to Eppilus. "Let's go and find Lukon. I bet he's with those ballistas."

He nodded. "I'll get the horses." He ran off.

"What will you do?" I asked Ganna.

"Protect my people and my temple," she replied. "Bring Lukon to me there, I haven't seen him for years. I'd like to catch up with him."

Caicer's men were standing around the statue of Nero, discussing how to knock it down. The sight of the young emperor brought back memories.

"Do you miss Rome?" asked Ganna.

"I miss the people. I miss my friends, and I miss Micipsa." I glanced around at the corpses and destruction. "But it's a lot safer here."

"Safer! But you almost got killed last night! What if I had told Cassie about you, and next day you died!"

"That was just bad luck. In Rome, people were actively trying to kill me. A lot happened after you left. Remember you dreamed of the ugliest animal? You were right, I met it in a race to the death. I'll tell you later. What about you, do you miss it?"

"I miss the temple, the priestesses, friends like Melanipa and Surus. I don't miss the politics. I heard that Agrippina's dead?"

"Yes, I was there. She's gone. You're safe from her."

"Is it safe for us to go back?"

"For you, probably. For me, it depends on what happens here. If the Romans find out what I'm doing here, they'll hunt me down. A lot depends on Melanipa."

"Melanipa! I've dreamed of her fighting in a great battle. Is she here?"

"I found her when we took a Roman fort. I couldn't let her be killed, so I called down from the fort walls and persuaded her to meet with the Queen. She escaped before I could talk to her face-to-face. I don't know if she recognised me."

"Where is she now?"

"Probably with the Ninth. Or with Suetonius. I'm not sure where she went."

Eppilus arrived with the horses, and I swung up into the saddle.

"Want to climb up and I'll take you back to the temple?"

"I have to see Roscius and Bitucus. I'll see you later."

"Be careful. Don't walk the streets alone."

"Baduhenna protects me. See you at the temple."

That night, we took Lukon to see Ganna. We sat around chatting, and Eppilus asked him about how he got here.

"I had to travel faster than the Ninth's infantry, so when another group of Teuhant's tribe arrived with more chariots, I persuaded them to drive me down here. I let them have some fun shooting the ballistas, then suggested it would be even more fun with live targets. They wanted to be here when the city fell, for the loot, so we rushed to make it in time."

"How did you get the idea to put the ballistas on chariots?" asked Trenus.

"I remembered Nero's games when he became emperor, and the wild animal chariot race. Sitting in the stands, watching Caz fighting, I thought of putting ballista on his chariot. I've had the idea in the back of my mind ever since then. I call it a carroballista."

"Tell Ganna the story. She hasn't heard it," said Trenus. So I told them of how Ganna's dream came true.

26

MADDENED BEASTS

The Romans love their games and sports, and the sport Nero loved above all else was chariot racing. When he became Emperor, of course he wanted the best chariot race ever. It had to have the fastest, biggest, most dangerous animals in Rome, and the biggest was Micipsa.

Centurion Gamus called me in to his office. 'You're riding Micipsa, not Surus,' he told me. 'This is going to get violent. Our spies have heard rumours of a lion chariot. You've fought lions before, Surus hasn't. So keep him out of it.'

'Yes, Sir.'

'These are the rules. Number one, no armour, for you or the elephant. Number two, no weapons. You're only allowed a knife for cutting the reins, and a whip for encouraging the animals to go faster. Rule three, it's a seven-lap race. The Circus Maximus is about a thousand paces per lap, so don't go off at a sprint and tire Micipsa out. Rule four, to win, you and your animal must cross the finishing line with your chariot. Questions?'

'Do we know what the other teams will be, Sir?'

'No, but we can guess based on what we've seen at the games before.'

'Wolves, aurochs, and lions.'

'There are twelve starting gates. If I was organising this, I wouldn't want any to be empty.'

'What about the chariot, Sir?'

'To make the race fair, and to prevent trickery like blades on the wheel-hubs, all competitors will get the same chariots, just adapted to your animal. The quartermaster is making one for you now to practise with, but the race one might be different. Any more questions?'

'Not at the moment, Sir.'

'Any race with lions and wolves in it is going to involve bloodshed. You're a warrior, shedding blood is what you're good at. Let me be clear. You are riding the Emperor's animal, in his first big public games of his reign. You'll be on the biggest, strongest animal there. The Emperor expects you to win. You are also the standard bearer of the Germanii. For our reputation and honour, nothing less than victory will do, by Hercules! In short, win or die trying!'

'Yes, Sir.'

'Then good luck. Do us proud.'

'Yes, Sir.'

'Dismissed.'

Melanipa, who was in Rome with her mother to swear Sarmatian allegiance to the new emperor, visited me on the evening before the race. An experienced wild animal hunter, she talked me through the likely animal opponents, their strengths and their weaknesses.

'People are betting on the race. Some guess there will be bears, and they're the best combination of speed, strength and ferocity. Some are betting on you, but others say elephants are too slow. Top of the betting now is the lions. If the charioteer cuts one or two loose, watch out for them. You don't have a lance.'

'Micipsa killed one with his tusks in Vinicius' garden.'

'Micipsa can only face one way at one time. Lions hunt in prides. Keep an eye out behind you.'

'I will.'

'Have you still got Ganna's amulet?'

'Here.' I touched my chest.

'Good. The priestesses at Baduhenna's temple are praying for you. Ganna told me she dreamed of you in a big battle, so your life can't end in a mere chariot race. You're going to be fine. Now go and get some sleep. You need to be on top of your game tomorrow.'

On the day of the race, a squad of Germanii cavalry escorted Micipsa and me to the Circus Maximus. Gamus was taking no chances, and racing fans had been known to ambush their opponents on the way to the competition before. Sure enough, there was a fire-breather in the crowds lining the street. He was just about to blow flames at us when one of our plain-clothes lads stabbed him in the back of the knee. He collapsed backwards, coughing, and set himself on fire. Micipsa's battle training paid off, and he calmly ignored it. I chuckled all the way to the arena.

The race was the highlight of the day, and was scheduled last, in late afternoon. That would give the cleanup crews all night to remove the corpses, I thought, then stopped myself. Thinking like that would get me killed. I had killed a whale before. I could do this.

The starting stalls are at the north-west side of the Circus Maximus. The attendants met me at the gates, and guided me to my stall. Some of the other competitors were already there. In stall one, to my surprise, was a giraffe. I had seen lions hunt giraffe in the arena before, and knew they have a vicious kick, but a pride can pull them down.

In stall two was a team of four zebras. They were wearing

blinkers to calm them down, but shifted around nervously. Zebras are almost untameable, and they would be hard to control, especially if they smelled lion.

A pair of camels stood chewing in stall three. Camels are never happy, and these two were no exception. Being African, they would be afraid of lions.

The next stall held war dogs. Their ears came up to my waist, and they growled when they saw Micipsa. Fortunately, they were not allowed their usual armour and spikes, but they were still fast and dangerous.

I laughed when I peered into stall five. A team of four ostriches, with their heads in bags, were jerking their heads around in confusion. I knew they were fast, and I'd seen one disembowel a dog with its claws, but they are still comical birds.

In the stall next to ours was a pair of bull aurochs. Although only half Micipsa's height, they had vicious horns that could do us severe damage.

We were shown into our stall, and the chariot was brought in and fastened to Micipsa's harness. It was a light, open racing chariot, with no protection from fangs or claws. I climbed in and sorted out the reins, which led from Micipsa's tusks back to me.

The stalls are like tunnels, and once you are in you cannot see what's in the others. But, twisting around, I watched the animals that passed behind us on their way to further stalls. They were mostly carnivores. First were a pair of tigers. That was worrying. I had seen a tiger jump over an arena wall and into the crowd before, and they were just as dangerous as lions. Next was a pair of bears, and after them, half a dozen cheetahs. The next animal was what Ganna had predicted, the ugliest animal I had ever seen. It was a hippo. It had massive teeth, and seemed totally unconcerned with the smell of tigers and bears. It did pause to breathe in Micipsa's scent, and shuffled a little away. I had only seen one in the arena once before, savaging a crocodile.

Finally came the lions. I was slightly relieved. In his quest for magnificence, Nero had chosen four males, large and dark-maned. I had seen lions in the arena before, and it's the females who are the main hunters. Four males might be persuaded to turn on each other.

Before the race it was time for the runner's parade. It did not go as planned. For chariot races the teams walk round side-by-side, but having zebras go side-by-side with lions was obviously not going to work, so this parade was one by one. The giraffe went first, tall and stately. After fifty paces it must have come into view of the lions, and one roared. The giraffe panicked, and burst into a run. It got to the far end of the oval course, and refused to return.

Next were the zebras. They too had heard the roar, and with alarmed brays, galloped from their stall along the sandy track. After two hundred paces they saw they weren't being chased, and calmed down.

With a hideous groaning the camels followed. Camels are fast, and they soon caught up with the other animals. The war dogs were next. I counted eight of them, in four pairs, like the cheetahs. They were well-controlled, and as a team appeared worryingly competent.

The ostriches were a disaster. The birds didn't want to go in the same direction, and started pecking each other. The circus staff had to re-hood them, and drag them around the track with halters round their heads.

The bulls and the hippo ambled forward, and plodded round the track. The charioteers tried whipping them, but they stopped and gave them an evil glare, then plodded on. They only picked up speed when Micipsa and I emerged, and they decided that they had better keep their distance from us. We were the best of the beasts so far: Micipsa was magnificent, stately, controlled, used to crowds from his many parades, and the pride of the Germanii. The rich and powerful in their seats at the front applauded. However, the poor and the plebs at the back of the stands were not so happy. They remembered Micipsa from the riot outside the palace, and rumours of his involvement in the deaths of popular personalities, such as Asiaticus and Vinicius. I stood in the chariot and saluted as I drove past the Emperor and his mother. Caratacus and his family were nearby, standing with Seneca as a demonstration of Nero's mercy.

The carnivores followed us. The giraffe was still at the far turn, refusing to move, but when the lion chariot appeared and advanced towards it, the animal realised that the only way to put distance between itself and them was back up the far straight, and it took off at a gallop. Eventually we all got round and back into the stalls, but it took a lot longer than expected, and the sun was dropping in the sky, casting long shadows over the course.

A hush fell over the crowd. Nero was a tiny figure in the distance. He raised a purple cloth, paused dramatically, then dropped it. Trumpets sounded, the gates sprang open, and we were off.

Fastest out were the cheetahs, but it didn't last long. Cheetahs are sprinters, and for them the chariot was heavy. Before they got to the first turn the lions had caught them up. Lions hate cheetahs, Melanipa had told me, and hunt them in the wild. They didn't stand a chance. The lions leaped on them, used their weight to pin them down, and savaged them to death. The crowd roared its approval, Nero cheering with the best of them. This was the spectacle he wanted. I decided to give them another.

The lions and tigers were my deadliest enemies, and here was a chance. In Roman chariot racing, a little pushing and shoving is all part of the sport. I guided Micipsa parallel to the hippo, and as we approached the lions, who were still mauling the cheetahs, I pulled Micipsa to the left and shoulder-barged it. It swerved, heading straight for the lions. The crowd gasped. The hippo sighted the lions and cheetahs, and got angry. It lowered its head, yellow teeth protruding. The lion and cheetah charioteers slashed their reins and jumped out of the way. The hippo smashed into the chariots and trampled the lions and cheetahs on the right side. Its own chariot smashed into the wreckage, and the harness broke, leaving the hippo free. It ran off, dragging the charioteer by the reins. He wisely slid along until he was well past the lions, then cut the reins and ran for the safety of the central divider.

I was now at the back of the field. Micipsa rounded the southeast corner and headed back up the track. I squinted ahead and saw the bears were in the lead, followed by the war dogs and the zebra. Elephants can run as fast as a human, but nowhere near the speed of the other animals in the race. They were turning the corner to complete the first lap, and I was only halfway along the straight, passing the Egyptian obelisk, when the first bronze dolphin lap counter flipped.

When I rounded the turn, the others were way ahead, but as they approached the lions and cheetahs, things changed. One of the lions that had dodged the hippo was free, and snarling. The bears and war dogs gave it a wide berth, but its instincts told it that zebra were food. It leaped onto the left-hand member of the team, grabbed it by the throat, and the whole team swerved as it was dragged along. They hit the central divider, and crashed over it into the central drainage canal.

That gave me an idea. I slowed Micipsa, and did what I had seen my father do at the Battle of the Medway, so many years ago. I edged forwards in the chariot, ran forward up the pole along Micipsa's side, then scrambled up the harness onto his neck. From there, above all but the giraffe, I had a much better view. We sped up again, and I guided him toward the cheetahs. One of the lions was savaging a survivor, so I leaned down and whipped him. He sprang away, and Micipsa trumpeted, so he ran off back the way we had come.

I was way behind the others now. Rounding the bottom turn, I looked back up the course. To my dismay, the leaders were at the other end of the track. The tigers, which are ambush predators, were tiring, as were the bears. The ostriches were in the lead, and came around the turn at a good speed, only to find themselves face to face with the lion going the other way. They tried to swerve, but not being used to towing a chariot, and already turning to get round the corner, it was a risky thing to do. Being long-legged and heavy-bodied, they toppled, squawking, to the sand, and the lion leaped on them. The charioteer cut himself free, and ran for the central divider.

Lap two, and nearly half my opponents were out. But I was still last. I urged Micipsa onwards. Behind the ostriches was the giraffe. It saw the birds being eaten by the lion, got frightened, and skidded to a halt. The aurochs, right behind it, had too much speed and weight to stop, crashed through the flimsy chariot, and hit the giraffe's rear legs. I heard them snap over the noise of the crowd, and the beast collapsed backwards onto the aurochs' chariot, smashing it just as the driver jumped clear.

The camels, dogs, tigers and bears saw the wreckage as they took the corner, slowed down and avoided it, but it delayed them. Time for my next plan.

We continued up the course, and as I rounded the same corner, the setting sun shone in my eyes. I pulled Micipsa to a halt in the shadow of the stand. The other charioteers were now down at the far end of the track, dust clouded the air from the crashes, and none of the racers saw us stop. They came running back up, rounded the corner into the sun, and Micipsa charged them. Just like ostriches, camels are long-legged, and top heavy. They don't corner well at the best of times, and seeing an elephant coming the other way, they lost it completely, and smashed into the wall. The bears were right behind them, and gripping the sand with their long claws, they managed to turn tightly, but not tightly enough to avoid the lion eating an ostrich in the middle of the track. Bears are not used to lions, and maybe don't see them as anything more than a big cat. To lions, however, anything smaller than a hippo is prey, and it jumped on them. The charioteer tried to whip the lion off, and it went for him. The bears ran off, and Micipsa and I charged the lion. It backed off, and Micipsa picked up the charioteer and threw him over the wall into the stands.

End of lap three, and only two opponents left, the tigers and the dogs. But they were over a lap ahead of me, heading down the track and nearing the far turn. How was I going to stop them? I clutched Ganna's amulet and prayed for inspiration. As the dogs reached the far end of the course, another lap marker was tipped. Each time a lap was completed, one more bronze dolphin's head was pulled down by a rope. Then I realised what the gods were trying to tell me.

I jumped down from Micipsa's back, took one end of the rein from his tusk and tied it to the gilded column on the central barrier that marked the turning point. Then I ran back to the camel chariot by the wall, and looped the rein around a wheel, then to Micipsa's tusk. I just managed to climb back up on his head when the dogs rounded the corner. Micipsa pulled the rein, and it rose from the sand to make a trip rope. The first dogs jumped it, but the ones at the back didn't see it in time, and went sprawling. They were dragged forward by the front dogs, but not fast enough. Under the chariot between the wheels they went, and were dragged behind. The charioteer slashed their harness, and he was down to four dogs. They were too slow. We dropped the rein, chased them down, and Micipsa got his tusks under the chariot, picked it up, then dumped it in the canal. Only the tigers left.

I checked around. The tigers were waiting at the bend. The charioteer had decided that the running had gone out of his beasts, and he was resting them in preparation for the fight. He cut one of them free, and it advanced towards us. Tigers and elephants are old enemies, and many tiger hunters have been killed by the predators leaping up to claw them down to the ground. I drew my knife, then thought of a better idea.

I reversed Micipsa back to the ostriches, the tiger following. The bird's neck had been half eaten by the lion, which ran off as we approached, and the smell of blood filled the air. We backed further away, and the tiger had to walk past the dead bird to get to us. It stopped, smelled the blood, tasted it, and as we backed further away, settled down to eat. Slowly and gently I guided Micipsa to the edge of the track, around the tiger, and then round the bend towards the tiger chariot. The charioteer knew that with only one animal pulling, he was going to be too slow, and as we charged him he jumped off and ran for the central divider. Micipsa soon caught up with the tiger and its chariot, and stomped the chariot into the dust.

"As a druid," said Ganna, "I'm horrified at the killing of all those animals. As a priestess of Baduhenna, I'm proud that my acolytes' prayers kept you safe. But we need to think about the here and now. Boudicca wants you to come up with a plan. What are you going to do?"

"I have a plan. All that we need, I learned that day. The Gods have used this temple and this memory to remind me. Tomorrow we crush the Ninth."

That night I dreamed I was on Micipsa, running round and round Camulodunum, pursued by Amergin and swarms of angry bees. I woke up sweating, and did not fall asleep until dawn.

Next morning Ganna, Eppilus, Trenus, Lukon and I went to see Dervalon. The war leader was in Boudicca's command tent with Caicer the druid. His pine marten was eating scraps again. "How am I going to feed this army?" Dervalon demanded, pulling his beard. "More tribesmen arrive every day. I need food for tens of thousands, for at least a month!"

"It's market day tomorrow," Ganna told him. "Most of the people of the city are dead or have fled. I can show you where the Romans kept the taxes. Use them to pay the drovers for their herds and the farmers for their crops."

"Excellent!" He looked at me. "Tell me your plan is as good as that one!"

"I can beat the Ninth, and get the Romans out of the temple, but you need to buy the animals for me first. Don't worry, you can eat them later."

"Tell me your plan."

"To get the Romans out of the temple, we'll use bees. The front of the temple has columns and a door, but the back is solid stone. Use siege ladders, climb up, take some tiles off the roof, and drop in some hives. The Romans can either stay and get stung by thousands of angry bees, or come out and fight. If they stay, set fire to the roof beams. Eventually the roof tiles will come crashing down on their heads."

He nodded. "Good idea. As for buying the animals, what's

that about?"

I explained, and a grin slowly spread over his face.

The Ninth legion, or what was left of it, arrived the next day. From my hiding place on top of the theatre, I spotted their scouts in the trees north of the river. To them, the city must have seemed strange. The road down to the bridge was clear, the bridge was undefended, and the road up to the north gate was unobstructed. The gate itself was closed. From behind the walls, plumes of smoke rose from burning buildings.

Soon sounds of chopping echoed from the woods, then the infantry emerged, carrying a battering ram and siege ladders. They marched across the bridge, screened by cavalry, and took cover along the southern river bank. Their commander, Cerialis, nodded to his Cornicen, who sounded the attack. The infantry charged forwards across the hundred paces between the river and the city walls.

I blew my carnyx, and its mournful cry echoed across the countryside. In the distance, strange sounds seemed to answer. Our warriors on the wall stood up, and raised the ballistas into place on small towers, like we had done at Durobrivae. They shot at the infantry burdened with the battering ram. Many fell as heavy bolts penetrated shields and armour, but more took their place.

A soft thundering sound came from the distance. The Roman assault teams reached the walls and lifted the ladders. Our men on the wall shoved them away with spears. Their cavalry took out slings and bows and started shooting at our spearmen.

The soft thundering grew louder. Roman infantry were climbing ladders, their comrades holding the bottom to make them difficult to push away. Across the river, one of Cerialis's scouts ran up to him and pointed to the west, where a cloud of dust was rising. The commander shaded his eyes, then snapped an order to the Cornicen. He raised his cornu, and sounded the retreat.

The infantry were half way up the ladders. They glanced back in astonishment, and then looked right, upstream. The thundering grew louder. They started to climb down, and the lower ones jumped. But too late.

A herd of cattle, led by the biggest bulls, rounded the corner of the city walls at full speed, herded by the drovers and Boudicca's cavalry. There were hundreds of them. They filled the area between the river and the walls with a torrent of bovine flesh. Like the aurochs in the Circus Maximus, they were unstoppable. The infantry ran for the bridge and the river, but it was too far, and they were trampled by a thousand stampeding feet. Those on the ladders fell as our warriors pushed them down, and were swept away in a tide of horns and hooves. Our cavalry speared any survivors. The Roman cavalry who had crossed the river fled, pursued by ballista bolts.

On the far side of the river, Cerialis sat helplessly on his horse as his infantry was destroyed before his eyes and his cavalry disappeared. Eventually his Cornicen spoke to him, and they cantered off to the east.

We had a grand feast that night, and just as Queen Boudicca was toasting our victory, a messenger burst in.

"We found Suetonius! He's ahead of us! He'll be in Londinium before us!"

27

Shipwreck

"War chiefs, to my command tent," ordered Boudicca. We followed her out, and Ganna and I slipped in amongst them.

Her tent was crowded, each of the tribes represented by their leaders, along with Dervalon and Caicer.

"Well?" demanded the Queen. "How did Suetonius get ahead of us?"

The messenger spoke up. "He's split his army. The cavalry have gone ahead and the infantry are following behind."

"How many cavalry? How many infantry?"

"About ten thousand altogether. Half are cavalry, a few from the legions, but mostly auxiliaries. The infantry are mostly legionaries from the Fourteenth and Twentieth."

"Dervalon, what do you think?"

"We've got them on the run," he replied. "Londinium isn't a military base, it's a trading port. The defences are worse than here. We can just follow them down, overwhelm the town, then turn on the infantry. Suetonius may even simply go through Londinium and head for the south coast, and sail away Gaul."

"Caicer?" asked the Queen.

"Same," the druid replied. "Let's keep our plans simple. Some of our warriors, like Teuhant's men, are experienced, but a lot of them are untried in battle. Best not try anything complicated."

"Teuhant?" she enquired.

"I see danger. If the Romans get to Londinium a few days before us, they can build defences. It's not a big place, and with five thousand troops they can put up walls and dig trenches. They can hold us off until their infantry arrive and attack us from behind. I've fought their infantry before, and most of Caratacus's men paid for it with their lives. We need magic. Magic like we saw here today. Cerialis' infantry were destroyed, and we lost no-one." Teuhant pointed at me. "We need his magic. I saw it work at Durobrivae. I saw it work here. The gods of war give him victory. Let him do it again."

Suddenly I was the centre of attention and expectation. But magic takes thought, care, and preparation.

"I'm merely a channel for the gods," I said. "I pray to them for guidance, and they send me signs." I played for time, to give the gods a chance. "Pray with me now. Druid Caicer, will you say the words, while we open our minds to their divine message?"

Caicer nodded, and everyone bowed their heads in silence while he called upon Andraste. I touched my war crown and prayed to the war gods Toutatis, Belatucadros and Cocidius. Ganna would be praying to Baduhenna.

There was silence, broken only by the distant cawing of seagulls. Tuneless birds, almost as bad as ravens.

When the prayer was finished, Boudicca looked at me. "Well?"

"The gods have spoken to me of the sea. Down-river from here is a port for supplying the city. We can raid it, seize the ships, and fill them with infantry. Sail south, then up the Thames, and attack Londinium from the east. If we catch the right tides we can beat Suetonius there. If not, he will build defences in the north of the city first, because that's where he expects us to attack. The other walls will be weak. Our cavalry can assault from the north, and we will catch him between two forces. To stop his infantry, we can use Lukon's ballistas. They proved their worth at the bridge here. Lukon can use the same hit-and-run tactics that the Parthians used to beat the Romans: charge into range, shoot, and get out before the enemy can counter-attack. As long as he has bolts, he can whittle them down. They'll need to carry their injured, because they won't want to leave them for us to kill. That will slow them down even further. If we can charge herds of cattle into them, so much the better."

Boudicca narrowed her eyes and regarded me suspiciously.

"You just want to get to Londinium first so you can save the civilians. I want to terrify the Romans so they never set foot on these shores again. Your soft heart invites them back. I won't have you leading my warriors."

Ganna stepped forwards. "I will command," she said. "As High Priestess of the war goddess Baduhenna, I will make sure that rivers of blood flow in her honour. The Thames will turn red, and corpses will wash up on the shores of Gaul to terrify the Romans."

Boudicca nodded approvingly. "Get the horses. We have a port to raid."

The next afternoon, Ganna and I stood at the prow of a captured Roman galley, rowed by ex-slaves that we had freed, fed, and offered the riches of Londinium as the spoils of war. Seagulls wheeled around us, as if guiding our ship to battle.

"You said that Agrippina was dead, and you were there," said Ganna. "What happened?"

So I told her of the death of the most powerful woman in the world.

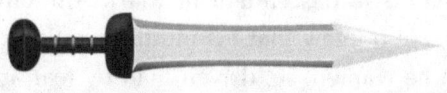

Seneca and Pallas's plot, that I had overheard outside the Mausoleum of Augustus, was to seduce Nero with an unsuitable woman, so causing a rift between him and his mother, allowing them to push her out of power. The plan worked at first, but then got totally out-of-hand.

The woman they chose was a freed slave from the east, named Acte. Nero fell in love with her, but when Agrippina found out, she was enraged. Nero wanted to marry Acte, but he was already married to Claudius' daughter Octavia. Agrippina was a noble, and for her son to want to divorce his illustrious wife, in favour of an ex-slave, was outrageous.

'Britannicus would make a better emperor than you!' she raged at him. Nero, his fragile young imperial dignity hurt, and a competitor revealed, had Britannicus poisoned at dinner, to the horror of Agrippina and Octavia. It removed that threat for him, but further soured relations with his mother. Octavia hated and feared him.

Claudius had given Agrippina the title of Augusta, and therefore she was entitled to her own bodyguard, which were taken from the Germanii. I was one of them. With all the enemies she had made, she needed protection. But there was one person who the Germanii couldn't protect her from.

Nero's relations with Agrippina got worse and worse. He exiled her from the palace to her villa in Misenum, on the bay overlooking Mount Vesuvius. He fired her ally Pallas from his job as treasurer, and deprived her of the powers that she held as Augusta. He also reduced her guard again and again, until I was the only one left.

There were rumours that she was part of a plot to replace him with Plautus, a descendant of Mark Anthony and Julius Caesar. Also, Nero knew that his mother would not let him be with women he wanted, so, driven mad by fear and desire, he decided to kill her.

Centurion Gamus sent me a coded letter, warning me that Nero was up to something. Three attempts to poison her were foiled by feeding her the antidote in advance. She ate the poisoned food and nothing happened, so Nero had the poisoner killed for incompetence, and decided to try something different. Therefore, when Agrippina called me in to her residence one day, I was on the alert.

'The Emperor has invited me to visit him in his palace at Baiae,' she told me happily. 'We will go there by ship tomorrow.'

That was a shock. Didn't she know? Wasn't she suspicious? Later, I got hold of the invitation letter from her secretary. It was polite, saying he regretted how things had become between them, and would like to make it up to her by throwing a dinner party in her honour. I found that very hard to believe.

The dinner party went well, and no-one tried to poison her. But as we were leaving, we were informed that there had been an accident down at the docks, her galley had been damaged, and that Nero would lend her one of his own ships to take us home. I don't believe in coincidences, and was sure it was a trap. But the dinner had gone well, and lulled her into a false sense of security, so she accepted the offer of Nero's vessel.

We boarded, and as we put out to sea, I escorted her and her friend the Lady Acerronia to the canopied command seat on the upper aft deck. I was on edge, and unarmoured, so I kept my hand on my sword and her within arm's length. I checked fore and aft, port and starboard, but no other ships were near. Above were only the sails and stars. I should have been more careful. Half way across the bay I was gazing at the distant lights of Pompeii when I heard a cracking noise from above me, and ducked just in time. The canopy collapsed with a tremendous thud, and we were only saved by the back of the seat holding it above us. The steersman beside me was crushed to death. It was a trap: a massively heavy canopy, made of lead. I struggled to extricate us, and when we finally emerged, we found that the crew had abandoned ship and the vessel was sinking fast. They must have scuttled it to hide the crime.

We crouched at the aft rail, and I shrugged off my cloak. Distant lights from luxury villas twinkled in the darkness. I had been trained to swim in full armour, but my companions were not warriors.

'Disrobe,' the Empress commanded Acerronia, stepping out of her gown.

'But I can't swim!' sobbed the lady.

'Find us something that floats,' the Empress commanded me.

I searched around, but the only things I found were the cushions from the Empress' chair, which held lots of air, but would soon get soaked and sink. With my sword, I cut bits out of the sail and wrapped them up to make flotation devices, like the Roman infantry had used to cross the Medway long ago. We slipped into the water and swam for the coastline.

The ship sank behind us, and the crew rowed their boat back to search the area for our bodies. Acerronia was struggling, and I was worried that she would give us away with her splashing around. As she tired, she lost hope of making it to shore, and decided that the treacherous crew were her only chance of survival.

'I am the Empress, save me!' she cried, and dog-paddled towards the boat. The rowers made towards her. But when they got to her, the crew bludgeoned her with the oars.

Agrippina and I stopped swimming, and floated silently in the darkness among the debris from the sunken vessel, hiding behind our flotation packs. The tide drifted us away, and we quietly swam off. It took hours, but the determination that had made Agrippina empress asserted itself, and we made our way towards the distant coast. Fortunately, the sea was calm and the water warm. When we arrived at the shore, Agrippina commandeered some horses from the surprised inhabitants of a nearby villa, and we rode back to her residence.

Her staff were shocked and horrified, but she gathered them together and addressed them.

'I hope it was an accident, and if not, I hope it was not the Emperor's doing. My life depends on it being one of those. Send a message to my son that by heaven's favour I have escaped a terrible disaster, and that I request that, even if he is worried about me, he visit me later, as for now I need to rest and recover.'

She paused, and sighed.

'But if it is as I fear, and his hand is behind this, I knew this night would come,' she told us. 'Years ago, I visited the astrologers, and they told me that my son would become emperor, and that he would kill me. I told them, "Let him do so, if that is the price I must pay." Now is the time that was prophesied. I will die with dignity. Ladies, prepare me to depart this world as befits an Augusta.'

She came to me and whispered, 'When the time comes, make it quick.'

'As you wish, Augusta.'

Nero sent a squad of marines, led by his naval commander, Anicetus, to kill her. They surrounded the house, broke down the gate, and massed outside her room. Agrippina's slave-girl opened the door, to reveal Anicetus, a captain, and a centurion of the marines.

'If you have come to see me,' said Agrippina, 'take back word that I have recovered, but if you are here to do a crime, I believe nothing about my son. He has not ordered his mother's murder.'

Her belief was soon proved wrong. The killers closed in on her. I did not get in their way. Nero was my emperor: my loyalty lay with him, not her. As Anicetus drew his sword, Agrippina drew herself up and commanded, 'Smite my womb.'

Anicetus stepped forwards and drove his blade into the source of her sorrows. As the sword went in, she gasped in agony. I swung my spear shaft, striking her on the back of the head. She died instantly.

The tide bore our ship up the Thames estuary, inexorably drawing us towards the destruction and death that was the fate of Londinium.

"What happened to you after Agrippina died?" asked Ganna. "Didn't Nero want all the witnesses silenced?"

"I was standard-bearer of the Germanii, and Nero didn't want to annoy us. I'd also saved his life twice, so he trusted me."

"Look," she said, pointing to a channel of silver-grey water on the left. "There's the Medway."

"Where we first met."

"We were on opposing sides. Now we fight together. It's better this way. I foresee a great battle. Baduhenna will bring us victory."

That night our ships landed us on the south shore of the Thames, opposite Londinium. The tide was in, and the river was about three hundred paces wide, so we couldn't be seen from the port. Each warrior made a flotation pack from sail cloth, stained it black with mud, and we swam the river and crept in through the docks. The buildings were unguarded, which was strange. No structures were allowed in the area around the walls, but piles of goods were stacked there. Obviously the rich merchants were bribing the guards to turn a blind eye. A military commander would have flogged those responsible, but Londinium was a civilian port.

We found a stack of lumber by the wall. It was oak, trimmed into beams. It might be a sign from the druid gods, but it might also be a trap. I touched the amulet, then sent the scouts forwards. They returned with good news: no guards were in sight, and the walls were unpatrolled. But where were Suetonius' five thousand men? I sent the scouts back with orders to go as far as the north walls if necessary, and watch out for a trap.

They were away for a long time, but creeping around quietly in the dark is a slow process, so I waited. Eventually, they returned.

"The only guards are on the north wall," said their leader. "No sign of cavalry, no patrols."

Maybe Suetonius hadn't reached the city yet. It might be a trap, but I couldn't dither, and we had to be ready to let Boudicca's cavalry in, so I made the decision to enter. I led my warriors forwards up the lumber pile, over the wall and into the city. All was quiet. We hid near the northern gates.

At dawn we heard the horns of our cavalry, so I blew the Horn of Cernunnos, and we assaulted the gates. To our surprise, they were practically unguarded, just a few old men who we easily swept aside. We threw them open, and the cavalry charged in unopposed. In the brightening light of day, we realised that the Romans weren't there at all. I grabbed a surviving gate guard.

"Where's Suetonius?" I demanded.

THE DRUID AND THE ELEPHANT

"Gone! He took everyone who could walk, and left."
"Where did he go?"
"They left from the west gate."

That meant he was on his way to Isca Dumnoniorum, to meet up with the Second Legion, and combine their forces against us. Their symbol is the god Mars. It seemed Ganna was right, this would be a battle between Baduhenna and the Roman god of war. I shoved the guard away, and went to find Boudicca.

28

Severed Heads

Boudicca was charging about in her chariot, setting fire to buildings and ordering executions. For an innocent civilian who had been abused, she had no problems doing the same to others. I doubted that her policy of butchery to scare the Romans from ever coming back to Britannia would work on Nero's advisors. Men like Burrus don't scare easily, and stoics like Seneca see death as inevitable. Her army was mostly an undisciplined rabble, and if Suetonius had seen them, he would have set an ambush and ripped them apart with his two legions. I went in search of more level heads.

I found Dervalon and Caicer in the town centre.

"One of the prisoners told me that Suetonius had been here, took all who could walk, and left by the west gate," I told them.

"Do you believe him?" asked Dervalon.

"Yes, but Suetonius isn't stupid. He wants us to think he's headed for Isca Dumnoniorum, but it's a long way, and our cavalry can catch him before he gets there. I believe he'll head back to his infantry. He'll go to Verulamium and collect the retired veterans who live there. Then he can either go west and meet the Second Legion at Corinium, or go further north and meet them at Venonis. He knows he can't run forever, so he'll collect all the forces he can, then find a good battleground for a final showdown. On his way down here from the Holy Isle, he'll have been keeping an eye out for suitable sites, and since that road runs through Venonis, I guess that's where he'll arrange to meet the Second."

"What do you propose?" he asked.

"First, we need to find out where he's gone. His army will leave a trail that our scouts can follow. If he's gone to Verulamium, Boudicca will want to sack it. We need to harry him: whittle down his forces with hit-and-run tactics. If he offers a battle, ignore it. Trap him and besiege him. Time and numbers are on our side. Next, we need to stop the Second Legion from joining him. I can take the ships from Camulodunum, add the ships from here, fill them with warriors, and sail around to Isca Dumnoniorum. Sailing is faster than walking. We can be there in a few days. We'll threaten the town, so that if the legion leaves, it will fall. Also, if we can convince their commander that Suetonius is already dead and his legions defeated, he will have no reason to leave."

"How are you going to manage that?" asked Caicer.

"Don't know yet. The gods will show me a way."

"What if Suetonius is really heading for Isca?" said Dervalon.

"I'll get there before him. I'll send scouts down the road to Londinium to warn me if he's coming. If he is, I can retreat to the ships and wait for you."

"How many men do you need?"

"The ships only have space for a thousand. But I'd rather take fewer men and more horses. Then, if the Second have left Isca already, I can send horsemen to find out where they are going, and to warn you."

Dervalon looked at Caicer, who nodded.

"Right," said Dervalon to me, "get the ships ready. I'll send you some cavalry who've sailed before. Tell me when you're ready to leave."

Four days later, we were prepared to set sail. Lukon, Trenus, and Eppilus had arrived with Boudicca's forces, and were coming with me. Lukon had moved his ballista chariots onto the ships, Trenus was fascinated by ships and wanted to come, and Eppilus was in charge of the horses. The steeds don't like sea voyages, and his expertise was vital for keeping them healthy for when we put ashore.

Ganna came down to the docks to see us.

"I can't come with you," she told us. "It's too far from Cassie, and the dreams of battle that Baduhenna sends me are not about the sea. Boudicca wants me to go with her to Verulamium."

"What do your dreams show you?" I asked.

"A huge battle, fields of corpses, me searching for you. I understand why Isca's important, but don't stay there long. That's not where fate leads you."

"Don't worry," said Eppilus with a grin, "we'll take care of him, and bring him back to you."

"Not just us," said Trenus. "The gods protect him. It was a miracle he survived the Parthian War. I was sure he was dead, and if I hadn't seen it with my own eyes, I wouldn't believe it. But here he is. Fate's not done with him yet. Or the gods."

"Why, what happened?" asked Ganna. So I told her the story of the saddest day of my army life.

Rumours were running wild around the Imperial palace. Furtive conversations stopped whenever the gossips saw me approach. People regarded me curiously, but looked away as soon as I made eye contact. I was not surprised when Centurion Gamus called me in to his office.

THE DRUID AND THE ELEPHANT

'The Emperor is returning to Rome,' he told me. 'He's emotional, unstable, unsure of his welcome by the senate and the people, and making unbelievable excuses about why he had to kill his mother. You were with Agrippina in the days before her death. If you claim she wasn't plotting against him, he's in trouble. That makes you a potential threat. So I'm getting you out of here. You're going to Armenia, with Micipsa, to support General Corbulo's war against the Parthians. He's planning to attack the capital city, Tigranocerta. Probably it will turn into a siege. Lukon's going with you. He's built a new war machine that can throw rocks a long way. Micipsa is the only animal strong enough to pull it. You'll need Trenus to help deal with the fortifications, and Eppilus is going because Micipsa will need protection from enemy cavalry.'

'Yes, Sir.'

'For the prestige of the Germanii, I want you to be an independent unit, answerable only to General Corbulo himself. Take what support personnel you'll need. You will be in command. Therefore, I'm promoting you to Centurion.'

'Yes, Sir. Thank you, Sir.'

'Don't thank me. A lot of powerful people are relieved that Agrippina is dead, and think you deserve it. But fortune is fickle, and this isn't over yet. The war is a chance for you to prove yourself. But beware. We've fought the Parthians before, and they are a powerful and dangerous enemy. They beat Crassus at Carrhae a hundred years ago. They use light horse archers to shoot our infantry, and heavily-armoured cavalry to smash through ours. They are fast and manoeuvrable. Take full armour for Micipsa. Rely on its protection and his strength. They also know about elephant warfare. Beware of fire.'

'Yes, Sir.'

'This is the first time the Germanii have been to war in a long time. Our reputation is on your shoulders. Only victory will suffice. Do I make myself clear?'

'Yes, Sir.'

'Then good luck, Centurion Decimus. See you next year at Corbulo's victory parade. Dismissed.'

The march to Tigranocerta was a nightmare, only made possible by two things. The first was General Corbulo. He marched every step of the way, and if a fifty year old could do it, his infantry wasn't going to appear weaker than him. Three legions followed him. The second thing was Melanipa. Corbulo had to find a way to handle the Parthian horse archers and heavy cavalry, so he employed the Sarmatians, who were even better at horsemanship. They brought along hunting dogs, good for detecting ambushes, and war dogs. What interested me most was Melanipa's tame hunting cheetahs.

'I'd like to see the Parthian cavalry try to outrun these beauties,' she said.

'How about their arrows?' I asked.

'Cheetahs are good at swerving when they hunt antelope. We train them to jink by shooting blunted arrows at them. They don't need to get too close, as the horses will spook at the sight of their charge.'

'How do you signal them where to move and when to attack?'

'They're trained to hunt alongside the dogs, who obey the hunt-master's whistle.'

She was right, and they kept the Parthian horse archers at a distance. Every morning we would break camp at first light and march as fast as possible until the heat became unbearable for the animals. The Sarmatians would go out scouting, and set the cheetahs and dogs on the Parthians if they got too close. Micipsa led the baggage train, pulling a wagon loaded with metal parts for Lukon's war machine. The horses and mules threw up clouds of choking dust. As Centurion, I couldn't just put my head down and march through it. I had to set an example, take care of my men and animals, and make sure everyone kept up the pace.

At night the Parthians would try to raid our camp. As a professional guard, I was often the guard commander. One night, Melanipa came to see me. Command can be a lonely position, so it's good to have someone to talk to who understands, and who you can share things with that you would never discuss with your subordinates. With her was her favourite dog, Alaunt.

We were walking the perimeter, checking the sentries were awake, when Alaunt stiffened and growled. I couldn't see anything, but dogs' senses are far better than humans by night, so Melanipa let him go, and he sped off into the darkness between the tents. We heard a growl and a thump, and ran up to find him biting the sword arm of an Armenian nobleman who was one of our allies.

'Get it off me!' he cried, furiously.

Melanipa and I pointed our swords at him.

'To the guard commander's tent, now,' I ordered.

Despite his protestations we marched him to the tent, searched him, and found a small dagger, with a blade that smelled suspicious. He tried to make a break for it, a stupid move when surrounded by the professional guards of the Germanii, and one that proved his guilt. We interrogated him by threatening to scratch him with the blade, and he confessed the plot and betrayed his fellow conspirators.

We bound him and dragged him to the command tent, where General Corbulo was still awake, organising the next day's march. Corbulo had the conspirators arrested, and they were all executed the next day. We left the bodies for the vultures, but took the heads on Corbulo's orders.

When we finally reached Tigranocerta, we surrounded the city, and Lukon's men chopped down pine trees and used the wood to build his war machine. He was immensely proud of it. It was a giant ballista, with a long wooden channel for guiding the stones. The stones were held on a sled that ran up the channel, so they would go straight regardless of their size, shape or weight. It was so powerful that the heavy metal parts were vital to stop it tearing itself apart. We all stood well back.

Corbulo came to watch the first shot.

'Let's send them a message. Throw the heads of those traitors,' he ordered.

Lukon loaded them into the sled, his crew cranked back the arms, and as they creaked under the stress, we all took cover in case something snapped. When it was at full stretch, Lukon ordered the crew away, and pulled the cord himself. The arms whipped forwards, and the sled shot up the channel. The heads flew high in the air, over the city wall, and disappeared among the buildings.

'Excellent!' commented Corbulo. 'Now aim for the towers on the walls. That's where their ballistas will be.'

Lukon set the infantry to bringing him suitable rocks, and started the bombardment. It wasn't long before the city gates opened and a delegation appeared.

'Stop shooting,' ordered Lukon.

The delegation was the city council. They had heard of Corbulo's policy of leniency towards cities which surrendered peacefully, but destruction to those which resisted. On seeing the severed heads, they had decided to open the city to Corbulo, and presented him with a golden crown. He ordered that no harm should come to them or their city.

Unfortunately, some hot-headed local youths decided that this was an insult to the honour of Tigranocerta, and they refused to yield. They assembled in the citadel, and slammed the doors in defiance.

We accompanied the council through the narrow streets to the citadel, a fortress built on a rocky outcrop, surrounded by a maze of buildings nearly up to its walls. The only way in was a gigantic door, at the top of a ramp which zig-zagged up to it.

The council pleaded with the youths to show some common sense. Corbulo surrounded them with our legions in a show of force. The defenders insulted him and the council.

Trenus was called forward.

'Give me options,' demanded Corbulo.

'The streets are too narrow to bring in a battering ram, unless we demolish the houses in the way. Getting a ram up that zig-zag will be a nightmare. There's not enough room to get up any speed. We need another way. The citadel's foundations are solid rock. Undermining them will take a long time. Too slow. Building siege towers would take about a week. Then we can assault the citadel at several places at once, and overwhelm them. We'd need to build them here, inside arrow range of the citadel, so we'd have to build wooden shelters first.'

'Time is not on our side,' Corbulo declared. 'We can't let our victory slip away. Others will join the revolt, and we'll end up being stoned by mobs. We need to get in there before resistance takes root.'

He gazed around for inspiration, and noticed me.

'Centurion, come here.'

'Yes, Sir.'

'Your elephant is a living battering ram. I want you to charge up that ramp, and break down that door.'

The honour of the Germanii was at stake, and I couldn't refuse a direct order.

'Yes, Sir. I'll get him ready. I request an assault team to follow us in, and archers to keep the enemy's heads down.'

'Granted. Get moving.'

I gathered Trenus, Surus, and Eppilus, and we discussed how to do it. Surus insisted on riding Micipsa.

'You need to command,' he pointed out. 'You won't have time to guide Micipsa, as well as look out and give orders.' So we dressed him in armour taken from one of Eppilus' horsemen.

'The danger is from above,' said Trenus. 'We can tie three layers of shields together, and put them on Micipsa's back. That should stop any arrows or stones. If we put a ridge pole on the platform from front to back, and attach the shields at an angle, like roof tiles, any stones should bounce off to the side. We can put straw underneath to cushion any blows.'

'Sounds like a good plan. Let's do it.'

An hour later, all was ready. Micipsa resembled a moving house. We practised running through the streets with the assault team, knocking down smaller doors, and making sure that everything was fixed and the shields wouldn't fall off. Surus and I decided not to ride Micipsa, because the citadel door wasn't tall enough for us to fit through. We would lead him from the front, under the cover of the assault team's shields.

Satisfied that we were as ready as we would ever be, we guided Micipsa back to the citadel. Corbulo was waiting for us with an assault squad and the archers. Behind them were the legions, waiting to charge in once we had cleared the way.

'Ready?'

'Yes, Sir.'

'Archers, forwards!' The bowmen moved out of the alleys, each hiding behind a comrade's shield, and prepared to shoot any enemy who showed their heads.

'Elephant, charge!'

THE DRUID AND THE ELEPHANT

We dashed forwards, Surus and I running in front, guiding Micipsa up the zig-zags of the ramp. Arrows and rocks rained down on us, but bounced harmlessly off the shields. At the top, Micipsa slammed his forehead into the door. It buckled and cracked.

'Again!' I shouted. We backed off a bit, then rammed the door again. I heard a beam on the inside crack.

'Again!' At the third charge the beam snapped and the double doors flew aside. We charged in, then frantically dragged Micipsa to a halt. In front of us was a short passage leading to a drawbridge. The drawbridge was up, and below it was a deep pit full of spikes. As we stood on the lip, arrows flew at us from loop holes above the drawbridge.

'Back!' I ordered.

There was a grating sound from above us. I looked up just as a huge portcullis fell. Iron-shod spikes on the bottom smashed through the shields and armour on Micipsa's back, piercing his ribs and knocking him flat. He let out a horrible trumpet. A waterfall of oil fell from the room above the portcullis, followed by a burning torch. The oil splashed through the broken shields onto the straw, and in a heartbeat he was on fire.

The poor animal was screaming in agony, trapped beneath the portcullis. I leaped up to his back and tried to put out the flames with my cloak, but the fire spread fast.

'Put it out, put it out!' I shouted, but there was too much fire and smoke. The assault team was in chaos. Then Surus made a decision. He leaped up beside me, and jumped onto Micipsa's head. From his belt he took an iron spike and a hammer, and with a terrible cry he broke Micipsa's neck.

I was horrified. Everything was a disaster. Micipsa was dead, the way into the citadel was blocked, and we were trapped. I suppressed the rising panic in my chest, and remembered my training. Look around, look up and down. Nothing but stone walls and a pit full of spikes. I looked up and prayed. Above me was the slot in the roof where the portcullis had come from, and the gap where the oil had been thrown. A head appeared, and dropped a rock, which bounced off a shield near me and smashed to pieces on the stone floor. Fear turned to anger. I wanted revenge. Suddenly I realised the portcullis was a grid of wooden beams, like a ladder. I screamed orders at the assault squad.

'Front rank: shield wall! Middle rank, plumbata at any heads above us. Rear rank: follow me.'

A centurion must always be first into battle. I ran to the portcullis, and started to climb. The head appeared again, and dropped a rock at me. The assault squad threw plumbata, but it was a difficult angle and smoke filled the air. They missed. The rock bounced off my shoulder armour. I got to the top just as the head appeared for a third time, and before it threw the rock, the plumbata flew up again, and hit. With a cry, the head disappeared. Reaching the top, I put my sword up through the hole and whirled it around, but hit nothing. Cautiously, I put my head through, to see a young man sitting on the floor with his face covered in blood. At the sight of me he pushed himself away across the floor.

I climbed into the room. The young man backed away, waving his arms and jabbering in a language I didn't know. In the guard we are taught never to leave a living enemy behind you, especially if you are on your own, and I was so angry about Micipsa and this young man's part in his death that I took out my anger on him.

Leaving his bloody corpse on the floor, I closed the doors into the room until the assault squad climbed up, in case the enemy had seen us through the smoke and were about to attack us. I guessed that the doors led to corridors that ran either side of the main entrance, and led to the drawbridge winch room at the far end.

'This is what we're going to do,' I told the squad. 'We need to get that drawbridge down. Half the squad will come with me along the right-hand passage, and half will take the left. When we get to the end, listen for my order to charge, and we'll take the drawbridge winch room from both sides. Kill anyone there, but the priority is to lower the bridge. After that we can clear the walls. Got it?'

'Yes, Sir.'

'Move now!'

We charged down the side passages, surprising a couple of archers, who looked round in confusion when we appeared, but who had no time to raise the alarm before we were on them. We slashed their necks as we went past at a run.

At the end of the passage, I took a quick peek around the corner at the drawbridge winch room. A group of bowmen were in there, shooting down into the gateway.

I gave my men a silent count-down with my fingers, and we charged. The first archer noticed me, his jaw dropping with surprise. I ran him through and shouted 'Charge'. The squad on the other side attacked, and in a few heartbeats, the defenders were dead. We ran to the winches and released the levers that dropped the bridge. The chains rattled round their drums, and the bridge crashed down, covering the pit.

'To the walls!' I cried, and we ran up the stairs to the parapets. The squad spread out left and right, charging into the enemy. They took one look at the bloodied legionaries coming at them, and fled.

I leaned over the wall and yelled. 'Attack!'

From below I heard Corbulo's order. 'Charge!' Our warriors cheered as they assaulted the gate.

That evening Corbulo was the new ruler of Tigranocerta. A few weeks later he installed a new puppet king of Armenia, Tigranes VI, and we attended the coronation. Tigranes rewarded me for leading the attack on the citadel by giving me the skin of a huge tiger, with its eyes replaced with semi-precious stones called 'Tiger Eyes' that made it seem alive. He dubbed me, 'The Tiger of Tigranocerta'.

Leaving a few thousand men to make sure the Parthians didn't take the place back, Corbulo left for Syria, where he was to become governor. Surus went with him, as Syria was his homeland, and he couldn't face going back to Rome without Micipsa. Before he left, we gave Micipsa a hero's funeral and buried him with full military honours. Three legions saluted his grave. At Surus's request, his tusks were mounted above the throne of Tigranocerta, so every visiting king, prince, emissary, and ambassador bowed not only to Tigranes, but also to Micipsa. I miss them both.

Corbulo sent me and my Germanii back to Rome. Without Micipsa he had no use for us, and Tigranes had his own guards. Melanipa came too. I asked her what she was going to do in Rome.

'Keep an eye on you,' she grinned. 'Ganna told me that you needed protecting, and every time I let you out of my sight, you get into trouble.'

"Well, she was right!" exclaimed Ganna. "Poor Micipsa. Poor Surus. I hope he finds another elephant."

"Corbulo wanted elephants for his army," I replied. "He asked Surus to come with him to Syria and get some. He's probably commander of a whole herd by now, and loving it. Maybe one day we'll meet again, and charge into battle at their head."

Footsteps sounded outside, and one of our captains put his head into the room.

"Tide's turning soon. Time to go."

The story of Tigranocerta had given me an idea, so before we boarded, I went to the Roman temples and collected a few souvenirs.

Our fleet sailed east from Londinium, then south between Gaul and Britannia, before heading west along the south coast, towards Isca. Boudicca sent Caicer and Teuhant with us.

"She still doesn't trust you, Caz," the druid told me when we were alone. "Londinium had far fewer Romans than she expected, and she thinks you might have warned them to flee. She took Teuhant aside and talked to him. I don't know what she said, but I wouldn't be surprised if it was about you. Her army is so big now, she thinks she doesn't need you anymore. My guess is that if Teuhant has any doubts about you, he's to kill you." His pine marten regarded me, as if curious how long I would survive.

"Thanks, I'll watch my back." Queens are just as treacherous as empresses. Even though Boudicca had been too young to be involved in the deaths of my father and brother, if she had ordered Teuhant to kill me, I would have to kill him and her, or I would never be safe.

We held a planning session on board. The Captain described Isca for us.

"It's on a river, about ten miles from the sea. There's a narrow mouth where the river runs into the sea. Upstream from there it's a thousand paces wide. About half way to Isca the river narrows to a hundred paces, and there's a fort on the east bank with a floating boom made of oak logs chained together to block entry at night. Isca's also on the east bank, and there's a dock just downstream of a bridge. At low tide it's a narrow channel with mudflats on either side. When the tide is in, the water's about seven feet deeper. I've seen war galleys dock there, and big cargo vessels."

"We don't have enough men to take on the whole Second Legion," I reminded them. "But we don't need to. Our job is to trap them there, so they can't join Suetonius. We need to convince the commander that if he marches out, we will sack his city and ambush his troops. Captain, has anyone tried to raid Isca before?"

"Yes, Druid, the Hibernian pirates tried it last year. They sailed up to the boom, and tried to break it. The fort there sent a signal to Isca, and the cavalry came down both banks. A galley full of marines rowed down the river alongside them. The pirates couldn't break the boom as the logs were too thick and the chains too strong. Bowmen among the cavalry rained arrows on the pirates. They gave up, and rowed off down river. The Romans released the boom to let the marines' ship through. When the pirates got to the river mouth, where it narrows, they were in arrow range again, and the Romans hit them from both sides. The wind was in the wrong direction for sailing, and they lost too many rowers to the arrows. The galley overtook them, and the marines killed them all."

"How do they open and shut the boom?" asked Trenus.

"The part of the chain on the west side floats on logs from the bank to the channel in the middle of the river. From there to the fort it's just a chain, with no logs, so it can sink. The fort has a capstan for tightening and loosening the chain. When they tighten it, the bare chain is pulled in, and it's above the water, so a ship can't pass. When they loosen it, the chain sinks, and ships can sail over it."

"How did the pirates try to break it?" I asked.

"They rowed up to it, then all ran to the back of the ship, so the prow was high above the water. They grabbed the chain with boat hooks, and tried to push it under the keel and drag the ship over it. But the Romans had pulled it so tight that it was above the water, and the pirates couldn't get over the chain."

"How thick is the metal?" asked Trenus.

"About like this." The Captain touched his forefinger to the tip of his thumb.

"It must be really heavy."

"Must be. It needs to be strong enough to withstand ramming by a ship."

"Oh, that's why they need logs," said Trenus. "Their capstan is only just strong enough to raise the chain out of the water. If it was any longer, they wouldn't be able to lift it. The floating logs use the tide to raise and lower one end of the chain."

"So?" I asked.

"If we can make the chain heavier, or break it from the logs, they won't be able to tighten it."

"Hmm. What about the town?" I asked.

"It's a normal Roman legion base," said the Captain. "Two main streets crossing in the middle, where the headquarters are. It's got a bathhouse, fed by an aqueduct, an exercise yard and a cockfighting pit. It's about three hundred paces along the river, and six hundred from the river to the far gate. The walls are a ditch and rampart. There's a gate that leads down to the bridge, and gates in the middle of the other three sides. The docks are close to the southern corner."

"How far from the river to the headquarters?" I asked.

"About three hundred paces. You can see the roofs from the river."

"And the civilian settlement?"

"On the north side."

"Any good beaches near the river mouth?"

"Along the coast, both east and west."

"Good. I need to pray to the gods for guidance. I'll tell you the plan tomorrow."

I went up on deck. Our galley had the sails up, and the rowers were resting. Around us was our fleet, blown along by a cold north-easterly breeze. My hair, grown long over the months since I had met Boudicca, was blowing in the wind, only restrained by the war crown. In the distance, gannets were circling, diving into the sea. Suddenly the waters erupted and giant mouths burst from beneath the surface. Fish leaped desperately to escape, but attacked from above and below, most didn't stand a chance. One fish leaped out of a whale's mouth, only to be seized by a diving gannet. Broad black backs carved the waters, and tails as big as sails rose, then disappeared beneath the waves. The gods had shown me the way.

A few days later we rowed our galley up the river to Isca, towing a smaller ship behind us. At the boom the fort signalled us.

"Tell them we are from Londinium," I told the captain, "with messages from the Procurator to the commanding officer." Lukon and I were on deck, wearing captured uniforms, and the legionaries in the fort must have believed me. Or maybe not, and they were waiting until we rounded the next bend before alerting Isca. Time would tell.

The boom was open. Logs lay on the mud, the chain vanished into the river, then re-emerged on the other side and entered the fort through a small hole in the wall.

We continued upstream, borne by the incoming tide. The

banks drew closer as the river narrowed. The Captain deftly threaded us along the winding waters, with a crewman at the bow calling the depths. Finally, Isca came into sight, the roofs of the headquarters visible in the distance. At the docks, a war-galley lay at anchor, along with a half dozen cargo vessels being unloaded. We halted in mid-channel, and let the current drift our stern upstream.

I waved at the ship behind us, and the crew steered around us and towards the docks. Once it was on course, the current pulled it onward, with no need for sails or oars. From the stern, the crew boarded a small boat and rowed back towards us. As we took them on board, a tendril of smoke rose from the ship. Closer and closer to the docks it drifted, the smoke growing slowly thicker. Cries of alarm went up from the cargo vessels, arms waved, and voices shouted.

"Now," I told Lukon.

His men pulled off the sailcloth covering their loaded and cocked ballistas, and with deep thuds they shot. Stone heads of Roman gods, my souvenirs from the temples of Londinium, arced over the ramparts, and smashed into the town. Recognising them, the commander would realise that Suetonius had failed to protect the city.

"Good shot! Reload! Oarsmen, get us out of here!"

There was panic on the docks. Our burning ship was well ablaze and drifted into a cargo vessel. Its crew ran, shouting. On the war-galley, heads appeared, and orders were yelled.

As we made off downstream, there was time for one final ballista volley. Our stones smashed into the waterline of the war-galley from short range, knocking holes through the planks. Alarms sounded from the walls of Isca.

We were moving slowly against the tide, and although Isca was behind some alder trees, there was a bridge in the distance. Give the Second Legion their due, the guard reacted quickly. With a drumming of hooves, a troop of cavalry emerged and thundered onto the bridge. When they got to the middle, Teuhant's charioteers, hidden on the east bank, shot their carroballistas, and the heavy bolts ripped into the front rank of horses, blocking the bridge with dead animals and thrown riders. From the west bank, behind the alders, I heard the thrum of more ballistas, and the neighing of panicked horses from the gates of Isca. It would be a while before any more cavalry could be saddled and pursue us down river.

The voyage back to the fort seemed like it took forever. As we approached, we heard alarms. On the river banks, our cavalry appeared, and their hoof-beats carried clearly across the waters. Rounding the bend, we saw one of our ships at the raised boom, with men pretending to be pirates hacking at the chain. At the sight of us they backed oars, and brought their ship around.

"Signal the fort to lower the boom," I ordered the captain. Would they believe us to be a Roman vessel sent to fight the pirates?

The captain waved his signal flags at the fort. Nothing happened. Time to make the pretence more believable.

"Ballista crew, shoot at the ship, but miss slightly to starboard," I ordered.

There was a deep thrum as the ballista arms whipped forwards. The bolt arced into the sky, and fell just off the side of the ship, opposite to the fort. Still, no response from the fort.

"Archers, break the heads off some arrows and prepare to shoot. Ballista, reload."

The range closed. The pirate ship was floating downstream, but the wind was light and it was slower than the rowing speed of our galley.

"Rowers, full speed!" At my command the drummer

increased the tempo, and the water churned under our prow.

The distance to the pirate ship closed. At a hundred paces I gave my command.

"Archers, aim just to the starboard of the ship. Blunt arrows, shoot!"

The arrows flew into the air, too fast for the fort's soldiers to notice their lack of arrowheads.

I touched Ganna's amulet for good luck. "Captain, signal again!"

He waved his flags, and this time a signal on the fort waved back. The guards, believing us to be the galley from Isca, slacked off the chain. It sank slowly. Then the alarms from Isca changed to signals. The message was clear: 'Stop galley.'

The chain tightened again, and rose out of the water. We were trapped.

"Captain!" I ordered, "bring us alongside the chain."

I raised the Horn of Cernunnos and blew the 'Come here' signal. Our pirate ship waved an acknowledgement, and backed oars.

The Captain had our galley drifting sideways downstream, and starboard side touched the chain, halting us in mid-stream.

"Ballista and archers, shoot at the fort. Keep their heads down!"

The ballista sent a tube of slingshots right into the hole where the chain emerged from the fort. I wouldn't have liked to be inside the capstan room with all that shot bouncing around. Our pirate ship reached us, and came alongside, on the other side of the chain.

"Captain, scuttle her and abandon ship!"

He yelled an order. Below, the ex-slave oarsmen took axes to the hull planking, hacking at the hated vessel that they had expected to row until their deaths. The water level in the bilges rose, and years of filth floated between the rowers' benches.

We jumped off the galley onto the deck of the pirate ship, like herring out of a whale's mouth, and when all were aboard, we shoved off and rowed downstream, leaving the sinking galley blocking the river. The tide was slackening now, and we made better time. On either bank, horsemen galloped.

"Row faster!" I ordered, but a ship can never outpace a horse. Our ballistas and archers killed a few, but with admirable discipline they spread out and kept coming. They caught us just as we rowed out of the mouth of the river, and their arrows arced across the water. But they were few, and we had brought shields as a precaution, so we escaped with only minor casualties.

The other ships in our fleet picked up Teuhant and the chariots from the beaches up and down the coast, and we put out to sea to plan our next move.

29

Prisoner

We held a council of war aboard. To my surprise, Teuhant argued that there was no point in staying.

"We've done our job," he said. "We know the Second is still here. They don't have time to march to Corinium, or Venonis, or Verulamium, or wherever Suetonius is going to make his stand. We've killed a lot of their cavalry, and by the time their infantry find Suetonius, it will be too late. But if we leave now, our chariots and cavalry can still be in at the kill. It will be the greatest battle this island has ever seen, and I want to be there, not at some distant blockade."

"What about the fleet, and our infantry?" I asked.

"The Captain says he wants to sail round the coast and north to Glevum. It's the headquarters of the Twentieth Legion, but most of them are with Suetonius. He thinks he can raid it and destroy any Romans there."

I wanted to be in at the kill, too, but for my own reasons. So I pretended to reluctantly agree.

We put ashore and rode north-east, following the road that the Second Legion would have taken to Venonis. One night, as we were cooking our meal, Caicer spoke up.

"Where do you think Melanipa is, Caz?" the druid asked, stirring some vervain into the pot. His pine marten ran off into the trees, searching for squirrels.

"Probably with Suetonius," I replied. "Why?"

"You seem to be concerned about her, but if you're right, and we do meet Suetonius' legions in battle, you're going to have to fight her."

"We'll find some way to avoid it."

"What is it about her that makes you value her so much?"

So I told him the story of how much I owe her.

When we got back to Rome, Melanipa took her cavalry to their usual stables, while I took my men to the palace guard commander to report in. Optio Hospes was in the guard room. He was wearing the insignia of a centurion.

'Centurion Hospes!' I exclaimed. 'Congratulations!'

'Centurion Decimus! You're back! I heard about Tigranocerta. Well done. Shame about Micipsa.'

I nodded. 'What's new?'

'A lot has changed. We have a new commander. The Emperor wanted a more famous fighter than Gamus as head of the guard, and he chose a retired gladiator. He's a good fighter, in favour with the Emperor, but with no experience of running a military unit. It was the Praetorian Prefect, Burrus's idea. He and Seneca advise the Emperor, now that Agrippina's dead. The Praetorians are taking more and more power. They're taking over the Germanii palace guard duties. Your century has been disbanded, and the men either retired or moved to other centuries. My orders are to tell you to report to Seneca on your return. If things go well, you'll be lauded as the Tiger of Tigranocerta. However, Seneca is worried that Corbulo is becoming too popular, and that's why he's been sent to Syria instead of being given a triumph in Rome. There's also a chance that Seneca will only consider how you fit into his plans, and he'll retire you like he did Gamus. Be very careful: one of our lads took violent objection to being retired, and ended up dead.'

I heard marching footsteps outside, and a Praetorian strode into the room. He ignored Hospes, and ordered, 'Centurion Decimus, come with me.' The lack of respect towards the Germanii was shocking. I wasn't going to take it.

'Did you hear something?' I asked Hospes.

'Remember what I just said,' he warned.

I looked out of the door, which the intruder had left open, and saw a squad of Praetorians, fully armed and armoured, outside. Objecting would be pointless, and only endanger our men, who were unarmoured and outnumbered. The Praetorians would surely retaliate on me for winding them up if the Germanii couldn't back me up.

'Keep an eye on the lads, will you?' I said to Hospes.

He nodded, and I followed the Praetorian out of the room.

We marched across the palace to Seneca's quarters.

The Praetorian announced me. 'Centurion Decimus of the Germanii, to see the Consul.'

One of the freedmen who serve Seneca looked up. 'He's busy. Wait here.'

We waited and waited. For hours a stream of visitors and aides went in and out. Finally, towards dusk, we were called in. Seneca seemed tired and old.

'Report,' he said.

'Centurion Decimus of the Germanii, Sir. We were part of General Corbulo's army that went to Armenia. We captured Tigranocerta, stormed its citadel, and put Tigranes on the throne.'

'Your orders were to take the Emperor's elephant to pull a

new war machine. What happened?'

'We pulled the war machine to the city, it shot the heads of some traitors over the walls, and the city council surrendered, Sir.'

'Where is the elephant now?'

'Dead, Sir. Killed in the assault on the citadel.'

'It wasn't a war elephant. Why was it assaulting?'

'General Corbulo's orders, Sir.'

'Did you object? Did you tell him it wasn't a war elephant? Did you tell him it was the Emperor's personal property?'

'I believe he knew that, Sir, and I don't question my General's commands.'

'The Emperor is annoyed that his elephant is dead. He blames you for getting it involved in the fighting, when those weren't your orders.'

I didn't reply. There's no point arguing with the words of an absent emperor.

'However, since you saved his life twice, he will be merciful. But he doesn't want to see you around the palace, because you remind him of his mother, so you can't stay here. Also, as your century has been disbanded, and you no longer have elephant-riding duties, you are surplus to requirements. You are hereby retired from service.'

I refused to acknowledge him.

'As you are now no longer a servant of the Emperor, you are no longer under his protection. When you first came to Rome, you rode the elephant and put down a riot, during which you demolished the front of some buildings.'

I remembered that night. We had charged the crowd, got bogged down in the streets outside the palace, and had been rescued by Melanipa's cavalry.

'I now own those buildings. You owe me money for the

THE DRUID AND THE ELEPHANT

repairs. Centurion Gamus paid off some of the debt from your rewards, but the outstanding amount is a hundred thousand sesterces. Can you pay that?'

'Of course not!' I was furious. 'I saved your life! Does your philosophy tell you nothing about honour and gratitude?'

'You saved the Emperor, I just happened to be in the same room. I owe you nothing. I am confiscating your retirement bonus to pay a portion of your debt. Until the outstanding amount is paid, you will be held in custody. Praetorian, take him to the cells.'

I was so angry I wanted to kill him on the spot. I had saved his life during the attack on Nero, and in return he was firing me from the guard and putting me in prison for a debt I could not pay.

The Praetorian grabbed me by the shoulders and kicked me in the back of the knees. As I fell, two others jumped on me, held me down, and tied my hands. Resistance would have been pointless, and just result in a beating, so I let them march me to the same cells where I had taken Caratacus, years before. As the cell door slammed shut I swore vengeance.

It's hard to keep track of time in the eternal darkness of the cells. I counted the meals and the changes of guards. It seemed like I was there for weeks. I dreamed of revenge, on Seneca, and on Rome. In my sleep I had nightmares about Micipsa, and dying pinned down in flames.

One day I was dragged out of my cell, chained, and taken up into the palace. The brightness of the daylight hurt my eyes, and I squinted against the glare. I was marched into Seneca's office, and thrown to the floor.

The voice of the man I hated most in the world spoke.

'Can you pay your debt?'

I shook my head, not wanting even to grace his enquiry with a reply.

The Praetorian kicked me. 'Answer when you're spoken to, barbarian.'

'No.'

'Look at me,' said Seneca. The Praetorian grabbed me by the hair and lifted my head. Seneca was seated at his desk. We were surrounded by a squad of Praetorian guard.

'I have news for you,' said Seneca. 'King Prasutagus of the Iceni in Britannia has died. He left half his kingdom to the Emperor. The nobles of his tribe borrowed four hundred thousand sesterces from me. The Emperor sees his death as an opportunity to expand the empire by taking over the Iceni kingdom. That makes the situation unstable, and my money is at risk.'

I was puzzled. What did this have to do with me?

'When I had you imprisoned, I read Pallas' intelligence report on you, to see if you had any useful skills, or if I should just sell you to gladiator school. He suspected from your treatment of Caratacus that you might be from Britannia. So I sent a slave from there to listen to you in the cells. When you have nightmares, you talk in your sleep, and you speak in a language of Britannia.'

I was horrified. My secret was out. They would see me as the next Hermann. Was that why the Praetorian squad was here? Were they my executioners? My torturers? His next words surprised me.

'Therefore, I have a use for you. Here is your mission. I'm sending you to Britannia to collect my money from the Iceni. If you can get more from them, you can use it to pay off your debt to me. Barbarian tribes usually try to rebel when the empire takes over, and they always fail. Their riches are forfeit to the conquerors. I want those riches, and you are going to get them for me.'

Now I understood why he had not simply had me killed. It was greed, pure and simple. The man had been a poor exile until Agrippina had brought him back. In Roman politics, money is power, and having money enough for bribes can be the difference between life and death.

'The Emperor has decided to send the Sarmatians to Britannia to put down any revolt. To avoid me having to pay your travel expenses, I'm hiring you out to them as a servant. When you get there, you will go and see the Procurator, Catus Decianus, and give him these letters with instructions to give you my money. Stay there until he does. Assist him to put down any rebellion. Then the Sarmatians will escort you back to Rome. If you fail at any step on the way, they have orders to kill you, slowly. But if you succeed, you can pay me and be a free man.'

He addressed the Praetorian leader.

'Take him and these letters to the Sarmatians. Dismissed.'

When we reached the Sarmatian stables, it was a hive of activity as they packed for departure. The Praetorians took me to Melanipa, and handed her the letters. She read them, nodded, and barely glancing at me, ordered, 'Go and help those men with the horses.'

Maybe she doesn't recognise me, I thought, but I was embarrassed by my own smell and unkempt beard from my time in the cells, and didn't want to say anything. I just nodded, and made my way through the bustling warriors to the men she had indicated.

They seemed familiar from the back. As I arrived, they crowded around me. Among them were Lukon, Eppilus and Trenus, and a bunch of other Germanii veterans from Britannia.

'What are you doing here?' I exclaimed in amazement.

'Did you think we'd let you go off to war without us?' said Lukon, grinning. 'Retirement is so boring without ballistas to play with.'

'And horses,' said Eppilus. 'Just look at these beauties!'

'I couldn't let you lot go off and play without me,' said Trenus. 'On the way there will be bridges and aqueducts and ships: all sorts of good stuff.'

'Come and see the horse Melanipa picked out for you,' said Eppilus. 'He's magnificent.'

It was true. He was. I almost cried.

"How," asked Caicer, "did she know he was coming?"

"Ah," replied Lukon. "We got discharged too. When Caz didn't come back, we went to see Hospes, who told us where he'd been taken. We still had friends in the palace, and they told us he was in the cells. When we heard from Melanipa about Seneca's loan to the Iceni, and that the Sarmatians were being posted here, we bribed one of the freedmen to suggest to Seneca that Caz would be more valuable here than in prison. Easy, really."

"Then what happened?"

"We rode across Gaul, got a ship to Rutupiae, then found the Procurator in Londinium."

"How did you get to the High Druid?"

"Sorry lads," I said, "but this is druid stuff." I took him aside and brought him up to date.

In Londinium, the Procurator read Seneca's letter, and shook his sweaty bald head.

'The Iceni may be muttering mutinously, but they haven't rebelled yet. If you demand Seneca's money back, it may tip them over the edge. We can't cope with a rebellion while Suetonius is away on campaign. I can't authorise this. Melanipa, take your Sarmatians north and report to Cerialis. The Ninth are spread out in the forts along the road to Lindum, you'll find him in one of them. Decimus, take Seneca's letters to Suetonius. If he signs them, I'll let you start collecting the money from the Iceni. There's a supply ship leaving on the next tide.'

The weather was bad and the supply ship was big and slow. It took weeks to get to the Holy Isle, and when we finally arrived, Suetonius had just left. Boudicca's revolt had started, and he'd been called back.

The island where I had trained as an apprentice druid was a nightmare. Unburied corpses lined the shore, women and men in black and white robes rotted in the open. Druids that I had known, friends I had trained with, and sages who had taught me. An overwhelming hatred arose in my heart, and I vowed revenge on those who had done this. Inland, the sacred groves lay in ruins, thousand-year-old oaks defiled and felled. That the Romans would do this did not surprise me, but where were our gods? Why had they not protected my people? Were Toutatis, Belatucadros and Cocidius weaker than Mars?

I had so many questions, and for answers I went searching for survivors. All day we searched, and found no-one. I touched Ganna's amulet, and prayed. Then I remembered the sea cave with the underwater entrance.

Leaving the lads searching other parts of the island, I went to the cave at low tide, left my clothes under a bush, and dived in. The water was freezing, the waves threw me around like a leaf in a storm. My lungs nearly burst before I finally got through the entrance into the cave.

As I staggered up the shingle beach, wiping the water out of my eyes, hands grabbed me, threw me to the floor and held a blade to my throat.

'Stop, wait, I'm a druid,' I cried. Then I realised my mistake. I should have said the password. 'Is this how you treat a brother, you troll? Did the Romans teach you manners?'

'Is that a beard, you walrus, or are those just bushy nose hairs?'

Ritual three-stage insults complete, the blade left my throat, and I was hauled to my feet.

'Who are you?'

'Cassibelanus, pupil of Amergin and Dubhtach, sent by the High Druid to learn Roman ways after the battle of Camulodunum. You?'

The quavering voice of a very old man spoke.

'I remember. Bring him here.'

I was escorted to the back of the cave. My eyes were getting used to the dim green light that filtered through the water from outside. Wrapped in a blanket, with a long white beard and wizened features, was the High Druid.

'I sent many men to Rome. Which one are you?'

'The green-and-blue eyed apprentice druid, who the priestess called "The Doom of Rome".'

'Oh, yes, the priestess. Ganna. Find her. Dubhtach can tell you where she is. Amergin's passed on though. One of Verica's courtiers betrayed him to the Romans.'

My old master: yet another druid killed by the Romans. I put my head in my hands, covering my face to hide my grief. Tears came into my eyes, and I knuckled them away.

'He'll be reborn.' The High Druid rested his hand on my shoulder. 'Balance will be restored. What did you do in Rome?'

'I learned their ways. I killed their Emperor. I know how to beat them.'

'Good. Your mission is not yet over. You need to find a way to make them withdraw the legions. You need to start a civil war.'

'A war has started, High Druid. Boudicca of the Iceni has rebelled. That's why Suetonius left.'

'Go and help her. Use what you've learned. Guide her.'

'Yes, High Druid.'

He nodded at the man who had held a blade to my throat.

'This is Segnorix. He knows Boudicca's druid, Caicer. He'll help you find the Queen. You need tokens to show my blessing. Segnorix, bring me the war crown and the horn.'

A short, thick-set druid went to the back of the cave, and returned with two round objects wrapped in cloth. The High Druid unwrapped the first. It was the crown.

'Put it on.'

It fitted as if it were made for me.

'This is the war crown of Toutatis, Belatucadros and Cocidius. Vow that you will not take it off until the Romans have left these lands.'

'I vow that I will not remove it until the Romans are gone.'

'And this is the Horn of Cernunnos.'

I unwrapped it, and found a mighty aurochs' horn.

'Good. There is one more thing you must do. The Romans stole the holy relics. The Cauldron of Ceridwen, the Spear of Lugh, and the Sickle of Nemausicae. Get them back. If Boudicca wins, bring them back here. If she loses, sacrifice them in Llyn Cerrig Bach. They will give you the power to destroy Rome. They are the most holy, powerful relics, gifts of the gods themselves. We can only sacrifice them once, so only do so if all is lost.'

He gripped my forearm.

'My time has almost come. I no longer have the strength to swim the passage. After the rebellion is over, come back and join the council to choose a new High Druid. I hereby declare that you are a full druid and council member. You can learn any skills you need from Dubhtach and Ganna later. Segnorix, give him the white robes.'

"Segnorix and I swam out of the cave," I told Caicer, "and I emerged a new man. No longer a centurion with a few years of druid training, but a full druid. We found the lads, I introduced Segnorix, and we left the Holy Isle. We galloped south along the old ways, and he set up the meeting with Boudicca for me. That's when I first met you."

"I remember."

"As we rode south, I scouted the route. There was a place that would be good for a battle: a narrow gorge, with steeply sloping sides. A small army might block it, and a bigger army would be bottle-necked, and only be able to attack on a narrow front. That's where I predict Suetonius will pick as his battleground, and that's where I'm taking us now."

"I just hope we're in time."

"So do I."

30

THE FINAL BATTLE

When we reached Venonis, where two great Roman military roads meet, we heard that Boudicca had pursued Suetonius to a nearby town called Lactodurum. As we approached them, the countryside became more rugged. We found the Queen's army camped near the opening of a gorge that led into thickly wooded hills. Her army was enormous, about the size of fifty legions. But far fewer were warriors, as entire tribes were present, with wagons of supplies grouped together like villages. We spotted Boudicca's command tent, and as we made our way towards it, children gawked at our chariots, and animals were herded out of our way.

The guards recognised Druid Caicer, and let us in. The Queen was talking to her war leaders, Dervalon and Tenvantius. I hadn't seen Tenvantius for weeks, and he seemed to have aged. His expression, normally sour, hardened further at the sight of me.

The Queen saw us.

"Caicer. How did it go?"

"Very well, my Queen. We raided Isca, and killed many. The Second Legion will not be joining Suetonius."

"Excellent. Join us. We are planning tomorrow's attack."

Dervalon had drawn a map of the area on the table with a

stick of charcoal.

"We're here, at the foot of the valley," he explained. "The Romans are here, in the gorge. There's a small river in the middle and pasture on either side. They've built a marching camp by the river, and dug trenches from side to side of the gorge, here and here." He drew lines across the map between the camp and us.

The Queen narrowed her eyes.

"Druid," she demanded of me, "you once told me you know how the Romans think and fight. Tell us how to beat them."

"The trenches are there to stop our cavalry and chariots. The warriors will need to cross on foot. There will be spikes under the water in the ditches, so we'll need the infantry to carry logs to make bridges. The Roman auxiliary slingers will be pelting them with stones, so they'll need shields. Our warriors must cross the bridges in large numbers at the same time, or else the slingers will shoot them, or the Roman cavalry will jump the ditches and charge them."

Dervalon nodded.

"I've already got men chopping down trees for the bridges," he said. "They'll be ready by tomorrow."

"That's the first ditch," I continued. "The second ditch will have their infantry fifty paces behind it. That's spear-throwing range. As we cross there, we will face not only sling stones, but also spears. We'll need bridges and shields again, enough to get a large assault force across the ditch. At thirty paces there will be another volley of spears, and then the Romans will be on top of a rampart of earth, protected by a final ditch, and spikes. Suetonius has got two legions of infantry, so we'll need three times that to assault the rampart, plus our slingers and spearmen to keep the enemy heads down. The assault teams will need ladders. Teamwork, timing and coordination will be critical. We must practise until every man knows what to do."

"What?" said Tenvantius, "no druid magic? No armies of animals? No elephant? No floods or forests? You're losing your touch!"

"The gorge slopes up too much for floods, and if you give me a few days, I can call the animals. But there is one thing I can do by tomorrow. I can make the Romans think we are attacking them from behind. Give me a wing of cavalry with horns and drums. If I leave now, I can march through the hills tonight, and get behind them by dawn. If they're under attack from the rear, it will pin them down so they can't escape. And they'll have to send their reserve to guard the rear, leaving less to face our assault."

"Typical dirty fighting tactics!" spat Tenvantius. "Sneaking about, stabbing in the back. I'm embarrassed to be in the same army as you. My Queen, I don't trust him. He'll run to the Romans and tell them our plans."

"Teuhant, go with the druid," ordered Boudicca. "Take enough men to attack the Romans from the rear. When you hear Tenvantius' assault begin, attack. Blow the horns. Let them know you're coming. We will crush Suetonius between us."

That night, with the help of a local guide, we circled the hills and climbed up behind the Romans. By dawn we were in position, at the top end of the gorge. I took my men aside and briefed them.

"We're not here for the battle. We have a more important mission. In the Roman baggage train are three sacred druid relics. Our mission is to seize them and take them to the Holy Isle. Lukon, search for the Spear of Lugh. Trenus, search for the Cauldron of Ceridwen. Eppilus, you find the Sickle of Nemausicae. I don't know what they look like, but they should be together, and they are ancient. When the order to charge comes, run in with the others, through the rearguard, but when you get to the baggage train, stop there and search. Find the relics, then come back here. If I don't meet you here by dawn tomorrow, take them to the Holy Isle, find Segnorix, and give them to him. I won't be with you because I need to scout forwards and give the signal to charge at the right time, depending on how the battle is going. But if Teuhant charges before my signal, go with him."

"Yes, Sir."

"Any questions?"

"What if we can't find them?" asked Lukon.

"Question the baggage train workers and the camp followers. We know the Romans took the relics; someone will know what happened to them. Anything else?"

"No, Sir."

"Right, the battle won't start for a while. Try to get some sleep. I'm going to talk to Teuhant."

Teuhant was organising his charioteers. When he finished, I took him aside.

"Our orders are to charge when we hear the sound of battle," I told him. "And we will. But battles take time, and we need to charge when the Romans feel threatened, so they will break and run. If we charge when they are still at full strength, they won't break. I'm going to scout forwards, find a place to watch the battle, and signal you at the right time. I'll take the guide with me as an escort."

"The guide isn't a warrior," he replied, "and the Romans may have sentries in the woods. I'll send one of my scouts with you as well."

He beckoned one of his men.

"Andoco," he ordered a short dark man in a green cloak, "go with the druid. Make sure no harm comes to him. Bring him to me after the battle."

Andoco nodded. "Best cover those white robes," he told me.

"Far too easy to see them in the woods." Teuhant gave me a brown cloak, and I wrapped it around me and my horn, pulling the hood up to hide the war crown.

Andoco and I left Teuhant and climbed into the hills to the right of the gorge. The forest was tense and silent, the birds and animals cautious of so many humans nearby. Our guide, a short wiry man with curly brown hair, dressed in leather and furs, led us silently through the deep undergrowth. Andoco brought up the rear. I was worried that he would try to kill me. Maybe Tenvantius had ordered it, or more likely, if I made any attempt to escape or to signal the Romans, he would attack me.

The guide paused to scan the trees in front of us. I crept up beside him.

"I'm Caz," I told him quietly. "What's your name?"

"Trasadasyus."

It was a name I had heard before, among the people of the forest, and it meant 'one who causes enemies to tremble.'

"Do you speak the old tongue?" I asked him in the forest people's language.

"Yes, Druid."

"I met Sego and Dia not long ago. Do you know them?"

"Yes. Few outsiders speak our tongue." He looked into my eyes and nodded to himself. "You and your deeds are known. Hush. I can smell Romans. Follow me quietly."

Trasadasyus guided us through the trees along the upper edge of the gorge until we came to an outcrop overhanging the valley. The view was magnificent. I could see all the way from where Teuhant was hiding, along the gorge, past the Roman army, to Boudicca's forces at the bottom of the valley. The smoke of the cooking fires drifted up as the warriors prepared their food. No point going into battle on an empty stomach, and this meal might be a man's last, so might as well eat heartily.

That reminded me, I hadn't eaten since the day before. In my bag I had some cheese, and I shared it with Trasadasyus and Andoco. Andoco had some bread, and Trasadasyus had dried venison. Then we took turns, one to guard and one to watch the gorge, while the third slept. When Trasadasyus woke me, it was mid-morning.

"They're moving," he said.

Down the valley, a chariot raced along the front of the army. In the clear morning light I made out Boudicca, exhorting her warriors. From the Roman legions a horse rode to the centre, and a man, probably Suetonius, waved his arms about as Roman noblemen are taught to do when giving a speech. At the end the Roman cornus blared, the warriors cheered, and beat their shields with the flat of their blades. From the Iceni, horns and drums answered, and shaken spearheads glittered in the sunlight. The war-cries echoed like thunder up and down the gorge.

The first Iceni warriors charged. Five bridging teams ran forwards towards the first ditch, led by their chiefs. From behind the Roman line there was the thrum of ballistas, and the bolts arced into the sky towards the middle bridging team. They didn't try to dodge or stop, but ran straight into the path of the bolts, shields held high. The heavy arrows fell among them, piercing the shields and the warriors beneath them. Unable to hold the weight of the bridge, the survivors dropped it. More warriors dashed out of the lines to help them.

The other teams had reached the first ditch, a hundred paces from the Romans. The auxiliary slingers stepped forwards and shot their lead bullets. I heard them whistle through the air, and a second bridging crew went down, dropping their burden. Again, more warriors ran forwards to help.

The three surviving teams lifted their bridges onto one end, and dropped them over the ditch. A second volley of slingshots ripped through one of the teams, but Boudicca's army were already charging. The whole mass of men, cheered on by their tribes who were watching from the wagons at the rear, rushed forwards. They flooded across the bridges and charged towards the second ditch.

Among them were new teams of bridge carriers, but burdened with their loads, they were slower than the leading warriors. At the second ditch, fifty paces from the Romans, the warriors had to choose, try to cross the ditch themselves, or wait for a bridge while being shot at by the slingers.

The sensible ones waited behind their shields, or used their own slings to try to keep the Roman's heads down. But the more impetuous tried to wade the ditch. Many found the painful caltrops hidden beneath the murky waters, and others discovered that the muddy back wall of the ditch was impossible to climb. While they waited or struggled, the legions threw their first pila high in the air. Our warriors were holding their shields in front of them to protect themselves from the slingshots, but the pila dropped straight down on them. Men screamed and died in the mud, but for each who died, a thousand were rushing forward to take his place.

The second wave of bridge teams reached the ditch. Many of the carriers fell to slingshots and pila, but there were so many warriors that willing hands stepped in, and the bridges fell over the ditch with a thud. A cheer went up, and the army charged.

Each bridge was a choke-point, a narrow way that concentrated the warriors. Slingshots and pila rained down on them. Ballista bolts pierced shields and bodies, sometimes penetrating one body and piercing through to the man behind. But still the hordes rushed on.

Horns blew from the Roman side, and drawbridges dropped over the ditches at the sides of the valley. Their cavalry galloped over them, lowered their spears, and charged. The Iceni had no time to stop and make a shield wall. The cavalry hit them in the flank, and rode over them. Heavy cavalry horses formed an armoured fist, smashing and trampling hundreds. I recognised Melanipa's Sarmatians among them. The line of horses swept from one side of the valley to the other, destroying all in their path. They wheeled and charged again, spearing any newcomers who had just crossed the bridges. The Iceni couldn't get enough men across the bridges to build a deep enough formation to resist them. Even when the cavalry had swept past a bridge, any warrior attempting to cross was met with a deadly barrage of slingshots and pila.

The warriors at the back couldn't see what was happening and pressed forwards. The men at the front were forced to choose between crossing the bridges or wading the ditch. Either choice was deadly.

The advancing warriors brought forward the two bridges that had been dropped earlier, and they crashed down across the ditch. With more ways across, more warriors charged, and some dodged the cavalry, sprinted forward, and reached the trench below the Roman rampart. Heavy stabbing pila thrust down at them, and a deadly rain of plumbata fell.

This was the critical moment, as our warriors were at the Roman ramparts. I took out the Horn of Cernunnos, and sent out a blast that echoed across the valley. In the din of battle, no-one below heard me, but the sound reflected off the cliffs on the other side, loud enough to reach Teuhant.

I peered up the valley, at the Roman rearguard. Behind them, Lukon's ballista bolts climbed into the sky. I heard the hooves of Teuhant's chariots, and they burst from the trees. A moment after Lukon's bolts hit the unwary warriors guarding the rear, the chariots smashed into them. Breaking through, they charged past the baggage train, and towards the rear units of the Roman army. By their boar emblem, they were the Twentieth Legion.

The Romans at the rear of the legion heard the rumbling of wheels, and spotted Teuhant and his men. Our warriors blew their horns, galloped forwards, leapt from their chariots, and charged in. The Romans got into formation just in time to meet them, and a vicious brawl started.

I cursed. Teuhant had hit the wrong target. The Twentieth were battle-hardened legionaries who had been fighting ever since the invasion. Teuhant should have gone around them, and hit the lightly-armoured auxiliaries on the flanks, clearing them away, lowering the drawbridges to give our army a chance to outflank the Roman infantry. But the Twentieth had defeated Caratacus, and Teuhant wanted revenge. He didn't have the numbers to win, and Boudicca's army was in serious trouble.

In the centre of the Roman legions, Suetonius glanced at the skirmish behind him, then returned his attention to the attack. He nodded to his Cornicen, who blew the signal to form up. The drawbridges on the flanks lowered again, and lines of infantry emerged, spreading out along the front of the rampart, clearing our warriors away with the help of the cavalry. They formed up three-deep, the wall of their shields facing down the valley.

The Cornicen blew the advance, and the legion stepped forwards. They were remorseless. The wall of shields marched down the valley, and short swords ripped into any of our unarmoured warriors foolhardy enough to get in the way. As the infantry approached the ditch, the cavalry galloped towards it, jumped over, and attacked the bridges from behind, clearing away any defenders. The infantry used the bridges to cross unopposed, re-formed into a line, and continued down the valley.

Boudicca's army was pushed back, and her superior numbers became a curse. Men at the back were still moving forward, while those at the front were pushed back. Many were crushed and trampled between, especially when the cavalry charged through. Any time a chief tried to rally his men into formation, the cavalry attacked.

The Romans crossed the second ditch as they had crossed the first. Men no longer moved forwards, and the retreat became a rout. The tribes at the wagons tried to hitch up the draft animals, but there wasn't enough time. The wagons formed a wall, and although many warriors scrambled over or under, more were crushed up against them, and the Romans waded forwards through a sea of corpses, stabbing viciously.

I looked to see how Teuhant's fight was going. All his warriors were dead, and the Romans were hurling pila and slingshot at the chariots, who wheeled, and made off up the gorge.

Trasadasyus and Andoco were watching the disaster unfold.

"No point staying here," I told them. "What do you want to do?"

Andoco's face was one of shock and horror. He gazed down at Teuhant's body. A Roman was ripping the golden torc from around his neck. Andoco's expression transformed to one of anger.

"Obey his last order," he said, pulling a dagger. "You can meet him in the afterlife!" He charged me. Trasadasyus leg-swiped him, and as he staggered, I punched him in the neck. Stunned, he teetered on the edge, and I shoved him off the cliff. He plummeted to the valley floor, far below.

"Thanks," I said to Trasadasyus.

"A pleasure. I didn't like him. He wouldn't even talk to me. Why did he have it in for you?"

"The Queen's war chief doesn't trust me. He thought I would betray them. No matter if this battle was won or lost, he wouldn't need me anymore."

"Well, he's probably dead now. What are you going to do?"

"There's a woman down there, a druid. I want to see if she's still alive. Then I'll go back to my men."

"I'll show you the way down. We'll go this evening. It's not safe now. Too many Romans."

He was right. I gazed down into the valley. Two armies of my enemies, that of the murderous Iceni, and that of the Romans who had massacred my fellow druids on the Holy Isle, were butchering each other. The forces of Boudicca's victory goddess Andraste fought the followers of Mars. I gave thanks to the druid war gods, Toutatis, Belatucadros and Cocidius. Then we retreated into the shelter of the woods.

At dusk we crept down the gorge to where the slopes were less steep, and made our way down to the valley floor.

"Stay here," I told Trasadasyus. "I'll go find her."

I crawled across the battlefield, moving only when clouds obscured the moon and the wind blew, bending the grass. Dark shapes inhabited the silence, wolves, ravens, and other carrion creatures. None disturbed me: with so many of the dead, why risk attacking the living? More dangerous were the corpse robbers: Roman camp followers, searching for gold and valuables. They all knew each other, and might attack a stranger.

Eventually I saw the figure of a woman in the moonlight, dressed as a priestess. She walked like Ganna, and was searching for something, not looting corpses. I let out three owl hoots with the correct pauses between that form a secret druid signal, and she made her way towards me. Standing to meet her in the middle of the battlefield would have seemed extremely suspicious, and given away the secret of the owl signal, so I retreated to where I had left Trasadasyus, and hooted again. She followed.

"Ganna," I called softly.

She came to me.

"Caz. Thank Baduhenna. My dreams never showed me if I would find you."

"This is Trasadasyus, my guide."

"Follow," he said, and led us back into the woods, along the slopes, to where Lukon and the lads were waiting. I thought of the woman by my side, and the men who followed me, trusted me, and depended on me. What would we do? Where could we go to make a life for ourselves? What about Melanipa, and my debt to Seneca? Ganna had dreamed of her and me on a ship, but a ship to where? Rome? Time to talk to the gods.

31

THE COUNCIL OF DRUIDS

At the northern end of the Holy Isle is a mountain, and on the summit is an ancient hill fort, with views across the sea to Hibernia. There we met Segnorix, who was now arrayed in the robes of the High Druid. With me were Ganna, Lukon, Trenus, and Eppilus. Many Druids had come to congratulate Segnorix, and debate what to do next. To my surprise, I saw Boudicca's druid Caicer among them, pine marten on his shoulder, and we went to speak to him.

"Caicer, good to see you!"

"Caz. Ganna. Lads. You all made it!"

"What happened at the end of the battle?"

"Boudicca led our chariots into combat to cover the retreat, and Melanipa's cavalry charged us. They wounded the Queen and killed her driver, so I took the reins and we escaped. The other survivors went home with Dervalon, but that's where the Romans would expect her to go, so we went in the opposite direction."

"And Tenvantius?"

"Dead. He was on one of the bridges, and a ballista bolt went straight through him. How about Teuhant?"

"Dead. Charged a wall of legionaries."

Caicer shook his head ruefully. "Such a waste. What are we

going to do now?"

"Let's hear what Segnorix has to say."

The new High Druid stood and walked to the middle of the ring of white-robed figures.

"Welcome. I am Segnorix. I will speak of what has come to pass, and what is yet to be. The Romans invaded us, and did their best to destroy us. But we are still here."

He paused and glanced around the circle of druids. Lifting his staff, he thumped it into the turf.

"We are still here because we cannot be beaten. They chopped down our sacred oak groves. We will regrow them. They murdered our brothers and sisters. We will raise a new generation. They stole our holy relics. We have taken them back. Bring them forth."

Lukon stepped forward and handed over a gigantic spear. The shaft was a narwhal tusk, twice the height of a man, and the head of polished copper, in the shape of a flame.

"Behold, the Spear of Lugh," said Segnorix, holding it high.

Eppilus was next.

"The Sickle of Nemausicae," intoned Segnorix. He held it up for all to wonder. The handle was of amber, and the blade of obsidian shards, set in gold.

Finally, Trenus carried forward a large item wrapped in his cloak.

"The Cauldron of Ceridwen." Segnorix uncovered a bronze vessel, with scenes of inspiration, transformation and rebirth hammered into its sides.

"To the Druid Cassibelanus," Segnorix told the gathering, "was entrusted the War Crown of Toutatis, Belatucadros and Cocidius. He vowed not to remove it until the Romans were gone from our lands. The Romans have now left these lands. No Roman foot fouls the Holy Isle. No Roman sandal defiles the kingdom of the Ordovices. These lands are now free."

He was right. The High Druid had never told me to free the whole of Britannia. I had taken revenge on Claudius. But I had not drawn away the legions.

"Also entrusted was the Horn of Cernunnos. Many a Roman died to the echo of its call. Cassibelanus, step forward."

I rose and removed the crown. It no longer weighed upon my head, or the responsibility on my mind. I handed the crown and the horn to Segnorix. Did this mean I had failed? Was he going to give them to my replacement?

"Now, let us speak of what is yet to come. The Romans are gone, but for how long? Our armies cannot defeat them, but who can? This island is not safe from them, but where is? I have prayed to the gods, and listened to the wisdom of the old High Druid before he left us. Here is my decision. The heart of the matter is who can defeat the Romans. The answer is, the Romans. The old High Druid saw that only a Roman civil war can cause them to withdraw their legions from this island. Druid Cassibelanus, long ago the gods declared you to be the Doom of Rome. Your sacred mission is to return there, kill Nero before he has children to succeed him, and set the contenders for the throne at each other's throats. To do this, you need the blessing of the gods. A powerful magic, never yet seen in the history of the druids. Tonight, we will sacrifice the holy relics to the gods."

He paused and looked around.

"But we also need a messenger, a human sacrifice to tell the gods of our intention, and gain their support. But who? A slave? Who listens to slaves? A prisoner? Who knows what lies they might tell? A druid? The Romans killed hundreds of us, but the gods did not heed our prayers. Who then? Who will the gods listen to? Who is willing to be our holy messenger?"

A voice spoke from the darkness.

"I, Boudicca, Queen of the Iceni, will deliver your message."

She stepped into the firelight, supporting her wounded body by clutching a spear shaft. The faint odour of gangrene told me that little time was left to her.

"The gods will listen to me. As Queen, I refused to let the Romans rule me. They do not rule me now, and I will never let them rule me. I gathered the largest army this land has ever seen, and with the blessing of Andraste, Goddess of Victory, I sacked Camulodunum, Londinium and Verulamium. Now the tide has turned against me, but I will not run, I will not hide, and I will not surrender. It was not my final battle. My body is bloodied and broken, but I can fight on in the afterlife. As Queen, I am responsible to my people, and I will do my duty. Caicer tells me that death is but a short sleep. We are all reborn. Your descendants will see me again, sword in hand, when I return. And however many lifetimes it may take, I will not rest until the Romans leave these shores. No better messenger will you find than I."

"So be it," said Segnorix. "Tonight is the night of the full moon. We will make the pilgrimage to the lake of Llyn Cerrig Bach. There, as our ancestors have done for a thousand years, we will make sacrifice. Our magic will be the greatest ever seen. None will be able to stand against us. We will fight on. Victory will be ours."

That night, a torch-lit procession crossed the Cymyran Strait to the island of Mona. On the sacred shores of Llyn Cerrig Bach we made our sacrifice.

"Gods of our ancestors," Segnorix prayed, "take these sacrifices as proof of our devotion and resolve. Heed the words of our messenger, Queen Boudicca of the Iceni, and bless our brother, Cassibelanus, on his mission."

Segnorix slit the Queen's throat with the Sickle of Nemausicae, and then hurled it out into the dark waters. Caicer caught her blood in the Cauldron of Ceridwen, then threw it into the path of moonlight on the lake. With the narwhal shaft of the Spear of Lugh I knocked her unconscious, then cast it like a pilum. It fell into the depths without a splash. With the Horn of Cernunnos I alerted the gods to our deeds, then cast the last relic, the war crown of Toutatis, Belatucadros and Cocidius, high out above the waters. In the frosty night sky a shooting star flashed across the heavens. Our sacrifice had been accepted.

A month later, Melanipa and I entered the office of the Governor of Britannia, Gaius Suetonius Paulinus.

He lifted his eyes from the piles of scrolls on his desk, and nodded to Melanipa.

"Who's this?" he demanded.

"Governor, allow me to present Decimus, ex-centurion of the Germanii, the Tiger of Tigranocerta, and currently representative of Consul Lucius Annaeus Seneca, senior adviser to the Emperor."

Suetonius raised an eyebrow.

"I see. What do you want?"

I handed over Seneca's letter. As Suetonius read it, he scowled.

"He wants four hundred thousand! No wonder the Procurator didn't agree. It says here that you are to stay here until he gives you the money. Well, Catus Decianus has gone to Gaul, and been replaced. You won't get any money from him. I'm the one in charge now, and I say who gets what. Second, it says you are to help put down any rebellion. I have already done that. I don't need your help. So why should I give you anything?"

"You've been searching for Boudicca for a month," I replied, "but you still haven't found her. The Iceni are still resisting. They believe she is still alive. So do you. You're offering a hundred thousand reward for her, dead or alive. Fighting will continue until you can prove that she is dead, and every day that fighting is costing you. You're losing money, but you can't put up taxes because you're worried that would rekindle the rebellion. If that happens, you're down to two legions. The Ninth was defeated and the Second won't follow you. Yes, you won a battle, but you lost three cities. The Emperor won't be happy. You need Seneca to put in a good word for you. Your position teeters on a knife-edge. But what if I put a stop to it? What if I give you Boudicca? What is that worth?"

"Ha! What do you think you are, some kind of magician? You want money to search for her, is that it? Well, no chance. My legions are taking care of that. I want results, not promises. Give me Boudicca and I'll get you Seneca's money. I'll even throw in the reward money. Otherwise, stop wasting my time."

"Oh, I'm not wasting your time, Governor. Believe me."

I shrugged off my backpack, took out a heavy cloth-wrapped ball, and dropped it with a thud on his desk. The wrappings fell apart, to reveal the severed head of the last Queen of the Iceni.

Notes

I have attempted to keep the story as true to written history as possible. However, there is always the possibility that after the date of writing, new archaeological evidence will add to our knowledge, and contradict the story. New battle sites may be found, and lost histories may come to light when the charred scrolls found in Pompeii are unwrapped and read. As a history lover, I look forward to it. The more we know, the better. Below you will find some notes on the individual chapters that I hope you will find interesting.

Boudicca
The name of the Boudicca is spelled in many different ways: Boudicca, Boudica, Boadicea, Boudiga, Bodicca or Buddug. It could come from Celtic, and mean 'victorious', but whether this is a name, a nom de guerre, or a title, who can say? Perhaps one day her grave may be found, with her name inscribed upon it. Until then, as long as the person you are talking to understands who you mean, and doesn't turn their nose up at your version, I don't think it really matters.

Ballista
The Ballista was an accurate long-range weapon, capable of shooting bolts or stones over five hundred paces. They look like giant wooden crossbows, but instead of a flexible bow, they have rigid arms with twisted rope springs to whip them forwards, and metal reinforcements to handle the forces. A skilled Roman

artillery crew could build their own ballista out of wood and rope.

The Battle of the Medway
While the use of chariots for warfare had died out in most of the classical world, it still continued in Britannia.

Monsters
The Emperor Claudius brought war elephants to Britannia, but it is uncertain if they were used before he arrived. However, in the archaeological documentary 'Time Team', during an excavation of a Roman fort near the Thames, the artist Victor Ambrus painted war elephants, so I have included them here.

Elephants are scared of bees, and farmers in Africa use them to scare elephants away from their crops.

The Battle of the Thames
The Catuvellauni Princes, Caratacus and Togodumnus, were real historical people, Caratacus becoming a famous resistance leader.

Ambush
Ballistas could shoot stones or bolts. There is no archaeological evidence of them shooting masses of slingshot bullets, but my fictitious character, Lukon, likes to experiment.

The Storming of Camulodunum
The Praetorian guard did accompany Claudius to Britannia.

The High Druid's Plan
Hermann defeated the Romans at the Battle of Teutoburg, known as the Varian Disaster.

The Imperial German Bodyguard were a personal guard for the Emperor, who mainly came from the Rhine delta region. Unlike the Praetorians, they had no links to the politics of Rome, and the Emperors valued them for their loyalty and reliability.

The Emperor's Parade
Claudius was not a well man. The historian Suetonius says that his knees were weak and his head shook. He would stammer, his speech was confused, and his nose ran when he was excited. Claudius claimed that he exaggerated his symptoms before he became Emperor in order to seem less of a challenger for the throne, and therefore less likely to be killed for it.

Micipsa the elephant is named after a King of Numidia who sent elephants to help a Roman commander in Spain.

How to Kill a Herd of War Elephants
The historian Cassius Dio states that Roman war elephants were used in Britannia, but they went out of use after that.

The Way to Rome
The Roman throwing spear was called a pilum, and the plural is pila. They could be thrown or used as spears against cavalry. They were designed to penetrate enemy shields and weigh them down, making them useless. They had soft metal necks, designed to bend so that the enemy couldn't throw them back.

The rope technique used in the story is based on the Greek amentum, a leather strap which allows a spear to be thrown over 50% further than by hand.

The Road South
The wide river that forms the boundary between Gaul and Germania is the Rhine. The banded mail armour that Decimus

is issued with is now called lorica segmentate, but what the Romans called it is unknown.

Fire, friend and foe
Caligae are Roman army marching sandals.

Roman cavalrymen wore metal masks covering their whole face, often in the shape of frightening faces.

Centurion Gamus of the Germanii swears by Hercules because the Roman historian Tacitus says that the Germanic people believed that Hercules visited them, and they sang his name when going into battle.

The Sarmatians were a people from the grasslands north of the Black and Caspian seas. About a fifth of Sarmatian graves contain women dressed as warriors.

Gods of War and Water
The Roman fort is at Great Casterton. The bridge is on what was later to be called Ermine Street. Lindum is now Lincoln.

A Test of Loyalty
A turma was a squadron of cavalry.

The Great Man's Garden
Durobrivae is Water Newton in Cambridgeshire, where Ermine Street crosses the River Nene. To the east of it is Longthorpe Roman Fort.

Death in the Garden
This Polybius is Gaius Julius Polybius, not the Greek historian. Seneca did write to him, in an attempt to return from exile. The Roman historian Cassius Dio claims that Messalina had Polybius killed when she tired of him as a lover.

Messengers of the Gods
Discovery of writing found on excavated pottery show that the town of Durobrivae was a vicus, a settlement providing support for a fort. However, the fort did not last long, and the town grew up around Ermine Street, on the closest dry land to the bridge.

The Emperor's Wedding
The tactic of building a double wall around an enemy position was used by Julius Caesar at the Battle of Alesia, and resulted in the Roman's taking over Gaul.

The Emperor and the Whale
The killer whale in Ostia was witnessed by Roman military commander Pliny the Elder, who says that the Praetorians attacked it with lances.

The Chieftain in Chains
Caratacus (also spelled Caractacus) was allowed to live on in Rome.

The Temple of the War Goddess
A carnyx was a Celtic battle horn, made of bronze, reaching several feet up from the player's lips to a mouth shaped like a snake or boar's head.

The River of Blood
The architect's dream, of an aqueduct fed by springs near Lake Bracciano, was completed in AD109, and called the Aqua Traiana, after the Emperor Trajan.

The Death of an Emperor
What caused Claudius' death is controversial. Seneca says it was

natural causes, Josephus says there were rumours of poison. Halotus went on to serve Nero and the Emperor Galba. Xenophon died in the same year as Claudius, but how is unknown.

The Theatre of Terror
The historian Tacitus writes of how the statue fell, and the theatre echoed with shrieks. Wealth was buried to keep it safe, for example the Fenwick Treasure of gold and silver jewellery.

Maddened Beasts
Cart-mounted ballistas were called caroballistas, and are shown on Trajan's column in Rome.

Shipwreck
Different historians retell different accounts of Agrippina's death. Tacitus tells of the lead ceiling, and the death of Acerronia. Suetonius tells of a collapsible boat, and Cassius Dio talks of a boat that opened at the bottom. By all accounts she survived, and Nero had her assassinated.

Severed Heads
Although the portcullis is typically associated with medieval castles, it was used by the Romans from about 200 B.C. It was called a cataracta, and there is one at main entrance of Pompeii.

Prisoner
The Iceni rebellion was partly Seneca's fault, according to Cassius Dio, as he did call in his loans.

The Final Battle
The site of the Battle of Watling Street, as it is now known, is

still uncertain. It was probably in the Midlands, although local legends place it anywhere from Warwickshire to Essex.

The Council of Druids
The manner of Boudicca's death and the location of her grave are unknown. Local legends place it anywhere from Wales to King's Cross Station. Tacitus states that she poisoned herself, and Cassius Dio says that she fell ill and died. I went with gangrene as that illness, and a death fitting her personality.

Acknowledgments

Publishing a book is a group effort. This book would not have been possible without the assistance of the following wonderful people: my publisher Graham and his team, my sister Jennifer and niece Bethany for being beta readers and for their encouragement, cover artist Betty Martinez, the Hong Kong Writer's Circle, and my friends of the Aberdeen University Dungeons and Dragons Club from the 1980s. I'd also like to thank some people on the internet for their advice on writing and history: Abbie Emmons, Daniel Greene, Elliot Brooks, Tim Hickson of Hello Future Me, Imperium Romanum, Jason Kingsley, Jenna Moreci, Jill Bearup, Lindybeige, Merphy Napier, the Metatron, Shad of Shadiversity, everyone at Time Team, Tod of Tod's Workshop, Garret Ryan of Told in Stone, and the team at the Writing Excuses podcast.

About The Author

Andy Morrall is a writer and university lecturer. From a young age he has loved fantasy, science fiction and adventure stories. On leaving school he became a soldier, but being a book lover, he went to university to study literature. Now he works in Hong Kong, teaching creative writing and language. He also enjoys hiking with his family, and painting animals and landscapes.

www.ingramcontent.com/pod-product-compliance
Lightning Source LLC
LaVergne TN
LVHW031609060526
838201LV00065B/4788